The Social Construction of Urban Schooling
Situating the Crisis

UNDERSTANDING EDUCATION AND POLICY

William T. Pink and George W. Noblit
series editors

Discourse and Power in Educational Organizations
  David Corson (ed.)

The Social Construction of Urban Schooling: Situating the Crisis
  Louis F. Mirón

Continuity and Contradiction: The Futures of the
Sociology of Education
  William T. Pink and George W. Noblit (eds.)

Good Schools: The Policy Environment Perspective
  Charles A. Tesconi

forthcoming

Stepping Back: Grounded Perspectives on Interagency Collaboration
  *Amee Adkins, Catherine Awsumb, George W. Noblit, and
  Penny Richards*

A General Theory for a Democratic School
  Art Pearl and Tony Knight

The Cultural Consequences of School Closings
  Maike Philipsen

Assessment and Control at Parkview School: A Qualitative Case Study
of Accommodating Assessment Change in a Secondary School
  Hilary A. Radnor

Talking About a Revolution: The Politics and Practice of Feminist
Teaching
  Cheryl L. Sattler

From Disabling to Enabling Schools
  Roger Slee, Mel Ainscow and Michael Hardman

From Nihilism to Possibility: Democratic Transformations
for Inner City Education
  Fred Yeo and Barry Kanpol (eds.)

The Social Construction of Urban Schooling
Situating the Crisis

Louis F. Mirón
University of California at Irvine

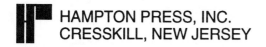
HAMPTON PRESS, INC.
CRESSKILL, NEW JERSEY

Copyright © 1996 by Hampton Press, Inc.

All rights reserved. No part of this publication may be reproduced, stored in a retrieval system, or transmitted in any form or by any means, electronic, mechanical, photocopying, microfilming, recording, or otherwise, without permission of the publisher.

Printed in the United States of America

Library of Congress Cataloging-in-Publication Data

Mirón, Louis F.
    The social construction of urban schooling : situating the crisis / Louis F. Mirón.
       p. cm. -- (Understanding education and policy)
  Includes indexes.
  ISBN 1-57273-074-9. -- ISBN 1-57273-075-7
  1. Education, Urban--Social aspects--United States.
2. Educational change--United States. 3. Education and state--United States. 4. Politics and education--United States.
5. Postmodernism and education--United States. I. Title.
II. Series.
LC5131.M56 1996
370.19'348'0973--dc20   96-21375
                                                    CIP

Hampton Press, Inc.
23 Broadway
Cresskill, NJ 07626

Contents

Preface	vii
Series Preface	xi
Acknowledgments	xiii
About the Author	xv

1. Understanding the Forms of the Current Crisis — 1

- Problematic Meaning of Urban Schooling — 2
- Deconstructing the Governance Crisis — 7
- The Cultural Politics of Inner-City Schooling — 13
- The Social Reality of the Urban School Crisis — 16
- The Measures of Constructed Reality in Urban Schools — 20
- Plan of the Book — 22

2. The Social Context of Urban Schooling — 25

- A Call to Action — 26
- The Ideological and Economic Bases for the War on Poverty — 28
- The Route Out of Poverty — 31
- The Legacies of Positivism — 33
- The New Federalism and the Conservative Restoration — 38
- The Excesses of the Free Market — 40
- Conservative Ideologies and the Ascent of the New Right — 47
- The Ideological Appeal of Head Start — 50
- The Possibilities of Postmodernism — 55
- A Break with the Past? — 64

3. The Perennial Quest of Ideological Control of Big-City Schooling — 67

- The Entrepreneurial Coalition and Consensus Building — 69

    The Ideological Strategies of the
        Entrepreneurial Coalition   72
    Summary   90
    The New Politics of Community   91
    The Social Production of Knowledge in the City   96
    Conclusion   98

4. Postmodernism and the Politics of Urban Pedagogy   101

    The Modernist View of Ethnic Identity   102
    Recasting the Politics of Ethnic Identity   108
    A Theory of Urban Pedagogy   116
    Border Pedagogy and the Politics of Difference   124
    Antibias Pedagogy as a Cultural Politics   128
    The Boundaries of the Urban School   132

5. Postmodernism, Identity Politics, and Student Resistance   135

    Student Resistance and Identity Politics   136
    The Struggle for Racial-Ethnic Identity
        in the Urban Context   142
    Research Design   145
    The Entrepreneurial Coalition's Drive for
        Ideological Hegemony in Louisiana   147
    Student Culture   151
    School Climate as Ordered Social Relations
        in the Classroom   157
    Interpreting Student Resistance   166
    The Social Construction of Racial-Ethnic Identity   169
    Summary of Identity/Cultural Politics   175
    School Work, Democracy, and the Politics
        of School Violence   176

Conclusion: The Lingering Quest of Democracy   179

    Conclusion: Breaking Through   183
    Taking Care of Business   185
    "Situated" Agency   187
    The Move Toward "Practical Intersubjectivity"   191
    Toward an Interpretation of Theory and Practice   193
    Understanding the Failures of Urban School Reform   194
    Hitting the Optimistic Note   195

Author Index   217
Subject Index   223

Preface

I have crossed borders all of my life, both literally and symbolically. This work is no exception. In 1953, my family emigrated from Guatemala City to New Orleans, LA. In Louisiana, where a new language and culture awaited, the strange quickly became the familiar, but not without struggle. I was always torn between the world of Central American Latino and Catholic culture at home and a deeply foreign Catholic culture in the parochial schools in New Orleans.

Similarly, when I first began to write this book over two year ago, I was struggling to get beyond the influences of an overly structural Marxist perspective I had acquired at Tulane University. I felt that structural Marxism simply did not leave sufficient space for agency. Ironically, I developed a structural perspective based on the writings of urban political economists, for example, Michael Smith, whose piece on postmodern social analysis I rely on heavily in the book. The postmodern perspective got me into the notions of instability, multiplicity, historical exigency, and shifting constructions of identity in the new urban social space. This postmodern view on the world frees me to hold true to the normative principles of Michael Apple's work, which cautions us over and over that "poverty is no sleight of hand" and, although subordinate groups' material conditions do not cause them to simply buckle under to dominant forces, there are limits to transformative possibilities. My drive in this work is to push these boundaries of possibility.

I seek to redraw the boundaries of structural limitations—hence, redefine the parameters of the discourses in the study of urban schooling—through the use of postmodern method of social analysis and practical criticism. In particular, I advance a *critical* postmodern perspective by exploring the possibilities for the reconstruction of urban schooling. The postmodern tenets of uncertainty, decentered power, practical intersubjectivity, and opposition to essentialism lay bare the mythology of the crisis in urban schooling. They also inform its social reconstruction. I remain, however, skeptical and self-consciously disciplined about the possibilities of student resistance, agency, and identity politics. Hopefully, I offer more than abstract discourse. In particular, I openly challenge the critique of a strand of neo-Marxist writers who argue (themselves without empirical support) that postmodern theorists lack a moral and political stance. I hope that my empirical chapter helps put this rather silly notion to rest.

I want to be more than a good scholar and researcher. I redraw the disciplinary boundaries of the study of urban schooling. These boundaries lack aesthetic sensibility. I believe that we in universities have much to learn from the performing arts and a cadre of talented performers who live and work in the city. Those of us in the university who still choose to live in urban centers and who wish to remain hopeful about the future of schools in these places need to listen to, and work with, artists like the new brand of jazz musicians who have mastered the past (the blues, be bop, and swing), but who have established their own style in the genre. Gifted artists, such as Wynton Marsalis and Terence Blanchard, believe that the tradition of jazz—as American art form—brings a message of optimism to youth in inner-city America. Marsalis's views on difference, interpretation, experimentation, collaboration, and improvisation, embedded in the following notes from *In This House, On This Morning,* is powerful metaphor for redrawing the disciplinary boundaries and discursive practices of urban schooling. This transition to the practice of art will eventually make possible the crossing of its borders and ultimate reconstruction. I begin this work with these images in mind:

> Overall what I wanted was to give musical structure in my personality to the communal elements that transcend any single place. Even though the form is definitely American, I wanted to open the interpretation up to all kinds of musical approaches. That's why the piece has the emotion of traveling and visiting many different kinds of services from the tightly refined all the way to the backwoods, way down the country. *In this house* moves from the feeling of the black American church to the study of Bach chorales, even the feeling of ritual in ancient religious forms and the sound one hears when in Middle Eastern countries. By using the blues as a fundamental element, I was able to ground the music in our culture while stretching it onto an international plane. But that's natural to jazz because it builds upon the blues and swing. (Liner notes: *In this House, On this Morning,* 1994)

My normative and aesthetic goals are to provide a cultural space for hope and optimism. I ground these attitudes, not in romanticism, but rather in the lived culture of marginal students and their self-representation of their hybrid identities and new subjectivity.

Series Preface

Books in this series, *Understanding Education and Policy*, will present a variety of perspectives to better understand the aims, practices, content and contexts of schooling, and the meaning of these analyses for educational policy. Our primary intent is to redirect the language used, the voices included in the conversation, and the range of issues addressed in the current debate concerning schools and policy. In doing this, books in the series will explore the differential conceptions and experiences that surface when analysis includes racial, class, gender, ethnic and other key differences. Such a perspective will span the social sciences (anthropology, history, philosophy, psychology, sociology etc.), and research paradigms.

Books in the series will be grounded in the contextualized lives of the major actors in school (students, teachers, administrators, parents, policy makers etc.) and address major theoretical issues. The challenge to authors is to fully explore life-in-schools, through the multiple lenses of various actors and with the anticipation that such a range of empirically sound and theoretically challenging work will contribute to a fundamental and needed rethinking of the content, process and context for school reform.

In this book Louis Mirón closely examines the context and substance of the reform of urban schools. Such reform is an attack on both citizens and educators in America's cities. His critique of the forces driving urban educational reform is central to the developing understanding of how reform has failed to serve children in urban schools even as it advances entrepreneurial corporate interests. We welcome this contribution to our series, *Understanding Education and Policy*.

Acknowledgments

This work has been a personal journey on several levels. I have enjoyed extraordinary support from many colleagues across the country, most especially George Noblit who was enthusiastic early on during the conceptualization of the project. As editor, George read the very rough first drafts and gave me much needed constructive criticism and feedback.

Early on my friend and colleague, Micky Lauria, kept a vigilant critical and skeptical eye on my moves into postmodernism. Spencer Maxcy wrote detailed comments on Chapter Four and encouraged my investigation into the multiple discourse locating identity. Michael P. Smith provided helpful comments on the possibilities of ethnic identity in the cities and in inner city schools. Gary Anderson of the University of New Mexico read early drafts of Chapters Two and Four. Over coffee in Albuquerque he and Patricia Irvine offered valuable suggestions on formulating empirical support for my theoretical work. Mike Apple and his students in the "Friday Seminar" at the University at Wisconsin stimulated my thinking on Identity Politics.

To my former colleagues at the University of New Orleans—Ira Bogotch, Alison Griffith, Ed St. John, Dick Elliott, Alma Young, Joe Logsdon, Mackie Blanton, Wilma Longstreet, Peggy Kirby and Bob Wimpelberg—I owe gratitude for long conversations. To my former doctoral students there (now colleagues), especially Vince Anfara and Joe Murry, Jim Garvin, Louise Olsen, and Leeta Haynes, I appreciate the chance to test my ideas in my course on power and politics in education. To Gail Lazard I am indebted for assisting in the interviews in Chapter Five. To my new colleagues at UC Irvine—Hank Becker, Dennis Evans, Alan Hoffer, Gil Gonzalez, Kathy Nakagawa, Mary Roosevelt, and Myron Simon, I appreciate the welcoming environment where I could complete this book. I want to thank Nancy Freedom for a thorough indexing of my book.

Finally, I owe my greatest thanks to three most important women in my life, Rose Ann, Devi, and Annalisa. They encouraged me through some difficult times during the life of the project. Without their active help and support, I would not have completed this book.

About the Author

Louis F. Mirón is Associate Professor of Educational Leadership and Director of the doctoral program in educational administration at the University of California at Irvine. He has published widely on the politics of urban school reform and has been active in Louisiana and California, advocating on behalf of teachers, students, and parents for local policies to empower local school communities. His new book, *Resisting Discrimination: Affirmative Strategies for Principals and Teachers*, will be published in Fall 1996.

Chapter 1

Understanding the Forms of the Current Crisis

There is little doubt that urban schooling is in crisis. Exactly what constitutes the nature of this crisis, however, is very much open to question. For practitioners, parents' groups, business and industry leaders, school reform advocates, and others, the crisis is one of the failures of governing bodies. Citizens perceive a lack of oversight of public education that best serves the interest of children and helps safeguard national economic security. This crisis of legitimacy (Smith, 1980; Young, 1988) is evident in the policy arena and at the community level of grassroots organizing. For example, the anti-incumbency mood of the national electorate was in part responsible for the ousting of former President Bush and the ushering in of more than 100 new members to Congress and the subsequent election of a Republican majority in the House in 1994. Yet, I establish in this chapter that elite groups have socially constructed the crisis in urban schooling. Thus, any attempts to arrive at technical or scientific solutions are problematic.

This chapter attempts to deconstruct the social mythology of the crisis in urban schooling. It examines the processes of common sense that gloss over new significant educational and social challenges emerging from the reconstitution of student demographics in inner-city schools. This chapter argues that dominant groups have attempted to set the parameters of the discourse that defines the crisis. The prevailing discourses in urban schooling engulf two aims. First, these attempts conceal the contradictions of the movement to reform urban schooling for ethnic minorities, whom economic and social elites view as a drain on the U.S. economy. Second, these actions reassert social control over public education in the inner city (Popkewitz, 1991) by equating urban schooling with social, academic (and ultimately, economic) problems in inner-city schools.

Substituting *problems* for *urban* in educational discourse necessitates, therefore, solutions (or problem solving) among elite groups, especially when demographic studies report that, by the year 2000, minority students will comprise one third of student enrollment. These are the same minority students who also reportedly lack sufficient basic skills to qualify for entry-level positions in sectors such as the grocery, medical, and hotel industries.

THE PROBLEMATIC MEANING OF URBAN SCHOOLING

The Historically Rooted Meaning of Contemporary Urban Schooling

There exists three ideological patterns in the discourses surrounding the current view of inner-city schooling as spawning a host of problems that educational leaders, spurred by social and economic elites, feel they must eliminate by the end of the century. These are the patterns of positivism (1965-1980), the conservative restoration between 1980 and the present (Apple, 1988b), and, finally, both the possibilities and the limits of the new social space of ethnic identity of the emerging postmodern climate. The obstacles alluded to here range from the perceived low educational productivity of so-called at-risk students to making inner-city schools safe from rampant crime and poor discipline. Following Popkewitz (1991), my intent here is to establish that the concept of *urban*, like the term *reform*, has no inherent definition or meaning. Its meaning is derived from its social context and is inextricably bound to dominant social and power relations, especially to the political uses of knowledge (Popkewitz, 1991) and official knowledge (Apple, 1993).

In general, I show here that, for ideological reasons, a loosely organized group I call the "Entrepreneurial Coalition" in major U.S. cities has succeeded in equating the social problems in the inner city with urban schooling. Briefly, I assert that this group constitutes a new social movement that has sought to build consensus in urban centers across America to reconstruct public education (Apple, 1993; Cuban, 1994; Gramsci, 1971). During the reform decade of the 1980s, a somewhat remarkable consensus emerged nationally among economic, social, political, educational, and governmental elites. Sparked by the publication in 1983 of *A Nation at Risk*, these elites produce a consensus that embraces the following two dimensions: (a) the United States had lost its economic dominance to global competition from Germany and Japan; and (b) a major cause of this loss of preeminence was the poor showing of its public education system. In the cities, the Entrepreneurial Coalition embodied the values of enterprise—it sought to improve public education in the inner city within the discourses, ideologies, and practices of corporate America.

I argue, however, that a more appropriate understanding of urban schooling in an emerging postmodern climate is embedded in the social construction of racial-ethnic identity (not confined to the inner city). The social space opened up by the reconstitution of student demographics (Smith, personal communication, June 10, 1992) has, both theoretically and politically, seriously challenged the idea of a single American identity. The implications for big city schooling are profound.

During the Great Society years of the administration of Lyndon B. Johnson, congressional leaders within Johnson's Democratic Party, civil rights groups, the Southern Christian Leadership Council, and a host of other national and local community-based organizations lobbied Congress successfully to fund programs such as Head Start to ameliorate educational problems in the urban centers in America. To be sure, leaders within these groups, like today, widely perceived the presence of rampant educational problems in the inner city. However, the focus then was on the resolution of these problems through the application of social science principles, resulting in the implementation of educational programs for socially and culturally disadvantaged students that, when properly funded by an activist federal government, would lead to the resolution of a host of cognitive and social ills in the inner city. The focus on *action* I call the legacy of positivism (interestingly, as I demonstrate in Chapter 2, the historical evidence does not point to the *economic* necessity of providing funding for such programs as Head Start; rather, the congressional leaders of the Great Society focused on the need to ameliorate widely perceived *social* ills in the inner city).

What remains are intended and unintended consequences of massive federal intervention of specially designed educational programs such as Head Start and Chapter One (then "Title One"). Researchers from both conservative and liberal political stripes have exhaustively documented the thorny implementation problems associated with federal mandating of educational solutions, which, themselves, were dependent on the willing cooperation of local teachers, principals, and boards of education in the inner city. For example, the unintended but clearly harmful effect of "pullout" remedial programs, a widespread strategy found in the federal Chapter One program through the early 1990s, caused students served by this program to lag further and further behind their academically better prepared counterparts enrolled in regular instruction (Levin, 1988). The continuation of federal intervention (action), although certainly well intended and based on matters of philosophical principles alone, justified creating a legacy of positivist problem solving. This legacy ignored the structural constraints inherent in any intervention strategy, especially a "top down" one, and ushered in a socially constructed vision of urban schooling. Both social scientists and the professionals defined social problems as real and relied on statistical evidence as measures of genuine success or failure to address these problems. The institutional holdover from federal and local educational policy and practice manifests itself today as society grapples with the latest reform— decentralization (Hannaway & Carnoy, 1993). For example, school-based management purports to provide school level personnel with greater decision-making authority in the hopes of improving instructional and other services to all children, although in city schools the financial resources are not sufficient to provide for the needs of poor and minority students (Kozol, 1991).

The conservative restoration of the 1980s and 1990s greatly succeeded in changing the parameters of the discourses of urban schooling from government action (read: increased federal funding) to a government and private sector partnership (Miron, 1992; Miron & Wimpelberg, 1989). Elites from both the private and public sectors, and within teachers' unions such as the American Federation of Teachers, supported the strategies of school-business partnerships, which were designed in part to garner private resources. School personnel deemed that additional funding could address the needs of inner-city schools during the 1980s recession. These partnerships also provided national *ideological* support for increasing business involvement in public schooling, especially in problem inner-city schools, whose students were reported to continuously lag behind their counterparts in the advanced industrialized nations of Japan and Germany. The following statement from Thomas Kearns, then president of Xerox Corporation, was in response to the crisis. In 1987, Kearns bemoaned to the Economic Club of Detroit: "Business will have to force the agenda, or we'll have to make it our agenda." Kearns later went on to become Deputy Secretary of Education in the Bush Administration.

Although Kearns's view did not necessarily reflect the entire spectrum of business and industrial leaders' attitude toward educational reform, his statement does accurately represent the aggressive spirit of enterprise marking the development of many school-business partnerships in the era of conservative restoration (Miron & Wimpelberg, 1989; see also Miron, 1992). The quotation illustrates the extent to which corporate elites, in particular, and the private sector, in general, defined the goals of public education as instrumentally preparing young adults for jobs in the workplace. In large urban centers the aims of the conservative restoration were even more narrowly focused: Business and industrial leaders devised a plethora of organizational and "market" strategies (school choice) to bypass what they unanimously agreed was a recalcitrant central office and school bureaucracy—an obstacle that would both undermine the accumulation quest for new capital and add fuel to the growing legitimation crisis of federal, state, and local governments (Habermas, 1975; Smith, 1980).

Potentially, in this context, the private sector is not simply a partner with urban public schools; rather, its role is transformed to that of a major policy actor during the reform decade of the 1980s. This new institutional role furthers a broader trend within the polity and society—a reemergence of new forms of social regulation of inner-city schooling and the control of perceived behavioral "deviancy" (Moynihan, 1993). The common-sense view broadly conceptualized learning deficiencies as those sets of behaviors, including a short attention span and field dependent learning, characteristic of ethnic minorities currently populating the large urban school districts of Los Angeles, New York, Chicago, and New Orleans in large percentages. The behavioral differences are dramatic when compared to a previous majority White middle-class student body. Clearly, there exists inherent tensions between the altered student demographics of inner-city schools and a school culture bent on transmitting a romanticized homogeneous vision of American culture.

In the present postmodern climate of urban ethnicity, the demographic transformations rapidly occurring in large school districts throughout the country has opened up a new social space (Smith, 1992), which may, alternatively, foster a new ethnic identity among inner-city minority students or, depending on the victor of the cultural struggle, relocate the less deviant (Moynihan, 1993) of these students to private schools through choice programs or to magnet schools. Magnet schools often offer distinctive curricula such as specialized course offerings in math and science, ostensibly to serve the productivity and capital needs of a globally dependent U.S. economy. The choice among ethnically affirming school strategies in inner-city schools and ethnically denying acculturation maneuvers will not only theoretically shape the contours of this and future discourses over urban schooling. More consequentially, the constructed character of urban schooling will, in all probability, determine whether the vast majority of these "underclass" students (Wilson, 1987) will ever learn to channel their social deviancy (Moynihan, 1993) into more constructive patterns benefiting their local communities.

This new social space briefly alluded to here is significant because, as Giroux (1983), Apple (1992), and others argue, schools are about much more than the technical features of instruction. Situated within two spheres—the administrative/political realm of the state apparatus and the cultural arena of the production and reproduction of knowledge—schools can transform their overly technical practices to sites of democratic praxis (Maxcy, 1991). In the inner city, the form of the quest for democracy is substantially shaped by students' confrontation with ethnicity and their own struggle to resist the representations of their personal identities that the mainstream school culture works to transmit (see Chapter 5; see also Everhart, 1983; Willis, 1977). While searching for ways to express their own identities in the cultural and ethnic kaleidoscope within the social context of urban ethnicity, my analysis of the qualitative data illustrates how African-American and other ethnic minority students resist, mediate, and at times politically transform school and family pressures to assume an assimilated, "modern" (economically functional) identity. I bring these struggles to life through a qualitative study that documents the political clashes between the dominant culture of the school and student ethnicity in two urban high schools (see Chapter 5).

DECONSTRUCTING THE GOVERNANCE CRISIS

The Reemergence of Social Regulation

In the 1980s this nation became a formal interdependent member of the global economy. Elite groups in the corporate, governmental, and education sectors became acutely aware of the loss of economic competitiveness among U.S. workers. These groups—the Business Roundtable, the National Commission on Excellence in Education, the Committee for Economic Development (whose members comprise the Entrepreneurial Coalition)—sought to improve the performance of the nation's public schools through a combination of market approaches and investment in human capital. Although virtually no one within these reform bodies believed that schools were *solely* responsible for the poor achievement levels of U.S. students compared to students in the advanced industrialized nations of Japan and West Germany, most agreed that worker productivity (hence, national economic competitiveness) would increase with better schools. There existed policy disagreements as to how to achieve this goal, whether through more funding, market incentives, or social regulation. Apparently, few elites who carried the reform banner were concerned with the global economic restructuring that was adversely affecting urban centers in America (Fainstein & Fainstein, 1983; Smith & Judd, 1983; Wilson, 1987). Thus, although few leaders of the reform movement of the 1980s blamed the schools entirely for the loss of the U. S. economic position, looking inward to poor business management policies and, deeper, within the logic of the global economic structure itself was neither ideologically nor practically feasible within the corporate community.

Schools in general are stubbornly resistant to change (Fullan, 1990; Sarason, 1982, 1990) and the worsening conditions in inner-city schools in particular during the decade of educational reform largely prevented significant education outputs desired by elite groups from materializing (Boyd, 1989; Levin, 1988; Maeroff, 1988; Miron, 1991; Miron & St. John, 1994). For example, some urban school districts such as the mammoth New York City system consistently maintained a 50% high school graduation rate or lower (Levin, 1987). Even when local school boards hire reform-minded superintendents, such as former New York City School Chancellor Joseph Fernandez, to improve performance levels, the potential benefits to ethnic minority students and other disenfranchised students (AIDS victims) pose apparently unacceptable risks to the status quo. The conservative restoration (Apple, 1988b) galvanized substantial ideological pressures to substitute market incentives (Chubb & Moe, 1990) in place of increased funding for public schools and forged a consensus among corporate and political elites alike to redefine urban school governance through the seizing of control from local school boards. School boards were widely perceived as corrupt, incompetent, and only interested in their future political and financial aggrandizement (Finn, 1992; Miron & Wimpelberg, 1992; Rand Report, 1992). With the cooperation of school officials, parents groups, and the news media (see Miron & Brooks, 1993), the consensus among dominant groups was cemented at the grassroots level and at the level of public opinion.

This focus on the reformation of urban school governance is primarily rhetorical (Cherryholmes, 1988). However, the effects on institutional arrangements, such as the election of community boards in Chicago (Wong, 1992) and the historically significant parents' movement to elect a new school board in New Orleans (see Miron & Brooks, 1993), marks the emergence of new forms of social control (Popkewitz, 1991) that regulate not only the policy outcomes of governing bodies. Such forms of social control, newly legitimized through public institutions attached to the state, also substantially regulate and control deviant student behavior and shape the discourse over urban schooling to satisfy the social and economic interests of elite groups concerned about the decline of U. S. economic competitiveness and dominance in the global marketplace.

Governance Reform as Common Sense

Faced with the prospects of despair over the nation's economic performance, as well as the failures of corporate management to mitigate global economic restructuring and the attendant deterioration of central cities social structure (Wilson, 1987, 1992), where can national and local policy actors make the most immediate impact over the intractable problems in inner-city schools? Given the ideological consensus among corporate elites and parent activists alike on the failures of urban school governance (Osborne & Gaebler, 1992), common sense dictates that changes in governance—defined as replacement or abolition of school boards, adoption of forms of school-based management, and decentralization of large urban school districts (Hill & Bonan, 1991) and school choice—are the most appropriate places to begin. Local elections of school board members usually produce little interest among the electorate as compared to, say, the national presidential elections. However, as witnessed recently in New Orleans, where a reportedly 70% of voters turned out to choose among a slate of reform candidates endorsed by a citizens' committee consisting of mainly parents (the Excellence in Education Committee), school board elections can serve as powerful forums for venting frustration. In addition, the traditions of democracy can be seemingly preserved if citizens, however rarely, are successful at ousting long-standing incumbents such as urban school board members. The chief idea is that citizens can exercise their constitutional rights and, if successfully mobilized, vote unacceptable urban school board members out of office and usher in new governing boards of education. This movement constitutes reform as Popkewitz (1991) conceptualizes it "as an ecological phenomenon" that ignores the history of reform and takes as its rhetoric the definition of change. The "common sense" of reform is to assume that intervention is progress: "A better world to evolve as the result of new programs, new technologies, and new organizations that increase efficiency, economy, and effectiveness" (p. 1).

Electing new school board members, as well as making an impact on establishing new governance arrangements (the local school councils in Chicago: see Lewis & Nakagawa, 1995; Wong, 1992), thus constitutes meaningful educational change for heretofore locked-out consumers such as parents and neighborhood associations and, more significantly, offers symbolic political and cultural "progress." Although there can be for now only cautionary optimism, as results on student achievement and the like will not be available in some cases until at least four years when the newly configured school boards complete their first terms in office in cities like New Orleans and Atlanta, the common-sense view is that coalitions of dominant social and economic groups and ordinary citizens have achieved educational improvement, however incremental and developmental, in the urban milieu. This meliorative view of progress is clearly appealing to the members of the Entrepreneurial Coalition, who believe that inner-city public schools are decidedly inferior to suburban public and private schools, in general, and are marked by rampant use of "drugs and constant fear of violence and disruptive youngsters, who are yelling and screaming and taking so much of the teachers' time that not much education is going on" (Shanker, 1992, p. 23).

The Contradictions of Governance Reform

It is clear that the apparent consensus among dominant and subordinate groups to change educational governance in cities carries an assumption that urban schools will change for the better. What is more difficult to uncover are the sets of institutional processes and discursive practices that give rise to curriculum forms, administrative systems, and governance practices that help maintain the status quo in the face of constant reform activity. Here, Apple's (1988b) work on the noninstructional purposes of schooling in advanced capitalist economies and Giroux's (1983) notion of cultural reproduction and resistance are informative.

The Noninstructional Purposes of Schools

Michael Apple's (1985, 1988b) work on the connections among schooling, the state, the economy, and cultural forms is helpful in understanding the contradictions embedded in the reform of urban school governance. For Apple, the common-sense perspective is such that schools are a neutral arena for both problem solving and amelioration for students seeking to become upwardly mobile. However, critical scholarship and urban school ethnography have both demonstrated that school practices are not neutral; rather, they are inherently political, the outcomes of which are unevenly bestowed rewards according to class, gender, race, and ethnic classifications (Anderson, 1992; Oakes, 1985; Pinar & Bowers, 1992). Schooling, in other words, largely helps shape who gets ahead and who does not in the already biased contest for economic and social advantage (Bowles & Gintis, 1976; Jencks, 1972). The effects of this patterned (Apple, 1985) unequal distribution of school benefits as a result of, for example, widespread tracking (Oakes, 1985) practices are particularly acute in inner-city schools. Obviously my intent here is not to recite a litany of the grim statistics documenting socially unacceptable school performance measures in inner-city schools. The goal of improving inner-city schools' academic performance through the reform of urban school boards is problematic at best because of these historically unequal power relations that may undermine *any* reform activity, especially one that aims at improvements at the top of the school hierarchy and ignores the schools' internal sorting, tracking, and grouping practices and, concomitantly, imports middle-class values on socially disconnected populations (see Miron & St. John, 1994).

Henry Levin's (1987) extensive research on the effects of remedial education for economically and socially disadvantaged students has established that such students (who are disproportionately ethnic minority and poor) frequently begin school behind their peers as measured by standardized test scores. Worse, on the same measures of student academic achievement as indicated by the California Achievement Test (CAT), disadvantaged students (increasingly at risk of academic failure or leaving school altogether) continue to fall further and further behind their culturally mainstreamed peers. At the end of eighth grade, they have on the average lost two years of achievement gains, and by the end of high school, four years. Moreover, the worsening fiscal and social conditions in inner-city schools (Kozol, 1991; Lemann, 1991) make it unlikely that gains desired by both the corporate and educational communities will materialize.

It is within this broader context of the political economy of urban schooling that the contradictory needs of the state for legitimation and accumulation (Apple, 1985; Smith, 1980) can be ideologically supported by the reforms of and interventions in the governance of urban schools and school districts (see Marcuse, 1981). Apple (1985) characterizes these noninstructional functions as *legitimation*, *accumulation*, and *production*. The ideological support of these functions in urban settings, thus, help serve the long-term interest of the political economy of the state and "local state" (Smith, 1980).

Legitimation

Schools assist in furthering the widespread beliefs and practices of dominant social groups in the classroom. Because the state contradictorily serves both an accumulation function and a legitimation function (Smith, 1980), public schools as sites of cultural contestation help engage their students in the struggle over what constitutes acceptable knowledge to sectors within the state and the economy. For example, the idea that abstract math is no longer practical for an expanding information economy is now debated in school curriculum committees, despite the poor performances of inner-city and more privileged students on math achievement tests (Osborne, 1993). The struggle over what constitutes "official knowledge" (Apple, 1993) is in fact a contest fought in the realm of the cultural politics of the classroom and the school organization. That schools give legitimacy to certain selective groups, for example, the New Right (Apple, 1992), is doubtless. However, of equal potential is the possibilities of creating democratic practices in the classrooms through critical pedagogy (McLaren, 1989), critical pragmatism (Cherryholmes, 1988; Maxcy, 1991), or moral leadership (Foster, 1986; Miron, 1991).

Accumulation

Like owners of multinational corporations, schools accumulate needed technical and administrative know-how to assist the state in meeting its capital goals and needs. The conditions for recreating an unequally responsive economy are partly established in schools through the forms of the curriculum itself (problem solving for identified gifted and talented students, basic math skills for at-risk students). The interests of dominant social groups within the state and corporations within the private sector can be secured through governance interventions in urban schools and school districts that make public administrative control over the curriculum feasible and private (New Right) regulation of curriculum standard institutional practice (Apple, 1988a, 1990).

Production

Finally, the production aims of schooling refer to the knowledge and ideologies that schools actually generate or reproduce. In the inner city, middle-class teachers of lower social-class students frequently seek to instill in their students the beliefs of hard work, discipline, respect for authority—all laudable values except when promises are made that employment lies "just around the corner" (see Apple, 1988b). Again, schools serve as the contested terrain of the hegemony of middle-class beliefs and attitudes about the workplace and about the correct way to behave and to live one's life. Schools do not mechanistically reproduce economic and cultural capital distribution unequally; rather, in the schools, as sites where knowledge is potentially generated, the curricula prepare students to assume their assigned stations in life and, simultaneously, challenge the arbitrariness of the social division of knowledge.

For example, the heads of Fortune 100 companies and small entrepreneurial businesses alike perceive that prerequisite job skills and attitudes are absent among students in the inner city. The common-sense logic described earlier makes reform of the governing configurations and practices a palatable, although greatly contradictory and contested, means of achieving social regulation of inner-city schools—and the diverse students they seek to educate. At the same time, ethnographic research conducted in inner-city and working-class schools (Willis, 1977) illustrates how human agency and the schools' informal culture works to reproduce class and social inequality (see Anderson, 1992) and to resist dominant school ideologies (see Chapter 5).

In this volume, I emphasize the *contested character* of the reemergence of social control over inner-city schooling and students and examine in further detail the contextually constructed realities of urban schooling as a contested arena of cultural/identity politics (see Chapter 5) generally, and specifically, the social space of ethnic identity. To do less is to succumb to the oversimplified theorizing of structural functionalism, which critical scholarship over the past 20 years has sought to overcome (Pinar & Bowers, 1992). Critical theorists would, therefore, miss the intellectual opportunities availed to them from postmodern and poststructural work because schools would (in an overly rational mode) mechanically meet the instrumental needs of the capitalist state (see Milliband, 1969).

THE CULTURAL POLITICS OF INNER-CITY SCHOOLING

I pursue in greater detail this issue of the "contested character" of the social regulation of inner city schooling. As critical scholarship has painstakingly established, schools are not simply neutral arenas for the dispensing of the technical function of teaching and learning. Indeed, schools, as Giroux's (1983) and Apple's (1985, 1990, 1992) work informs us, are culturally contested arenas that serve as host sites for struggles over the forms of legitimate knowledge, the production and reproduction of dominant values, and the definition of socially acceptable behavior and discipline. Within the newly contextualized terrain of ethnic identity, in particular, these issues dramatically unfold at the intersection of two stages: the global political economy (see Wallerstein, 1980) and the cultural struggles of inner-city schools and classrooms. To explore these heightened tensions, the book draws on the theoretical assumptions embedded in Poulantzas's (1978) notion of the "relative autonomy" of the state, city, and, as I analyze later, city schools.

The Relative Autonomy of Inner-City Schools

As vulnerable as inner-city schools might be to the ascendancy of conservative forces and coalitions of reform-minded citizen groups, they do not mechanically act as instruments of a capitalist state or passive enclaves of imposed knowledge, ideology culture, or technology (Althusser, cited in Giroux, 1983; Glucksman, 1982). Put simply, like all cultural and state institutions of advanced capitalist economies, schools vary in their reproductive, mediative, or transformative roles. However, because they are institutionally separate from the economic sphere (Poulantzas, 1978), school personnel and students can act generally within a degree of relative autonomy (Apple, 1985). Specifically, inner-city schools produce forms of differentiated knowledge that contribute to social and economic inequality as a consequence of large urban centers' restructured position in the global economy (Fainstein, 1983; Smith & Keller, 1983). They also, through much conflict and struggle, produce knowledge that *may* improve the life chances of inner-city students by validating the knowledge and lived cultural experience students bring to the school and classroom, thereby redefining student success (Haynes, 1993). Furthermore, inner-city schools (like other social institutions that enjoy a relative amount of organizational autonomy) may engage in democratic processes such as student representation in school governance and discipline proceedings. These possibilities for political and civic renewal (Glickman, 1993) hold especially profound implications in the urban context because the tensions between the global and the local are especially acute and the well-known effects of these tensions so potentially significant for students, families, and their communities. My point here is this: Despite the intractable social and economic ills besetting inner-city schools, and the unlikelihood that job prospects will improve for families—and future generations of children enrolled in them

(Garvin, 1994)—these schools have the capacity to mediate hegemonic practices of dominant groups and the possibility of transformation through critical pedagogy and student/community empowerment always looms in the backdrop of the cultural/ethnic politics of the urban school.

The Milieu of Urban Ethnic Politics

Large urban school districts possess two distinguishing characteristics that enable schools situated in the inner city to pursue political struggle in its hallways, administrative offices, and classrooms, almost unabated. These characteristics are: *decentralization* and *bureaucratic isolation* (Wong, 1992). Schools in the urban landscape vary widely in their degree of governing arrangements, parental involvement, and, of course, funding. However, precisely because the large school districts in urban centers in America vary widely among these dimensions, it is virtually impossible to impose neat organizational order to control schools administratively (Weick, 1976). On the surface, decentralization appears to hinder inner-city schools in their attempts to gain attention and support from the central office and from affluent parent and corporate groups. However, in practice, as parents and community groups in cities like Milwaukee, Chicago, New Orleans, Miami, and New York have come to realize, the "benign neglect" (Smith & Keller, 1983) distressed city schools have endured dialectically enables these schools and their school communities to engage in political struggle that mediates the need to receive institutional nurturing in the first place. In particular, the ethnic conflict that seems to engulf so many large urban school districts, such as the Los Angeles Unified School District, embrace new forms of unofficial knowledge and ethnic expression for which the schools can potentially provide legitimacy.

Bureaucratic isolation inside the large district organization shields historically abandoned inner-city schools from close monitoring, traditionally associated only with rural public schools and private schools. I assert that the deskilling of teaching (Apple, 1992), a by-product of technical control over teachers and their curriculum, is in practice and in theory virtually impossible to sustain on a day-to-day basis in the classroom. Although social reproduction exists, teachers and students resist. The curriculum cannot be so neatly aligned, for example, so as to eradicate the desires of teachers, principals, and parents to care for their students and children. Occasionally it is impossible. In

16   Chapter One

New Orleans, as in other cities, the abysmally low funding for textbooks and student supplies, coupled with an apparently out-of-control bureaucracy that literally locks up student texts in understaffed warehouses, makes a mockery of efforts to closely monitor the implementation of the "expected learning outcomes" of the district's curriculum and the standards set by state and local school boards, and would thwart even a national curriculum currently advocated by national business and teachers' union leaders alike (see Goals 2000, 1994; Ravitch, 1995).

This new social space of ethnic identity, which I develop relationally and ethnographically in subsequent chapters, potentially gives rise to liberating practices such as the multiethnic curriculum development in New Orleans, the "African American Infusion Program," bilingual community education in Milwaukee, and the development of community councils in Chicago. Of course, it is important to avoid the trap of romanticizing the actual worsening conditions of the inner-city school and conclude that these will simply all disappear under the cultural storm of postmodernism or liberating qualities of poststructuralism. The struggle over ethnic identity has only recently commenced. The outcome is uncertain. As we know from the research on school restructuring in the urban context (see Boyd, 1989; Miron & St. John, 1994) school and community change is never simple. To avoid the "discourse of despair" (Giroux, cited in Pinar & Bowers, 1992, p. 69), the normative focus of this project lies in the realm of possibility. Only qualitative analysis of the lived culture and experience of students in urban communities currently experiencing restructuring can ascertain whether the theoretical expectations of "what this all means" for schools and their students can shed ultimate light on whether our speculations are based on romanticism or genuine hope.

THE SOCIAL REALITY OF THE URBAN SCHOOL CRISIS

No one denies that problems exist in inner-city schools. There is an abundance of statistical evidence documenting the high percentage of high school dropouts, inordinate suspensions of Blacks as a percentage of total district enrollment, schools in which violence appears rampant, and so on. We need not recant these data here. What needs to be unpacked, however, and empirically demonstrated is the extent to which the *proportionally* small amount of social and educational problems in urban versus suburban milieus—which are largely confined to *inner, central city-*located schools and neighborhoods attached to public housing developments (Kozol, 1991; Lemann, 1991; Wilson, 1987)—is now taken for the common-sense understanding of the failures and misery of all (or most) urban schools. This is what I define as "the social construction of urban schooling." In the remainder of this chapter, I sketch the intellectual roots of this approach in Berger and Luckmann's (1966) seminal treatise on the sociology of knowledge, *The Social Construction of Reality* and, in Chapter 2, develop the theoretical framework from a critical /postmodern sociology of knowledge (see Noblit & Pink, 1995) based on the work of Thomas Popkewitz, Michael Apple, and others to establish the ultimate project of this text: situating and interpreting the crisis of inner-city schooling at the nexus of the relationships between the global political economy and the emerging social space of ethnic identity.

Constructing Social Reality

The ordinary view of many individuals is that ideas are "real." That some problems exist in the inner city translates uncritically for many publics as: *Most urban schools have failed their students.* In a nutshell, this illustration represents the concept of socially constructed reality. Berger and Luckmann's (1966) theoretical project on the sociology of knowledge concerns the processes and institutional contexts in which this construction actually happens in the larger society. By "reality," these authors refer to that which occurs outside the will of human beings or, put differently, "independent of their own volition" (p. 2). "Knowledge" thus consists of the positive purporting—the certainty of that phenomena—as real, possessing discernible characteristics. An example is now called for.

It is customary in New Orleans, as it is in other large cities, for parents to "camp out" at magnet schools, for reasons of academic reputation as well as distinctive course offerings (Eason, 1992), during periods of open registration. Enrollment at these schools is selective according to diverse criteria (test scores, special talents such as performing arts or math and science aptitude, and racial quotas). There is keen competition for available slots among parents. Local newscasts give prominent coverage of what has become a yearly ritual and tradition—sleeping overnight (or longer) on school grounds in the company of hundreds of other parents seeking admission for their children in the socially coveted slots. Significantly, the media cover only a handful of public magnet schools (in New Orleans, there are typically three elementary schools). The social reality, therefore, is illustrated in the following comments I have paraphrased from a parent recently interviewed on camera in February 1993: "Of course, we (other parents) don't mind the waiting. We all know that there are only a few good public schools remaining in the city." Put plainly, public perception—social construction fueled by broadcast media coverage—has become social reality (Waters, 1994).

Ideology and Social Reality

A central interest of the project of the sociology of knowledge is the concern with ideology. Berger and Luckmann built on Mannheim's (1936) classification of three types of ideology—the particular, the total, and the general concepts of ideology. Mannheim's typology of ideological thinking embraces ideology as constituting a segment, the whole of an opponent's thought, and characteristic not only of an opponent's thought, but of one's own thought as well. At the general level, Berger and Luckmann argue that the level of the sociology of knowledge is reached—the understanding that no human thought is immune to the ideological influences of its social context. Furthermore, Mannheim's theory removed ideology from its previous strictly political sense as "false consciousness," theoretically situating the concept as a problem of epistemology and historical sociology.

Similarly, in this work I am advancing the theoretical question of what general society knows and how it decides what constitutes authentic knowledge. What characterizes the lived cultural experience of producers and consumers of knowledge, generated socially? I refer, then, not only to the abstract sphere of ideas, but to the postmodern everyday practices of "common sense," embodied in the widely held perception noted earlier that large urban school districts contain only a handful of good schools (in the previous example, three magnet elementary schools). For example, what are the everyday experiences and perceptions of parents, students, teachers, and principals of magnet urban schools, and how do they contrast with more traditional neighborhood (that is, the majority of ethnic and underachieving students) schools?

I contend that the sociological analysis of common-sense knowledge is a study of that knowledge that serves as a guide to the strategic conduct of everyday living. Therefore, the social world is analogous to the natural (biochemical) world in that both are epistemologically ensconced as "givens," confronting the lived cultural experience of individuals who uncritically embody this reality and knowledge. Such an uncritical acquiescence of both the historical architecture (Foucault, 1972) and the ideological engineering of socially constructed reality has obviously devastating consequences in the inner city. Scoring below the international average on standardized achievement tests passes off as real failure for many students of poverty. Being "wrapped too tight" (Fine, 1991), many of these ethnic minority underachieving students either drop out or, more pervasively, simply get pushed out of inner-city high schools. The social perception becomes sociologically self-fulfilling phenomena! In the more abstractly sophisticated vernacular of critical theory, mainstream society reproduces official cultural forms through the production of ideas.

In the words of Berger and Luckmann (1966):

> It is important to keep in mind that the objectivity of the institutional world, however, massive it may be, appears to the individual as a humanly produced *constructed objectivity*. The process by which the externalized products of human activity attain the character of objectivity [we term] objectivation. The institutional world is objectivated human activity, and so is every single institution . . . , despite the objectivity that marks the social world in human experience, it does not thereby acquire an ontological status apart from the human activity that produced it. The paradox [is] that man is capable of producing a world that he then *experiences* as something other than a human product. . . . It is important to emphasize that the relationship between man, the producer, and the social world, his product, is, and remains, a dialectical one. That is, man . . . and the social world interact with each other. *The product acts back* upon the *producer* [and] the producer can transform the product. (pp. 61-62; emphasis in the original)

The Legitimation of Ideas

These institutional processes demand societal acceptance. Because social institutions (hence, social reality) are historical products of human agency, powerful social groups periodically seek to justify their existence and explain the necessity of maintaining support for their continuation. This involves the process of legitimation, that "activity concerned with the establishment and defense of patterns of belief" (McLure & Fisher, cited in Apple, 1990, p. 7). Legitimation processes are socially organized and originate from the historical patterns of group action that may range from a narrow utilitarian need to defend their social, economic, and political interest to the protection and reinvention of general patterns of ideas defining comprehensive worldviews, outlooks, or what Berger and Luckmann called "symbolic universes" (Apple, 1990, p. 20). In Chapter 3, I analyze the political and civic activities of the Entrepreneurial Coalition with regard to the legitimation work cited earlier.

At the general level of symbolic meaning, nothing less than the survival of social groups who have historically given rise to institutional life in support of their own dominance is at stake. However, the means by which survival is maintained and dominance recaptured is problematic. Hegemony, thus, is never a certainty. It is a process by which dominant groups gain ascendancy primarily by providing moral and intellectual leadership (Gramsci, 1971). Dominant groups provide such leadership to those interests who compete for hegemony and to subordinate groups who cooperate in their own domination (Everhart, 1983; Willis, 1977). Such universal acceptance at the general level of ideology marks the completion of the legitimation process and the beginning of hegemonic practices. In institutional life these discursive practices demand reinvention. During the current crisis in urban schooling, they take the form of social and academic problems and a seemingly obsessive focus on altering governance arrangements and "reinventing" schooling (Osborne, 1993).

THE MEASURES OF CONSTRUCTED REALITY IN URBAN SCHOOLS

Most writing on urban schooling has assumed a social problem perspective (see Davis & McCaul, 1991; Freedman, 1990). The empirical issues associated with urban (inner-city) schooling such as student underachievement, high school dropout rates, and teen pregnancy have been the focus of much research and scholarship. Both liberals and New Right conservatives recite similar laundry lists of abysmal statistics throughout the country.

What purposes do these interminable incantations fundamentally serve? Messages of hope they do not convey. Clarion calls for reform usually fall on deaf ears as local school boards and their chief executives are ideologically prone to either defend actions already taken as purported remedies or to cite money as reasons not to embark on new actions (First & Miron, 1991; First & Walberg, 1992). Although there is some truth to both of these responses, they mask the practical effect of substituting unrealistic remedies for (largely constructed) measures of student academic failures. Finally, at the levels of school culture and student culture, these data have lost their meaning except to reinforce negative self-images of the students identified as having failed "to measure up."

That the empirical data are socially constructed remains hidden from most casual observers. Indeed, across the spectrum of ideological postures, the socially architectured reality is, at both a universal level and psychological level, construed for reality. The numbers do not lie. However, the process of situating the endless (increasingly nauseating) recitation of the academic and social problems at the nexus of the global economic and legitimation crisis and the cultural struggle for ethnicity unearths the hidden purposes. The global crisis exports (or more technologically voguish) "downloads" these global crises to the city, specifically to the distressed inner-city schools. These schools may (or may not) impassively "receive" the crisis. I repeatedly stress that it is not without struggle. Situated at a historical kairo of the new social space of postmodern ethnicity (Smith, 1992), cultural forms of resistance such as "rappin' and cappin'" (Dashner, 1992), Black on Black crime, and cocaine trafficking are labeled "new deviance" (Moynihan, 1993). More hopefully, the actions can be interpreted as forms of cultural/identity politics embedded in students' search for their own ethnic identity.

The sets of social relationships, as well as the interactions between macro and micro forces, are dialectical in character (Miron, 1992). Just as the hegemony of dominant social groups is never a guaranteed outcome of historically significant ideological clashes, so does a romantic picture of life in inner city schools remain an abstraction. In one sense, the statistics may not "lie"; however, the conditions of neglected inner-city schools, as Kozol has recently chronicled, have deteriorated. Precisely forecasting the human outcome of downloading the crisis is problematic and presumptuous, understanding the complex sets of dialectical relationships and painting the picture of the struggle for ethnic identity more realistic, and ultimately more satisfying

My broad concern in this undertaking is to contribute to that significant, but limited, discourse, which seeks, as Michael Apple (1988b) describes, to "combine a structuralist focus on the objective conditions within a social formation and the culturalist insistence on seeing those conditions as ongoingly built, and contested, in our daily lives" (p. 24). Apple's structuralist focus provides the theoretical and normative backdrop for this work. However, I intend to venture into the terrain of the postmodern challenge that questions the assumed rationality of material and social structures. Even within the tight reins of capitalistic logic, structuralist relations are, nonetheless, abstract ones. Structuralism, as an intellectual treatise, is often ahistorical; at times, a dangerously self-fulfilling prophesy. For me, the struggle for human agency remains paramount, and a theory of praxis/action remains the intellectual challenge that postmodernism offers theorists and practitioners alike.

PLAN OF THE BOOK

I take up these theoretical tensions in substantial detail in Chapter 2. In it I move beyond Berger and Luckmann's seminal work outlined in this introductory chapter and rely substantially on Thomas Popkewitz's reinvigoration of the concept of social regulation to establish a theoretical framework for understanding the basis of the social construction of the crisis in urban schooling. Leaving the universal plane of symbolic meaning behind, my immediate focus in Chapter 2 is on the political/institutional processes currently in place to regulate the reconstitution of student ethnicity in inner-city schools. Also, in Chapter 2, I present an historical/ideological analysis of the social context of the concept of urban schooling, tracing the roots of the current crisis to the legacies of positivism of the Great Society and the "focus on action" (Giddens, 1974) through the conservative restoration of the 1980s (Apple, 1988b), culminating in contemporary postmodern conceptualizations of the new social space of ethnic identity (Smith, 1992).

My aim in pursuing this historically grounded ideological analysis of the social context of urban schooling is to establish that the current form of the crisis—the crisis of legitimacy of school governance —is socially constructed. Furthermore, the crisis in urban schooling is exacerbated owing to the social derivation of academic problems such as below par student achievement on national (and increasingly, international) standardized norm-referenced tests. In short, the technology of testing measurement, coupled with the indicators of achievement, to a large extent constructs an educational epidemic of sorts in schools located in inner-city neighborhoods and public housing developments (see Garvin, 1994).

In Chapter 3, I analyze the ideological roots of the current crisis and locate its origins in what I describe as the "ideological strategies of the entrepreneurial classes." Among others, these strategies include school choice (vouchers, magnet schools), state regulation and state takeover of statistically underachieving inner-city students and schools, shared (or self) governance, and school closures. Entrepreneurism and widespread economic and civic boosterism have staked out legitimacy claims in the neopopulist calls for the "reinvention of government" (Osborne & Gaebler, 1992), which echo from the Washington beltway to jam-packed chamber of commerce meetings and governmental steering committees (Osborne, 1993).

Although radical, critical scholarship in the tradition of the new sociology of education has contributed much to our theoretical understanding of the relationships between dominant ideologies and political ideological movements and unequal educational outcomes, only lately has a serious attempt to study these relationships commenced (see Apple, 1988b, 1993). In particular, how ideological processes and the formation of legitimate knowledge actually plays out in schools is not widely understood. I hope to lay out both a theoretical and practical understanding of the incorporation of dominant ideologies in curriculum, administrative, and disciplinary practices.

Chapter 4 embraces postmodernism and scholarly writing in urban ethnography to come to grips with the social space of ethnic identity (Marcus & Fischer, 1986; Smith, 1992). In this chapter I try to self-consciously avoid any innate tendencies to romanticize the embedded cultural formations of inner-city schooling. However, I intend to argue that it is precisely the new social space theorized by postmodernism and documented by urban ethnographers that makes ethnic formation conceptually and ethnic self-identity existentially a distinct possibility in the reconfiguration of inner-city schooling. The tone of this chapter, and indeed throughout the text, is decidedly hopeful and optimistic. Again, my intent is to ground this optimism not on a glorified view of what life in ghetto schools is like, but rather on one that links the possibilities emanating from postmodernism and poststructuralism with an insider's ethnographic perspective on the dialectic interactions between the lived culture of students and the reified experience of the culture of the school organization.

Chapter 5 presents my analysis of interview data from two ethnically diverse high schools. The goal of the qualitative analysis is to produce narratives of student life in inner-city schools, especially as such accounts highlight the struggle for ethnic identity within the cultural sphere of the school. This research takes the critical scholar both into the intellectual and political domains of what might loosely be termed the culture of marginality.

Secondary sources indicate that the dual themes of racial and social segregation pervade life in desegregated schools (Logsdon & DeVore, 1991; Miron & St. John, 1994) in the Deep South. In other regions, for example, the desert Southwest, the contours of ethnicity and the cultural struggles for racial-ethnic identity (Anaya, 1992) serve to heighten social, academic, and political tensions emanating from the global fiscal crisis (O'Connor, 1971). Paradoxically, these give rise to multiethnic/multicultural curriculum movements, which foster resistance and social reconstruction.

Chapter 6 concludes the project and offers a new vision of urban schooling, which is grounded in a historical understanding of the social contexts that previously defined the term. This new vision or image embraces a postmodern understanding of ethnic difference, moving the conversation away from a crisis (problems focus) to a community praxis that emphasizes freedom. Although not necessarily condemning rationality, the critique moves reason beyond utilitarian aims of amelioration to suggest an ongoing process of human development for ethnic minority (soon to be ethnic majority) students in large urban centers throughout the nation.

I term this perspective a *community development* view of urban schooling (Miron, 1995), one that defines the quest for good inner-city schools, however constituted, as embodying the goals and values of democratic communities dedicated to serving the mutual goals of freedom and social justice for all groups. This long path begins in Chapter 2, in which I come to grips with the constructed nature of urban schooling generally and with the forms of the current crisis in particular.

Chapter 2

The Social Context of Urban Schooling

As I argued in Chapter 1, the idea of "urban," like other socially derived concepts (e.g., reform) has no inherent meaning. The epistemological understanding of the term *urban* depends on the social context in the wider society. It is a socially constructed reality. In this chapter I analyze the historical development of the social context of the crisis in urban education.

Specifically, I examine three important "periods": the Great Society, the New Federalism, and the current postmodern climate. The first two periods I view conceptually as parallel, although ideologically dichotomous, domains of modernism (see later sections); the third, of course, I view as a paradigm shift to a "postmodern" social analysis. I do not intend for these periods to read as linear progressions or the accounts of individual presidents and their policies during the past 30 years. My purpose here is not to debate the pros and cons of the political philosophies of U. S. presidents or their administrations. Rather, I wish to demonstrate, through historical and policy analysis, that such political philosophies discursively translated into a set of coherent political ideologies and strategic choices, both of which provided the intellectual backdrop for the current crisis in urban schooling. They mark substantive contexts out of which federal policies, procedures, ideologies,and other processes shaped the social construction of urban schooling in this country.

My purpose in looking at these three periods is to demonstrate how the crisis in urban schooling is embedded in the historical ideologies and public policies of the past 30 years. To understand the fundamental nature of this crisis, thus, one has to understand the social context in which it is historically and politically embedded. I begin with the Great Society.

A CALL TO ACTION

The Significance of the Great Society

Just a few days after he was called by fate into the office of the presidency, following the assassination of President John F. Kennedy, Lyndon B. Johnson addressed a joint session of Congress. There, he laid bare the weight public education would carry in launching the ambitious social welfare program of the Great Society. Stressing the urgency of federal action to move the education agenda forward, he pleaded with Congress: "This is no time for delay. It is a time for action—strong forward-looking action in pending education bills to help bring the light of learning to every home and hamlet in America" (*Congressional Record*, 1963, pp. 22, 839).

Doubtlessly, the expansion of federal funding for public education during Johnson's term in office between 1964 and 1968 marks one of the most significant developments in the history of public education in the United States. This expansion was part and parcel of the expansion of the welfare state during the Johnson Administration. As such, to understand the nature of growth in federal education during this period and, by extension, the broader social and political contexts of the current crisis in city schooling, it is imperative to examine the educational policies, ideologies, and programs of the Great Society. Rulon (1981) captures the significance of the educational agenda of Johnson's Administration. The strategists of the architects of the Great Society "proposed to to use teaching and learning in addition to legislation to ensure equal justice, to provide equal opportunity, and to increase the gross national product so that a larger economic pie could be split by all, regardless of age, creed, or national origin" (p. xii).

At a commencement address at the University of Michigan, on May 22, 1964, President Johnson first publicly referred to the programs and ideological basis of his administration as the Great Society. Johnson clearly was bent on attacking the problems of poverty while using the built-in constituents of the poor and minority groups to shore up his political base. Moreover, it was the call to action in the form of federally funded education programs that were to be his vehicle. Ginzberg and Solow (1974) argue that the Johnson Administration set out to use the powers of the federal government "to speed changes on the domestic front that would help those who were encountering difficulties in taking care of themselves in the competitive arena" (p. 6). The historical record is clear on the issue of a call to federal action. This call would crystallize in the goals of improving education for the nation's poor. The push to sustain economic growth (then averaging approximately 6 % per year) would become the ideological incentive.

For example, on January 28, 1964, Johnson addressed the national Planning Committee of the Non-Partisan League. He emphasized the commitment of his administration to compassion for the downtrodden. Leaders from the White House, the Academy, and the Congress argued that only through a healthy economy could Johnson live up to the principles of the "Golden Rule." Improving public education throughout the country, but especially among the inner-city poor, would assume a central role (Rulon, 1981). Historically, the forging of a national consensus to nurture healthy economic growth for the benefit of all social groups would in turn foster ideological commitments to specific elite corporate groups in urban centers such as Cleveland and New Orleans (see Miron, 1992; Smith & Judd, 1983; Swanstrom, 1985). Johnson felt that it was the responsibility of the federal government to ensure that it removed the barriers to economic prosperity for all Americans. This would "give every American a life as rich and productive as his talents would allow" (quoted in Rulon, 1981, p. 201). As will be discussed later, economic growth would become the ideological cornerstone of both liberals and conservatives.

Of the three places where Johnson wanted to build the Great Society, two are relevant to our purposes—the cities and the classrooms (the other was in the countryside). Johnson felt that, much like today, the cities must be rebuilt in order to restore a great nation. However, his was a call to action by the public sector, whereas under the economic growth strategies of the New Right the cities were to be rebuilt through privatization. In education, during Johnson's term, the federal government's ideological call lay in activism: "Learning must offer an escape from poverty" ("President Johnson's design," 1965, p. 3).

THE IDEOLOGICAL AND ECONOMIC BASES FOR THE WAR ON POVERTY

A Calculated Risk

Widespread poverty, especially among ethnic minorities in the city, was not in the public consciousness in the early 1960s. To the contrary, the U. S. economy was in a state of rapid expansion, and most Americans' income levels climbed to the highest in history and unemployment remained at a politically acceptable level of 5% (Levitan, 1969). In a Cabinet meeting of July 2, 1964, President Johnson acknowledged the golden political opportunity (fueled by economic prosperity): "There is every likelihood that the economy will continue to move towards greater prosperity—from an economic standpoint we can afford to move boldly where new programs are called for" (quoted in Rulon, 1981, p. 213). Why would Johnson risk such a strong economic position and move to build a national consensus to attack poverty—through improvements in urban schooling—in the nation's cities?

Tyler (1974) argues that Johnson's Great Society campaign moved the American public to accept the harshness of the hidden problems of urban (and rural) poverty: "We were an affluent society, yet millions of Americans were in dire poverty, living in city or rural slums, without gainful employment" (p. 167). The American public recognized the paradox of rapid economic growth and increasing poverty. Also, through the Johnson campaign, the general public perceived poverty as a *social*, not a personal tragedy. The president therefore seized on the political opportunity to reward his minority constituency in the cities and to shore up his political base.

In 1963, Congress moved to place the issue of poverty before the public agenda. The chairman of the Council of Fiscal Advisors, Walter Heller, lead the charge. Having worked on this issue in the Kennedy Administration, Heller approached Johnson the day after Kennedy's assassination and convinced the new president to maintain the policy commitments of the prior administration. Politically, Heller was very successful as exemplified in Johnson's (1986) first *State of the Union Address* in which he stated that his administration "here and now declares unconditional war on poverty in America" (p. 114). Kantor's (1991) assertion makes clear the link between the improvement of public education and the goal of the elimination of poverty in the cities and rural communities: "The expansion of federal education policy in the 1960s was based on widely held assumptions about the role of the state in relation to the economy" (p. 51).

The Attacks on the Culture of Poverty Thesis

In 1961, anthropologist Oscar Lewis published *The Children of Sanchez*, in which he laid out his controversial culture of poverty thesis. Lewis made two fundamental points about the nature of poverty. First, a distinctive set of behaviors, attitudes, and personality traits marks poverty in various cultures. Second, these traits are intergenerationally transmitted. Thus, Lewis seemed to imply that the children of poor families could not escape this culture of poverty. These assertions proved highly controversial, and their attacks helped fuel a consensus, first within the confines of the Johnson Administration and second within the wider society that believed the federal government must eliminate poverty.

Lewis apparently took his thesis to the extreme of cultural determinism. He asserted that poverty had noneconomic factors and therefore could not be eliminated solely by income redistribution. Only through a social movement that organized the poor and that fostered "solidarity and a sense of identity with larger groups" would poverty be eradicated (Lewis, 1966, p. 191). In fairness to Lewis, he recognized prior to the advent of community action programs (Peters, 1978) that neighborhood groups could (and should) provide social support to people living in poverty. That is, a powerful cultural dimension to poverty could not be ignored. This insight was largely unnoticed, however, as other social scientists understandably attacked the "blame the victim" implications.

Social scientists close to the Johnson Administration were aghast at the suggestions that the causes of poverty were located within individuals and poor people's culture. Such a conclusion obviously dismissed the structural (economic) roots of inequality and, of greater consequences to the architects of the Great Society, virtually eliminated any interventionist role for the federal government.

Specific competing arguments derived from social scientists such as Herbert Gans (1969), who argued that poverty was an individual "adaptation" to the structural inequalities in the economy and wider society. He wrote that the poor constitute "an economically and politically deprived population whose behavior, values, and pathologies are adaptations to their existential situations" (p. 205). Gans and other social scientists such as Lee Rainwater (see Westinghouse Learning Corporation, 1969) were influential with the Johnson leadership team and waged the federal attack on poverty early in his administration. Rainwater's point was that any careful analysis of the causes of poverty must contain an account of those social conventions that work against systemic changes in the lower socioeconomic class populations. These conventions would certainly include "the almost total unwillingness of conventional society to admit its complicity in the suffering and exclusion that lower class [sic] people experience" (pp. 247-251).

Policy leaders within the Johnson Administration such as Walter Heller exploited the attacks on the culture of poverty thesis to press the case for improved public education in the city (and poor countryside). While the liberal social science community attacked Oscar Lewis and his cultural determinism thesis, policymakers ironically focused on the need to change the poor's behavior through education (Aaron, 1978, p. 20). It was felt that if the poor could simply acquire the "proper" (i.e., dominant) skills and attitudes the federal government (with the aid of social scientists and social welfare professionals) could break the cycle of poverty. Aaron is clear on this point: "By providing the poor with skills, the government could reduce poverty without blaming the poor themselves or initiating potentially more disruptive struggles over the organization of the American economy" (pp. 20-21; see also Mead, 1986, pp. 55-56). Governmental action on the education front became an ideologically acceptable tool to aid the poor. In the cities especially, programs such as Head Start, ESEA, and Title One (see later section) enjoyed the support of a political consensus fostered by Johnson and his cadre of advisers.[1]

---

[1] Today well-financed federal educational programs, such as Chapter One and Head Start, include organized parental and community advisory committees, who are effective advocates for continued funding and expansion.

THE ROUTE OUT OF POVERTY

The Consensus for Federal Action

On January 25, 1965, in a joint message to the House and Senate, the Johnson Administration made clear its priority on improving education to win the war on poverty. Johnson (1986) told the joint meeting that education "is our primary weapon in the war on poverty and the principal tool for building a great society" (p. 94). He had earlier referred to knowledge as "a cure for the ills of this age" (in a speech before the 200th Anniversary convocation of Brown University, cited in Rulon, 1981, p. 10). Johnson was proud of making the link between a quality public education and the escape from poverty. The chairman of the Council of Economic Advisors, Walter Heller, was familiar with the voluminous studies on educational inequality (e.g., Jencks, 1972). Heller's position was that "education is at the core of any successful sustained campaign against poverty" (quoted in Patterson, 1981, p. 186).

Finally, the 1964 *Annual Economic Report to the President* mentioned the importance of taking federal action to ensure equal educational opportunity for the children of poverty. The social context of urban schooling, thus, engulfed the massive federal call to action to eliminate poverty. Eliminating poverty in the cities, therefore, became a major policy goal of the Great Society. Improving public education was the politically acceptable vehicle to accomplish what history would judge as an overly ambitious goal.

The passage of the Elementary and Secondary Education Act of 1965 (ESEA) symbolized the federal government's commitment to improving public education in the inner city. ESEA broke through the long-standing resistance to federal aid for public schooling.

Moreover, it focused attention on taking *public* (governmental) action to meet the educational needs of poor, minority children in the inner city. For example, the Act established standards to encourage local school districts to provide more equitable treatment of disadvantaged students (Thomas, 1975). Such optimism was soon dashed as it was learned, as discussed next, that there were powerful limits to this activist role of the federal government.

The Limits of Federal Action

During the expansionist phase just described, a conservative coalition organized opposition to federal aid to education. This coalition feared that federal monies would move the nation closer to a socialist economic system. In the 1960s, socialism was ideologically equated with communism (fear of "reds"). Religious opposition was part of this coalition and centered in the demand for federal funding for private and parochial schools. The issue of separation of church and state also drew a wedge between the liberal-democratic Johnson Administration and the conservative resistance. Johnson was able to win over the Congress for important legislation such as ESEA; however, scholars point out that opposition based on fears of racial educational parity lay dormant (Rulon, 1981). These forces would gain support from a more ideologically congenial president, Ronald Reagan.

All told, Johnson gained the passage of 60 education-related bills during his terms as president. The successful legislation encompassed a wide scope of federal activity, ranging from preschool assistance to support for graduate school. Johnson had hoped that the Great Society, and the improvements to public education that would become the political mechanism to implement policy, would result in progress in the arenas of economic growth, social justice, and liberation of the individual (see Rulon, 1981). However, what soon would become obvious is that sustaining economic growth would become a limit to accomplishing these social goals. The economically better off citizens would be called on to help the nation's poor and socially disadvantaged people. Sustained economic growth was a prerequisite to the federal government's assuming its role as a "compensatory government" (see Brinkley, 1989). It was obvious that external events, however, would pose a drain on the economy and cause eventual distress for President Johnson. It would become difficult to sustain the rate of federal funding for public education, which climbed from $2 billion to $6 billion at the end of his term in the White House.

By the end of the Johnson Administration, the crippling political effects of the Vietnam War had taken their toll on the president. Domestic violence and a climbing inflation rate were issues that were also on the collective minds of the general public. Continued funding for education programs established during Johnson's administration was jeopardized by the drain on the economy resulting from the war and from internal pressures. As Jeffrey (1976) stated the liberal consensus of the Great Society "disappeared under the strains of the country's frustrating Vietnam involvement, deep divisions within the black community, race riots, and violence" (p. 24).

THE LEGACIES OF POSITIVISM

The Positive Use of Knowledge

Popkewitz's (1991) analysis of educational reform of the 1960s provides an ecological perspective on the social construction of educational change. He wrote: "The call for reform in the 1960s can be seen as a response to at least four elements in the transformation of a society: increased professionalization, an increased emphasis on science, a dynamic economic expansion, and a spiritual hope brought about by the end of World War II" (p. 137). I discussed earlier the point that a growing economy played a strong role in the unprecedented expansion of the role of the federal government in public education generally and in urban schooling particularly. Public education became Johnson's political vehicle for mobilizing public support for the Great Society. Here, I draw attention to the technical/scientific means his administration employed to justify governmental activism. This scientific application of professional/technical knowledge and wherewithal will have profound implications for the perceived failures of liberalism. The epistemological basis of Johnson's approach lay in the assumptions of positivism.

I do not enter into a critical analysis of the tenets of positivism. Rather, following Anthony Giddens's (1984, 1987) work, I focus on the assumptions of a science of society and a theory of social action, which are embedded within a positivist paradigm. It is my contention that many of the scientific assumptions underlying the programs of the Great Society, specifically federal educational intervention in the cities, were faulty. Giddens concisely lays out three assumptions of positivism and its application in the helping professions such as education. These are: (a) that the procedures of natural science can be imported by social scientists to the study of social action; (b) that the outcome of social science research, like that of the natural sciences, takes on the properties of natural law; and (c) that social science research can be applied in a value neutral manner. I extend Giddens's argument and claim that the application of positivism assumes political (ideological) dimensions when applied to the resolution of social problems. Specifically, where the context is the professional delivery of services such as public education, who determines who receives those services (and who is eliminated) is embedded in the unequal power relations in the client-professional relationship. Values are very much a part of the allocation process; they also undergird the particular "treatments" a needy population should receive.

Problem Solving as Scientific and Professional Action

The historical evidence is clear on Johnson's and a legion of social scientists' naive importation of positivism. For instance, on May 11, 1966, Johnson quantified his faith in an educated elite to solve the social problems of the country. Speaking at Princeton University, he noted that (among the) "371 appointments I have made in the last two and one half years, they collectively hold 758 degrees" (quoted in Rulon, 1981, p. 244). Johnson drew on the tradition of the late 1950s to rely on the advice of social scientists in the political matters of public policy. The belief was that social scientists would not only analyze the problems of society; they would also advocate solutions in the political and policy arenas. This advocacy ruins the value-free assumptions previously cited. Not surprisingly, this descent into the policy/political arena involved education. Mosteller and Moynihan (1972) observed that "social science had come to the aid of the widest range of causes and not the least that of educational equality" (p. 31). The value of equality could not be made more visible than in the poor quality of inner-city public schools.

Social scientists found a gold mine to apply their training and knowledge in the establishment of national councils and task forces. The country became aware of the invisible social ills such as poverty and the poor quality of urban schooling. They joined Johnson's call to action. The nation called on social scientists to bring systems analysis and computer applications in hopes of resolving these problems (see Apple, 1990; Cherryholmes, 1988; Popkewitz, 1990).

On the education front, Johnson relied on the use of specially created education task forces to secure consent for (and ultimate approval of) 60 pieces of education-related legislation. The task force mechanism brought to bear the knowledge of the social sciences to effect professionally organized education programs for the poor and socially disadvantaged students. He organized groups within the Departments of Health, Education, and

Welfare, the Bureau of the Budget, and congressional leaders, all of whom were very sympathetic to an activist role in public education by the federal government. Johnson called these task forces his "brain trust" (Johnson, 1971). Rulon (1981, p. 244) noted that "these individuals (the task force leaders) were more academic than political and more Ivy League than Texas. Only two, in fact, earned college degrees in the Lone Star state. Five sported sheepskins from Harvard, three from Yale, three from Columbia and two from Princeton." A phalanx of social scientists lead education's flank against the war on poverty. A large focus of the campaign was the improvement of city schooling. I illustrate this point in detail when I discuss Head Start.

Johnson appointed 16 education task forces between 1964 and 1968. Divine (1981) counted a total of 135 federal task forces that served as the think tank of the Great Society. Politically, these task forces were able to "short circuit the normal central clearance process of legislative agenda formulation. They interrupted the normal bureaucratic process, combated the inertia and boundary maintenance of existing federal agencies and maximized the president's leverage over the entrenched political bureaucracy" (p. 158). Most significantly these task forces provided scientific assurance and faith that the programs of the Great Society—especially federal support for inner-city schooling—would achieve positive social results.

The positive application of social science is best illustrated with the education task force of John Gardner, former head of HEW. The membership comprised three university presidents, three professors, two business executives, one foundation president (Carnegie's Gardner), one mayor, one magazine editor, and other federal officials (Graham, 1981).

Recalling Gardner's task force, Johnson wrote that "early in 1964, I had asked John Gardner . . . to head a task force that would take a searching look at the problem of education and make recommendations for action." The report of Gardner's task force in 1981 confirmed the crisis in American public education and stressed the urgent need for taking (federal) action (cited in Graham, 1981, p. 208). Thus, the social roots of the current crisis in urban schooling were sown as early as 1964. Johnson was convinced that the federal solutions to social problems would derive from an educated elite. The principles of social science, like the laws of natural sciences, could be positively applied to the problems of society. As discussed next, the Reagan Administration and the New Right would would turn this ideology upside down.

The Critiques of Positivism

The end of the 1960s brought a critique of positivism, specifically to the faith in social science application. The social sciences became synonymous with the rationalization and legitimation of existing power relations and the unequal distribution of financial and human resources. Ironically, the radical critique of value-free research, and its positive deployment in federal policy, spawned the rise of the New Federalism and, later, the ideological victories of the conservative restoration (Apple, 1993). Two influential reports, one written by James Coleman, the other authored by Christopher Jencks, both of whom were generally sympathetic to Johnson's program, ironically provided ideological fuel for the conservative attacks on the uses of social science.

In 1964, under the auspices of Title IV of the Civil Rights Act, the Office of Education hired James Coleman to conduct a national study on the availability of equal educational opportunity. Although the report was officially entitled the "Educational Opportunity Report" (EEOR) and had multiple authors, the report became widely known as the *Coleman Report*. The results of Coleman's regression analysis suggested that, when compared to family background and other socioeconomic factors (SES), in-school factors could explain only a small percentage of lower academic achievement of minority students. The sources of the problem of low-achievement levels for minorities lay largely outside the influences of the school and the classroom. Coleman's (1966) summary of his findings are worth noting in detail:

> The sources of inequality of educational opportunity appear to lie first in the home itself and the cultural influences immediately surrounding the home; then they lie in the school's ineffectiveness to free achievement from the impact of the home, and in the school's cultural homogeneity which perpetuates the social influences of the home and its environs. (pp. 73-74)

Spawning a flurry of school effectiveness research,[2] Coleman explained that providing equality of educational opportunity meaningfully "implies not merely equal schools, but equally

---

[2] Ron Edmonds's research on effective schools for disadvantaged students spawned a generation of "effective schools" research. For an excellent review of these studies, see Wimpelberg, Teddlie, & Stringfield (1989).

effective schools, whose influences will overcome the differences in the starting points of children from different social groups" (p. 72).

Christopher Jencks went much further in challenging the positive application of school intervention as a means of remedying the social malaise of poverty. Jencks was adamant in his belief that educational reforms were inadequate to reduce economic and social inequalities. I quote from his equally influential study, *Inequality: A Reassessment of Family and Schooling in America* (Jencks et al., 1973):

> We have seen that educational opportunities, cognitive skills, educational credentials, occupational status, income, and job satisfaction are all unequally distributed. We have not, however, been very successful in explaining most of these inequalities. The association between one variable of inequality and another is usually quite weak, which means that equalizing one thing (schooling) is unlikely to have much effect on the degree of inequality in other areas. (p. 253).

The demise of the liberal consensus forged through the programs of the Great Society laid the groundwork for the ascent of New Right forces. The New Right gained ideological ground with the election of Richard M. Nixon and flourished under the auspices of the Reagan Administration, its most powerful sympathizer and advocate.

During the advent of the New Federalism, a major ideological pendulum swing took place. It was marked by the reemergence of twin forces that, through its leaders in state government and in the private sector, would jointly seek ideological control of inner-city schooling. The first of these social forces is the flourishing of the ideology of privatization (see Miron, 1992). The second is the ascendancy of the state's regulation of local control over public education. In the next section I lay out the policy contours of this pendulum shift. In the subsequent chapter I analyze the broad ideological underpinnings of the quest for control over urban schooling.

THE NEW FEDERALISM AND THE CONSERVATIVE RESTORATION

The Privatization of Answers to the Crisis

Richard Nixon was the political precursor to the Republican Party's philosophy of the New Federalism. Although the marked ideological shift characteristic of the administration of Ronald Reagan did not occur during Nixon's term, it became evident early on that the federal government opposed the role of compensatory action such as Title One programs. As part and parcel of the ideology of local control over matters of education policy, Nixon eschewed a strong federal role and sought to return decision-making powers to state and local governments (Kantor, 1991). (As discussed later, Reagan succeeded in redefining the federal role in social problem solving by implementing block grants, replacing the categorical programs of the Great Society.) The cities were the eventual losers in this strategy as state governments groped to identify revenue streams from reconfigured federal sources (National League of Cities, 1993). Because funding for categorical programs was lumped under the block grant umbrella, a net loss of federal funds resulted. Perhaps of greater consequence was the loss of control over these funds by locally elected public officials and community-based organizations (see Peters, 1978).

Under the *Education Revenue Sharing Act of 1971*, Nixon proposed the consolidation of federal educational programs. Congress ultimately consolidated 77 educational programs into nine new or modified block grants, as part of the massive Omnibus Budget Reconciliation Act of 1981 during the Reagan Administration (*Congressional Quarterly*, 1989 p. 46; Hartle & Holland, 1983).

Reagan's theory was that block grants would provide the mechanism that would reduce costs for public education, as well as those of other entitlements of the welfare state (see Wilensky, 1975), by standing "on their own as a federalist tool for transferring power back to the state or the local level" (cited in Verstegen, 1987, p. 539).

Many scholars have, of course, disputed the idea that the procedural tools of federal devolution (see later discussion) and the mechanism of block grants would return decision making to the local level of ordinary people. For instance, Gittell (1981) wrote:

> Since many of the categorical grants now provide federal funds directly to local districts, the shift to state control will undermine local control and is blatantly contradictory to Reagan's rhetoric. Shifting discretion and/or control to the states . . . placed educational decisions in the political arena of the state capital. *That arena has a historical bias that does not bode well for urban school districts.* (p. 6; emphasis added)

As early as 1981, then, scholars anticipated Popkewitz's later work on the reemergence of state "steering" and the political space that state regulatory authority over public education opened up for urban entrepreneurs, which is a concern of this work. Briefly, education entrepreneurs in the inner city were able in subsequent decades to exploit the regulatory role of state government. Arguing in behalf of choice programs, for example, statewide business groups helped enact voucher legislation in states such as Minnesota (see Mazzoni, 1987).

In 1981, the beginning of this new social and political space was vividly portrayed in the redesign of the Chapter I program of the Education Consolidation and Improvement Act (ECIA). At the time, many in the liberal educational establishment considered the passage of the Act as synonymous with a repeal of the Elementary and Secondary Education Act, passed during the Johnson Administration and a hallmark of the Great Society. The existing ESEA "Title I" program provided much of the federal dollars that went to school districts that served large percentages of poor and minority students. A contradictory outcome was that overall federal funding for public education actually *increased* during Nixon's term in office (Alkin, 1992). For example, Congress approved new funding for environmental education and ethnic heritage programs. Although Congress appropriated these funds, they were not in accord with Nixon's political philosophical principle that "the time had come to sort out the appropriate roles and responsibilities of each level of government" (Barfield, 1981, p. 53). This political philosophy, which would have profound implications for city schools, crystallized under the popular presidency of Ronald Reagan.

Reagan changed the requirements of the ECIA in 1981 and reduced overall federal funding when he consolidated 44 categorical programs into a single block grant to state governments. Total federal outlays for Chapter I were reduced by almost 40%. (The original legislation and sets of federal regulations provided that a minimum of 80% of the federal assistance would be targeted to local education agencies (LEAs), depending on enrollments in public and private schools.) Under the revised guidelines, 6% of the total appropriation would be reserved for discretionary programs of the Secretary of Education. These included arts in education, and drug and alcohol abuse.

THE EXCESSES OF THE FREE MARKET

During Reagan's 1980 presidential campaign, his recurring theme was the promise to get (the federal) government off the backs of the American people. Arguably, Reagan enjoyed the greatest degree of popularity of any U. S. president. More significantly, Reagan's widespread public appeal permitted him to unleash the ideological forces of privatization and the free market. Reagan used his polished media skills to convince the American public (and Congress) that the federal government was the cause, not the solution, to the country's woes. By investing in the free enterprise system through tax credits and the loosening of federal regulations, Reagan believed the economy would prosper and the country's optimism grow.

In the Reagan epoch, the net consequences of this Administration's ideological strategies and policies were that the (ever increasingly tax resistant) public began to view city schooling as an economic and individual problem. The poor achievement levels, coupled with the aberrant behaviors of many inner-city students, were viewed as a drain on the economy and, eventually, on the entire social fabric of the country. This widespread belief represented an 180-degree ideological turn in the discourse over public education that marked the Johnson era. It signals the power of efforts to construct the social reality generally and urban schooling in particular.

What was politically palatable during the Great Society—an activist federal government willing to resolve educational problems in the inner city—was tossed to the winds of the free market and private enterprise. This marked shift in the social context paved the way for the ideological strategies of the Entrepreneurial Coalition. I assert that this group of loosely organized national elites constitutes a new social movement that sought to reconstruct urban schooling to assist economic growth (Miron, 1992). The group focused on urban school reform, for instance, school-business partnerships, decentralization, and school choice, now hallmarks of the conservative accords of the

New Right. These activities would help cement the ties between global economic competition and an educated cadre of workers in urban centers across America. I discuss the ideological/discursive strategies employed by the Entrepreneurial Coalition in detail in the next chapter.

To understand how this shift was accomplished, I discuss next the use of "procedural tools" (Astuto & Clark, 1992) during the Reagan presidency. The Entrepreneurial Coalition converted these tools into what I have elsewhere called the "privatization of the public interest" (Miron, 1992, p. 281). The deployment of procedural tools is an attendant process of social construction advanced by the architects of the New Federalism. Ironically, while shunning the intrusion of big government into the everyday lives of ordinary citizens, the elites within the Reagan Administration were skilled technicians in the use of government to accomplish their ideological/discursive aims.

The Tools of Privatization

Astuto and Clark (1992) identified the procedural tools used to achieve the goal of the devolution of federal power and authority in social and civic life in the Reagan Administration. In this context, *devolution* refers to the reduction in the size, scope, and authority of the federal government. These tools are decentralization, deregulation, diminution, and disestablishment. My interest here is to examine the relationship of these tools to the processes of the the social construction of urban schooling. These institutional procedures of the New Federalism became the governmental mechanisms whereby President Reagan accomplished his philosophical and political vision for the country.

Under Reagan, *decentralization* involved the transfer of federal authority to implement educational policy and programs through state governments. Central to the educational goals of the New Federalism was the passage in 1981 of the Educational Consolidation and Improvement Act (ECIA). ECIA established block grant funding for federal educational programs and designated the states as the vehicles to disburse federal dollars *according to state criteria*. Block grants served as (a) a precondition for the new federalism, (b) the dismantling of the categorical (and politically popular federal aid to the cities) programs of the Johnson era, (c) the removal of the necessity of federal monitoring and evaluation, and (d) the formal transfer of leadership and program management to the state and local levels.

Deregulation meant the reduction of federal control over the implementation of most educational programs and policies (the exceptions were for special needs cases such as the handicapped and the limited English proficient). Although some conservative scholars asserted that the number of specific deregulation activities were relatively few (Finn, 1988), the effect was to signal a reversal in the activist role of the federal educational apparatuses in public education. Coupled with the global economic fiscal crisis and the restructuring of cities (Fainstein & Fainstein, 1983), deregulation left city schools vulnerable both to state regulation (see Lauria, Miron, & Dashner, 1994) and economic distress (see Crowson & Boyd, 1992).

Diminution reduced federal funding for educational programs. Conservative forces in Congress and in the public at large argued for less federal dollars to support public education, while pushing for tax credits and vouchers for financing private schooling. Ideologically, these arguments were strong. Citing the criticisms of the educational programs of the Great Society and the general failures of liberalism, these forces wanted to dismantle the welfare state. Apple (1993) wrote that "the gains made by women and men in employment, health and safety, welfare programs, affirmative action, legal rights, and education must be rescinded because they are too 'expensive' both economically and ideologically" (p. 19) for the goals of the conservative restoration.

Examples of specific dollar reductions dramatizes this tool of the New Federalism. In FY 81 and FY 82, *total outlay reductions were about 20%*. At the end of Reagan's eight years in office, the percentage of GNP allocated to public education dropped from 0.6% to 0.4% (the effects of the reductions on city schools were more dramatic; see Kozol, 1991), declined from 2.5% of the federal budget to 1.8%, and reduced the overall share of federal dollars for elementary and secondary education from 8.7% to 6.2% (Clark & Astuto, 1989).

Disestablishment aimed to eliminate the position of the Secretary of Education as a cabinet-level appointment. Reagan had originally opposed the creation of the federal Department of Education (given cabinet status under President Jimmy Carter) because of his perception that it was "a mere creature of the left wing National Education Association" (Dugger, 1983, p. 318). This measure ultimately failed. However, de facto disestablishment happened. In 1985, for example, the Department of Education lost nearly 2,500 employees owing to a reduction in personnel force measures. Ultimately, reorganization, budget cuts, and elimination of programs altered the influence and operations of the federal Department of Education (Clark & Astuto, 1989).

The transformation in the discourse over public education began when Reagan's Secretary of Education, Terrel Bell, acting in accordance with the president's wishes, proposed to replace the Department with an educational foundation modeled after the National Science Foundation. However, Congress quickly cooled to the idea. Even Reagan ally (and future chief of staff) Howard Baker and Human Resources Committee Chairman Orrin Hatch were outspoken in their opposition to the dismantling of the Department of Education (Clark & Astuto, 1989; Dugger, 1983). Eventually, the issue died during the confirmation hearings for the next Secretary, William J. Bennett. I assert, however, that the largely symbolic defeat of this proposal to abolish the Department provided ideological fuel for the fire that would ignite the country and the educational establishment, with the publication in 1983 of *A Nation at Risk*.

From Procedural Tools to Educational Ideologies

What characterized the Reagan Administration's view toward public education was the contradictory attitudes toward policy development. Terrel Bell, Reagan's first Secretary of Education, underscored this point when he noted in 1986 that, during his four-year tenure, no comprehensive public policy was ever created to guide legislation and administrative proposals in public education. Indeed, many vaguely articulated proposals, for example, a reduced federal role and White House endorsement of universal school prayer, were contradictory (Finn, 1988). Bell (1986) cogently summarized the contradictions when he noted that "during my tenure the administration moved for advocating reduced funding and the phasing out of many educational programs. The President would then turn around and endorse a new math, science, and technology bill" (p. 493). I should note that Reagan's sanctioning of these measures supported the increased role of state governments in the promotion of educational standards and proficiencies as an economic development measure (Lauria, Miron, & Dashner, 1994). Also given birth were the goals of consensus building for the restructuring of urban schooling to meet the production needs of the global economy. Although Bell and Reagan undoubtedly paid only rhetorical attention to improving public schooling, their ideological stance sowed the seeds for the social construction of the current crisis in urban schooling.

In particular, Bell (1986) noted six educational goals of the Reagan era. These goals marked the development of the ideological strategies of the Entrepreneurial Coalition. I assert that a loosely organized new social movement (see Apple, 1993) forged a new consensus in urban centers to reconstruct schooling around the vision of entrepreneurial values and organizational forms of a restructured corporate America (see Miron, 1992). I discuss in detail these ideological strategies in Chapter 3. These educational goals were: (a) to reduce the levels of federal funding, (b) to strengthen local and state control over public schooling, (c) to maintain a limited federal role in the sponsorship of programs that would build the capacity of state governments to assume their historical responsibilities, (d) to enact legislation that would offer greater parental choice and that would increase competition for students among schools adhering to the discipline of U.S. business, (e) to reduce the levels of federal judicial activity, and (f) to abolish the federal Department of Education. In addition to Bell's recollection, another important ideological aim of the Reagan Administration was the authorization of school prayer in public classrooms (Anfara, 1993).

The push to allow prayer in public schools marks a fundamental contradiction, and the rhetorical nature, of Reagan's views toward public education. He wanted to reduce the federal role in public schooling and sought passage of several decentralization measures. As I noted earlier, as part and parcel of the philosophy of the New Federalism, the Administration advanced proposals to abolish the Department of Education, deregulate rules on spending federal dollars, and allow for parental choice. Simultaneously, Reagan supported federal legislation that would authorize school prayer and initiate steps leading to a national curriculum. These ideological proposals, together with their political mobilization among New Right groups such as Phyllis Schafly's Eagle Forum, would extend federal benefits to already advantaged groups as well as extend federal control in specific arenas (Boaz, 1988; Finn, 1988). In Chapter 3, I examine in detail the strategies of the Entrepreneurial Coalition, who is the beneficiary of the New Federalism. I argue that these ideological strategies create the space for the social production of knowledge in the city and, thus, *potentially* control city schooling through ideological (and ultimately) epistemological means.

The Reemergence of State Regulation

The influence of the states over educational policy increased dramatically during the Reagan years. However, state governments in general had already positioned themselves to assume their role as "pass through" agencies for the dispersal of federal dollars. For example, in anticipation of the policies of the New Federalism, they had already modernized their governmental machinery, improving accounting and budgeting systems (Hartle & Holland, 1983). This increased fiscal capacity, accelerated with the advent of block grants, would pave the way for an unprecedented flurry of state activity in the formation and implementation of educational policy (Mueller & McKeown, 1985). Verstegan (1987) provided the following summary documenting the heightened financial role of the state following the election of Reagan:

> While the flow of financial aid from Washington has been decreasing, state governments have been expanding old taxes or enacting new ones. As a result, state tax revenues as a percent of the GNP have kept pace with the growth of the economy, rising from 4.0 percent of GNP in 1964 to 5.3 percent in 1982, and 5.5 percent in 1985. Federal tax revenues as a percent of GNP were 15.0 in 1964, and then dropped to 13.2 percent in 1982 and to 11.7 percent in 1985. (p. 545)

Primarily aimed at reestablishing the state's authority over educational standards and the setting of a professional climate for classroom teachers, political, civic, and education elites coalesced to launch several reforms in public education. Researchers labeled these reforms as the first and second "waves" of educational reform.

Wave one was a top-down push to increase the standards of teaching and learning. Elites marshaled political support on state legislatures to force accountability in public schools, specifically in moving away from cafeteria-style curricula to college preparatory courses. Principals and classroom teachers would measure the performance levels of their schools by comparisons on standardized test scores.

Wave two aimed to learn from the difficult lessons of achieving top-down change. Its designers (mainly professionals from K-12 institutions or college and universities, together with allies in corporations and foundations) sought to improve the labor conditions of teaching. The broad aim was to establish teaching as a profession comparable to others such as law and medicine.

Although there is sharp disagreement on the ultimate effectiveness of either first-or second-wave reforms, these measures helped to produce the following specific outcomes. Thirty-eight states enacted career ladder or merit pay programs. Thirty-nine states required teachers to pass competency tests like the NTE; 44 states raised certification requirements and 29 states raised standards for teacher preparation programs in colleges of education. In addition, 20 states increased instruction time, and 48 states raised high school graduation requirements (see Clune, 1989).

Of course, this frenetic reform activity at the state level would have negative, unanticipated consequences for city schools (see Giddens, 1982). Verstegan (1987) noted that the states lacked the "initiatives designed to address special needs students and the goals of equity and access in elementary and secondary education" (p. 546). As a result, in the early 1990s, a host of state finance litigation would be filed in the state supreme courts of New Jersey, Kentucky, Texas, and others that would seek to equalize funding for at-risk students, many of whom attended poorly funded inner-city schools. Significantly, Verstegan cautioned that upholding the values of equity and access were legitimate domains of the federal government and to abandon those, as Reagan did, would precipitate a crisis in urban schooling. As early as 1986, she cited demographic data indicating that one out of every four children lived in poverty. Such data would foreshadow the chronic impoverished conditions of many of the nation's children in urban centers. As I illustrate in Chapter 3, such harsh economic realities would be largely overlooked as elites in the corporate, governmental, and educational sectors would coalesce to focus the discourse of the crisis around issues of governance and parental and student choice of public schools.

The Disadvantaged Position of City Schools

It is clear that city schools suffered under the block grant mechanisms of the New Federalism. Nationwide, the percentage of federal support for K-12 schooling dropped from a total of 7.4% of the federal budget in 1970 to 5.8% in 1988 (*Statistical Abstracts*, 1992).

At the same time, the worldwide drop in oil prices caused the unemployment rate to climb to a record 12% in cities like New Orleans in 1983 (it has hovered around 7% in metropolitan

New Orleans since then); consequently, sales and property tax revenues also declined during this period.
City schools, however, suffered more than financial losses. The historical anti-urban bias in state legislatures—fueled as much by racial as well as ideological factors—resulted in the passage of legislation (cf. stricter graduation requirements). These state legislative measures negatively impacted the largely African-American population enrolled in large urban school districts.
The concern with equity, characteristic of the Johnson Administration, gave way to the push for excellence in the nation's public schools (see Thompson, 1976). Big-city school systems lacked the financial and organizational resources to adequately cope with the excellence movement (Crowson & Boyd, 1992; Kozol, 1991).

CONSERVATIVE IDEOLOGIES AND THE ASCENT OF THE NEW RIGHT

The Rallying Call of the New Right

The ideology of educational excellence galvanized public support for the policies of the New Right and helped lay the groundwork for the conservative restoration. The impact of *property rights* on poor and minority students is potentially deadly. Michael Apple (1993) underscores this assertion: "We are, in fact, in danger of forgetting the decades of hard work it took to put even a limited (compensatory) vision of equality on the social and educational agenda and of forgetting the reality of the oppressive conditions that exist for so many of our fellow Americans" (p. 41). Clark and Astuto (1986) conceptualize the transformations in political philosophy. They argue that the mood of the electorate has shifted from concerns with equity to excellence, from needs and universal access to ability and selectivity, and from social and welfare concerns (person rights) to economic and productivity issues (property rights, see later discussion).
On one of the few occasions that President Reagan chose to address the issue of public education, he articulated the philosophy of the New Right and presaged the discourse of the Entrepreneurial Coalition. Speaking to an audience at Seton Hall University in the spring of 1983, Reagan argued that the answer

to our educational problems was to demand excellence and to improve the quality of the teaching force (Clark & Astuto, 1986). Echoing the position of the influential federal Department of Education report, *A Nation at Risk: The Imperative for Educational Reform*, published the same year, Reagan espoused the belief that the nation must demand better outcomes from its public school students and teachers. Importantly, *A Nation at Risk* called for no new federal dollars; rather, the authors renewed the call for state and local governments to accomplish the ambitious goals. That strategy foreshadowed the present-day call for the implementation of national curriculum standards in math, science, history, and language at the community level. I pursue the discussion of national educational goals further in Chapter 3.

The Educational "Market" as Equalizer

The New Right's successful completion of the ideological transition from equity to excellence embraces a historical movement, which leads to a renewed quest for ideological control over city schools (see Chapter 3). Apple (1993) argues that the New Right has redefined the term *equality*: "Equality, no matter how limited or broadly conceived, has become redefined. No longer is it seen as linked to past group oppression and disenfranchisement. It is now simply a case of guaranteeing *individual choice* under the conditions of a 'free market'"(p. 19; emphasis added).

Viewed within this perspective, failure to achieve educational excellence is an individual shortcoming, not a societal problem, as Johnson's Administration argued in the 1960s. In the cities, therefore, the social construction of urban schooling has moved from societal action to be taken to the problems of individual students and their families. Unlike the political philosophy of the Great Society, however, the federal government is largely viewed as the source of the problem. The free market (choice) is the solution.

A conceptually more sophisticated explanation is contained in the distinction between *property* rights and *person* rights alluded to earlier. Gintis observes that "what we are witnessing today is nothing less than the recurrent conflict between property rights and person rights. Therefore, dominant (corporate and entrepreneurial) groups have consistently defended the prerogatives of property" (Gintis, quoted in Apple, 1993, p. 18). Gintis's conceptualization of the distinctions between the two kinds of rights underscores the ascendancy of New Right forces and the consolidation of the conservative restoration. I assert that this movement is constructed at the expense of the liberal discourse for the activist role of the federal government in the Great Society. Gintis's (1980) theorizing is worth noting at length:

> A property right vests in individuals the power to enter into social relationships on the basis and extent of their property. This may include economic rights of unrestricted use, free contact, and voluntary exchange; political rights of participation and influence; and cultural rights of access to the social means for the transmission of knowledge and the reproduction and transformation of consciousness. A person right vests in individuals the power to enter into these social relationships on the basis of simple membership in the social collectivity. Thus, person rights involve equal treatment of expression and movement, equal access to participation in decision-making in social institutions, and reciprocity in relations of power and authority (p. 193).

It is helpful to analyze these important conceptual distinctions for their "ideological loading" on the current crisis in urban schooling.

Positivism as Paradigmatic Legacy

It was unlikely that, even under the social democratic consensus in the Johnson Administration, the protection of person rights reached the level of "reciprocity of power and authority." Nonetheless, the expansion of the welfare state (see Wilensky, 1975) created the social conditions for the protection of person rights in federal policy. As I argued earlier, during the Johnson Administration, the educational conditions in the nation's inner cities were not viewed as intractable problems; rather, Johnson viewed the improvement of public education in the city as a golden opportunity not only to reward his constituents in the minority community, but as a means to shore up politically inexpensive popular support for the attack on poverty. The consensus was that good public city schools were essential to a healthy economy and the nation. The role of the federal government was to insure that this ideal would be met.

With the ideological switch to the protection of property rights, the discipline of the free market would be touted as the vehicle to eliminate grossly unacceptable levels of social deviancy and academic underachievement. These New Right messages would greatly influence public perception that inner-city schools were, indeed, beyond repair. The solution to the disfunctionality lay not in intervention and funding by the federal government, but only the wholesale breaking up of the intractable school and district bureaucracy would rid public education of its misery (see Chubb & Moe, 1986; 1990; Finn, 1992; Ravitch, 1974).

I emphasize here the importance of placing the crisis in urban schooling in its wider social context. By situating the crisis in the changing conceptions and images embedded in political ideologies, public policy, and the opinion of the newsmedia, we establish its social construction. History, however accurately chronicled, is not a linear development. Although the liberal consensus forged during the Great Society largely eroded during the Reagan and Bush terms, the Head Start program not only survived the budget cuts of the 1980s; it actually prospered. Although some public policies survived (even prospered), the social context of urban schooling underwent transformation. The meaning of *urban* changed dramatically.

The interpretation human agents derive from social action is largely contingent on the context in which such action is carried out. Public policies, and the ideologies that often undergird their formation and implementation, are forms of social action. Social actions carry with them a multiplicity of interpretations, regardless of whether the author is known or "absent" (see Foucault, 1969). The story of the Head Start program well illustrates this phenomena. In particular, it highlights the primacy of the contextual underpinnings of the construction of meaning and the interpretation we ascribe to events as they unfold historically (see Giddens, 1987).

I illustrate here the complexities of the changing social context of urban schooling by tracing the history of the popular appeal of Head Start in both liberal and New Right ideological camps. Its appeal as social safety net (Zigler & Muenchow, 1992) highlights well the ideological complexities, material conditions, and discursive practices that constitute the backdrop for the social construction of urban schooling.

THE IDEOLOGICAL APPEAL OF HEAD START

The Head Start program originated from the recommendations of an interdisciplinary federal panel, which Robert E. Cooke, a professor of pediatrics at Johns Hopkins University School of Medicine, chaired. The purpose of the panel was to investigate effective programs the federal government could fund that would increase academic achievement levels for the poor and thus improve their future economic opportunities. The panel focused its attention on the preschool-age population.

Cooke's panel recommended a comprehensive preschool program that would provide an array of social, medical, and educational services to poor students. Thus, from its inception, the Head Start program offered a range of services not normally associated with traditional preschool education. These included medical and dental care, emotional development, school readiness, and home-based social services. Head Start was able to achieve its goal as a comprehensive preschool program, providing many noneducational services that greatly affected the disadvantaged child's ability to perform in the conventional classroom, by its model of service delivery. Head Start was organized by hundreds of community-based centers, which coordinated delivery of these comprehensive services (Valentine, 1979).

In 1965, Congress appropriated $17 million to serve approximately 100,000 poor children. Owing to a national advertising campaign, a far greater number of applications were received from families than the federal government had anticipated. The Office of Economic Opportunity (OEC), the federal agency responsible for the awarding of funds, greatly expanded the numbers of eligible children it would support to about 560,000. These additional children who were initially funded by OEC enrolled in 11,000 Head Start centers in the summer of 1965, the same year that witnessed the passage of the Civil Rights Act.

Local Community Action Programs (CAPs) administered the funds for Head Start, although the various Head Start Centers were separate organizations with their own staff and program guidelines. Its early success can, therefore, be attributed to its founding in the philosophy of the Great Society of "citizen participation." This meant that the recipients of comprehensive, federally funded programs such as the preschool Head Start program (the poor and socially disadvantaged) should be involved in the planning and implementation of federal programs.

The focus of Head Start was, of course, on the child and her or his immediate family. A focus on meeting both the individual needs of children and that of the family necessitated tight programmatic coordination among federal and local governmental and community action agencies. A result of this need for coordination between the federal and local governments was the proliferation of community-based, nonprofit organizations such as Total Community Action, with its multitude of affiliates (food stamp distribution centers and utility conservation programs). Ideologically, Head Start's community-based organizational model fit well into the political goals of mobilizing Blacks and other minority groups for public support of Johnson's War on Poverty. In fact, the director of the Office of Economic Opportunity, Sargent Shriver, viewed Head Start as a vehicle that could dispel local hostility, especially in the minority community, on the community action agencies that helped launch it (Valentine, 1979).

Initially, Head Start was caught up in a variety of contradictions. On the one hand, its model of service delivery through community-based organizations accounted for much of its early success. On the other hand, the same growing bureaucracies (CAPS) that administered Head Start preschool programs also fostered local hostilities among its poor constituents for alleged corruption and inefficiency of service delivery (see Peters, 1978). It is unlikely that had Head Start not focused on helping families, thus winning ideological support from conservatives in Congress, it would enjoy the levels of federal funding it receives today.

In 1969, Head Start was in danger of losing its federal funding. During the administration of Nixon, the Westinghouse Learning Corporation (WLC) conducted an evaluation study of Head Start and included among its nine findings that:

> The Head Start children cannot be said to be appreciably different from their peers in the elementary grades who did not attend Head Start in most aspects of cognitive and affective development measured in this study with the exception of the slight but nonetheless significant superiority of full-year Head Start children on certain measures of cognitive development" (Westinghouse Learning Corporation, 1969, p. 8).

The most positively stated of the nine findings concerned the strong level of parental approval of Head Start and the parents' perception of its positive impact on their children.

As a result of some of the negative findings of the WLC evaluation, the strong endorsement for reauthorization of Head Start funding, which Nixon's Administration had planned, was altered. Instead the Administration described the program as being in its experimental stages (Steiner, 1976). Edward Zigler, the former director of Head Start during the Nixon Administration, reported that when he took over the program the impact of the WLC study was so detrimental that much of his work focused on simply keeping Head Start afloat. In fact, between 1975 and 1978, the national news media ran several stories alluding to the elimination of Head Start (Zigler & Rescorla, 1985).

Head Start was, of course, ultimately refunded and remained enormously popular on both sides of the aisle in Congress. Since publication of the WLC evaluation, several favorable studies on the impact of Head Start on children and their families have been published (cf. Committee of Health and Human Services, 1980). In addition, powerful lobbying groups such as the National Head Start Association (NHSA) have won congressional support from conservatives who would normally oppose federal funding for education. For example, Moral Majority leader Senator Jeremiah Denton of Alabama, as chairman of the Subcommittee on Education, Arts, and Humanities, endorsed the reauthorization of the program when the Head Start funding bill came before the Senate Education Committee. According to Zigler and Muenchow (1992), "Denton was a family man all the way and he saw Head Start as a family program" (p. 202). New Right leader, Republican Senator Orrin Hatch, became a convert to Head Start's cause because he believed in the rights and responsibilities of parents to educate their children (Head Start included a strong parental involvement component).

Zigler (1985) attributed Head Start's widespread success in Congress to five factors: (a) public support by parents, staff, and advocacy groups such as the Children's Defense Fund and the NHSA; (b) positive news media coverage; (c) bipartisan support in Congress; (d) favorable evaluation findings that demonstrate its long-term cost effectiveness; and (e) powerfully located converts from within both the Reagan and Bush Administrations.

In 1986, none other than the champion of the free market system, President Ronald Reagan, praised the program, declaring that "Head Start has demonstrated its worth and effectiveness over the past two decades" (quoted in Zigler & Muenchow, 1992, p. 203). Reagan's endorsement of Head Start signaled its future stability in the halls of Congress.

Significantly, business leaders in the Entrepreneurial Coalition such as CEOs of Proctor and Gamble and AT&T (see Chapter 3) have praised its cost effectiveness and advocated for similar investments in human capital. In 1988, Head Start was so popular on both sides of the aisle in Congress that the party platforms of both the Republican and the Democratic conventions contained language calling for expansion of funding to include all eligible children. In 1990, the Head Start program received its largest budget increase in its history, and both President Bush and Congress pledged their support for full funding of Head Start. The Clinton Administration hopes that this funding goal will be accomplished in the year 1998 (*Congressional Quarterly*, 1993).

Summary

The legacies of positivism, thus, account both for the perceived failures and successes of a liberal democratic agenda in the sphere of city schools. Head Start almost lost its funding because preliminary quantitative studies failed to demonstrate measurable differences between achievement levels of students who attended its programs with those who did not. Put plainly, the intractable social problems of inner city poverty were ill suited to the laws of social science and their attendant policy recommendations. In broader terms, on the failure side, the bloated governmental bureaucracies were perceived by the public to limit the creativity of the classroom teacher. Fed up with the education delivery system, business, education, and civic groups forced state legislatures to enact questionable topdown policies to mandate change.

On the success side, programs such as Head Start, paradoxically, grew enormously popular owing to both the perceived involvement of community groups and its family values. Globally, the consensus gained for a societal safety net for protection against hunger, homelessness, and an array of social services—all important dimensions of inner-city students academic success—for the moment appear to have survived even the attacks of the architects of the *Contract with America*, House speaker Newt Gingrich and his circle of Republican public relations consultants. In other words, multiple interpretations of programs such as Head Start, and the use of positivism more generally, abound in the modernist periods of liberalism. Although largely undone by the New Right, some vestiges of the liberal democratic agenda remain in vogue.

The discourses of failure largely won out during the ascent of the New Right and gave rise to the influence of market forces and educational ideologies, for example, excellence. Lest we sink into what Henry Giroux characterizes as a discourse of despair (Giroux, in Pinar & Bowers, 1992) I now enter into a discussion on the possibilities of the emerging postmodern paradigm. The controversies surrounding this paradigm notwithstanding (see

Beyer & Liston, 1992), a new climate is upon us. It behooves those of us interested in the social construction of reality to investigate the prospects of this method of analysis for an understanding of social realities such as educational crises.

THE POSSIBILITIES OF POSTMODERNISM

One way to think about the negative consequences of the legacies of positivism is to place both the Johnson and Reagan eras firmly in the intellectual camp of modernism (see Giroux, 1991). It is plain that the confidence Johnson held in the capacities of professional knowledge and social science to solve educational problems in the city was largely misplaced. Equally misplaced, if not more socially damaging to inner-city students and their families, is Reagan's positive trust in the free market to provide the discipline in public education "required" by the economy. Both political philosophies, those of the Great Society and the New Federalism, subscribed to the positive belief in objectively verified knowledge as the basis for educational policy. For example, leaders in both political parties used the same litany of education statistics as proof positive of the crisis in city schooling. The difference is that, during the Johnson years, the context was domestic. Students in the city supposedly fared worse than students in the suburbs. These students were testing much below the norm on national standardized tests. As a result, they (and the education delivery system) became easy targets for an ailing nation.

In the 1980s and early 1990s, the context and competition are global. Students in the cities (and throughout the country) fare worse than students in the industrialized countries of Japan, Germany, and Taiwan.

Education critics presently argue that public schooling has been notoriously vigilant in holding on to the positive paradigm (see Doll, 1993; Stack, 1993). While all around us in literature, architecture, film, and video the postmodern paradigm is evident, in public schooling, especially in inner-city schools, a cultural/theoretical lag exists.

Skeptics in the educational research community are correct to bristle at the suggestion that simply changing cultural and epistemological paradigms will do much to help schools, especially when the ideas are as vague and abstract as those embedded in postmodernism appear to be. I want to specify here what I mean by the term. I limit my use of the term *postmodernism* to a form of social and political analysis and pragmatic criticism (e.g., deconstructionism and poststructuralism; see Cherryholmes, 1988; Maxcy, 1991). Urban theorist Michael Smith (1992) articulates well both the passion and intellectual emphasis in postmodernism as a *method* of social analysis and critique. He observes that as a method postmodern analysis "constitutes a revolt against rigid conventions of language and method in intellectual discourse and textual representation. [It extends] into a deconstructive critique of the closed systems, grand narratives, and totality theories of modernism itself (e.g., liberalism and Marxism)" (p. 3; see also English, 1993). Simultaneously a method of social analysis and social/cultural critique, the emerging paradigm of postmodernism embraces a significant, although limited, number of theoretical tenets.

Postmodern Tenets

In an otherwise unsympathetic treatment of postmodern social analysis, Beyer and Liston (1992) nicely summarized these tenets. The first tenet is against metanarratives. Postmodernists embrace a "pluralism in languages" by which subjects create meaning and interpret human experience and local culture. Postmodern analysis rejects realism as an epistemological category because of its essentialism in pointing to material causes as the basis of social understanding and cultural meaning. Reality "can never be unambiguously known" (pp. 373-383). Only through a careful analysis of *local practices*, not macro-level structures, can meaning be qualitatively ascertained in its true mutidimensionality.

Beyer and Liston assert that the second tenet of postmodern analysis, antirepresentationalism, is closely related to the emphasis on locality and the rejection of metanarratives. This emphasis stands in opposition to the

> notions of cumulative knowledge, scientific progress, and objectivity. The more characteristically postmodern thesis of the intertwinement of and the symbiotic relationship between power and knowledge amounts to an outright rejection of the possibility of validating scientific method or knowledge on independent, ahistorical, gender- and race-free grounds: hence the dismissal of the time-honored aim of the sciences as the representation of an inviolate and unmediated cultural and natural reality. (Kiziltan, Bain, & Canizares, quoted in Beyer & Liston, 1992, p. 376).

The significance of this passage lies in its explicit renunciation of the assumptions and excesses of positivism. Specifically, postmodern analysis disputes the common-sense, taken-for-granted view that there exists an externally verified reality that can be positively known, verified, and measured. For example, both liberal and neoconservative groups for over three decades have relied on the use of standardized achievement tests to propose alternate policies and strategies to solve problems in city schools. The positive use of tests results presupposes that such instruments accurately describe and measure the social reality of student achievement.

Beyer and Liston characterize the third tenet of postmodern social analysis as the orientation to the "other," rather than a search for commonality. Here, the postmodern concern is with systems of domination and exploitation. The commentators note that "postmodern writers repeatedly emphasize a concern for the 'other'—those who have been oppressed or exploited. Women, people of color, prisoners, children, and the economically underprivileged have, on this view, been left out of reason's (Positivism's) grand equation" (1992, p. 379). What Raymond Williams (1961) has called the "selective tradition" has in the curriculum and in the schools generally disenfranchised nondominant students (ethnic minorities, limited English speakers, students of poor families). Nicholson (1989) commented on the implications for discursive practices in education

> We must listen to those who are telling stories about what it means to be excluded from a conversation or a community because their "heroes" or "heroines" are different from those of the dominant group. We need a "rainbow coalition" of postmodernists, feminists, and educators who are committed to the task of making sure that no serious voices are left out of the great conversation that shapes our curriculum and our civilization. (quoted in Beyer & Liston, 1993, p. 380)

As discussed in Chapter 3, owing in large part to the process by which the discourse on national educational goals is developing, Nicholson's call is going unheeded. Postmodern social analysis is highly abstract and in danger of become jargon-laden. Its potential to redefine the educational conversation to incorporate the absent voices of inner-city students, parents, and teachers may be lost unless sympathizers can make its discourse more concrete and its criticism pragmatic. Yet it also offers us a way to reinterpret existing ethnographies and inform critical urban ethnography. I now turn to this task.

Social Reproduction in Paul Willis's "Learning to Labour"

I deliberately overstate Paul Willis's case of social reproduction. My purpose here is to draw a contrast between postmodern social analysis with those critical scholars' interpretation of Willis's research. In particular, I rely on Michael Apple's relational analysis to highlight the possibilities (and benefits) of multiple interpretations. In brief, Apple's (1985) relational analysis of informal student culture focuses on the *limits* of student resistance to dominant culture. In particular, it is the working-class students' (active) reproduction of social class, at the heart of Willis's study, that Apple argues is essential for the legitimation of public schooling. Relationally, students' creation of culture inside of the classroom remains inextricably bound to class and social relations outside of the school, in the shop floor.

Critically oriented scholars have analyzed the pathbreaking work of the British ethnography of Paul Willis. His contribution to the development of a critical theory in education has been to painstakingly demonstrate how working-class students, maneuvering through the relative autonomy of the lived culture of the school, have assisted in their own social reproduction. Put simply, it is not only oppressive, abstract structural forces that predetermine working-class students' timely entry in an unequal economy. It is the students themselves, who, rejecting the "mental labor" of the formal curriculum, virtually guarantee their position as manual laborers in relatively low-paying jobs. Michael Apple's (1985) relational analysis of Willis's ethnography in *Education and Power* is illuminating for the embedded macro-level assumptions.

> The response of the working class students (the 'lads')[3] to
> lived conditions both inside and outside of the school, ones

---

[3]Paul Willis's (1977) ethnography in *Learning to Labour* focuses mainly on the differences in outlook between two groups of working-class students. The first group, the "lads," consists of a group of students who largely resist the formal curriculum of this secondary school located in a working-class neighborhood in England. The "lads" ridicule the second group, the "ear'oles", whom Willis describes as complying with the demands of the curriculum and the policies of the school.

experienced by the lads at home, on the shop floor, within the school culture, and elsewhere . . . is an informal cultural response to the ideological and economic conditions and tensions they confront. *And while it holds out the possibility of economic and political awareness, it remains relatively disorganized and unguided.* (p. 100; emphasis added)

I contrast Apple's perspective with that of postmodern anthropologists George Marcus and Michael Fisher: Culture "mediates all human perceptions of nature and . . . *understanding these mediations is a much more important key to explaining human events than is mere knowledge of ecological and material limits*" (quoted in Smith, 1992, p. 5; emphasis added). Although both of these passages contain a high level of abstraction, I hope to concretely illustrate the marked difference in emphasis. Put simply, Apple is concerned with the students 'disorganized' lack of political action or sophistication. Apple perceives this deficiency as limiting the potential to alter oppressive structures (unequal capitalists economy and hegemonic ideologies); realistically, within this framework, such potential remains virtually nil. Postmodern analysis, however, is potentially more optimistic because, in the words of urban theorist Michael Smith (1992):

> The language which [subordinate student groups] possess and the circuits of communication in which they are implicated are resources as well as limits. They constitute [dialogically] the terrain for the contestation, as well as the reproduction of cultural meanings, for resistance as well as accommodation to dominant structures of power and ideology. (p. 5)

In short, by altering the arena of discourse through language and other forms of communication, student culture mediates the reproductive patterns of school and society, thereby potentially "modifying global structural and cultural processes" (Rosaldo, quoted in Smith, 1992, p. 24).

Apple's (1985) emphasis, in brief, is on the "partial reproduction" of an unequal society (p. 106). The orientation of postmodern methodology, however, is on the mediating power of culture to potentially alter unequal micropower relations through discursive practices and the use of language. The following lengthy passage from Apple's (1985) *Education and Power* underscores the limitations of student resistance and student culture.

60 Chapter Two

> What actually seems to happen is that the somewhat more progressive setting sets limits on and enables students to develop within their own day to day lives in school an array of working class themes and attitudes which give them strength and can act against the ideological values represented by the school. Resistance, subversion of authority, working the system, creating diversions and enjoyment, building an informal group to counter the official activities of the school, all of these are specifically brought out by the school, though all of these are the exact opposite of what the administrators and teachers want. . . . At the same time, however, the limitations are clearly there, limitations that just as clearly end up tying such working class youths to a labor market and preparing them for generalized and standardized work. (p. 101)

Contrasting Assumptions

It would be helpful to examine in some detail the underlying theoretical and normative assumptions embedded in this passage. Exposing both of these sets of assumptions would then enable the researcher to tease out the subtle, yet significant, differences in orientation between a postmodernist analysis and a modernist view, which I define here as any paradigm that employs technocratic rationality to postulate a "master narrative" (see Giroux, 1991). Apple's neo-Marxist theoretical framework, although highlighting some important limitations of simple reproductive theory, seems clearly lodged in this master narrative (or modernist camp).

First, it is clear that his interpretation ultimately rests on a social class analysis. Although culturally mediated by the resistance that is "brought out by the school," class and social reproduction occur, even as the "lads" own "resistance" paradoxically fosters such reproduction, "tying (them) to a labor market and preparing them for generalized and standardized work." Within this neo-Marxist perspective,[4] local (student) culture is not a

---

[4]Neo-Marxism broke ground with classical, instrumental Marxism with Poulantzas's (1969) insistence that the political and cultural spheres maintained a degree of relative autonomy from the economy. Much critical scholarship since approximately 1970, then, sought to demonstrate the contradictions of schooling in capitalist societies. Reconceptualizing the school as sites of cultural politics, scholars such as Michael Apple and Henry Giroux sought to radically move away from simple reproduction theory, which held that schools instrumentally functioned to replicate the economic order.

resource that enables "local ethnicities . . . *to both modify global structures and cultural processes and reinvent themselves*" (Sahlins & Rosaldo, quoted in Smith, 1992, p. 24; emphasis added). On the contrary, culture becomes a subtle, yet particularly insidious, commodified instrument of the forces of capital.

Second, the day-to-day practices of the "lads", that is, their lived culture, is undermined. Following Willis, Apple's analysis assumes a natural subordination of student culture to that of an "'informal group' to counter the official activities of the school." The emphasis on the informal constitution of the student's lived culture, ironically, refocuses our interpretive attention on the dominant macrolevel economic structures and power relations, rather than on a focus on the understanding of the students' everyday experience of marginality. It is my contention that theorists and researchers must push the boundaries of marginality sufficiently in order to "discern the formation of new 'subject positions', grasp emergent counterlogics to the prevailing modes of domination in society, and give voice to the polyphonic patterns of accommodation and resistance to domination" (Smith, 1992, p. 4). I attempt to do just that in Chapter 5. The focus on a close study of marginality is an explicit project of postmodern social analysis. As Smith (1992) observed: "Current efforts in the debate on postmodernity to subordinate cultural processes to the master discourse of Marxist political economy also downplay the ontological and epistemological challenge which poststructuralist philosophy poses for all forms of essentialism" (p. 4).

Third, the school's contradictory role of facilitating both cultural and discursive mediation and social reproduction, a central concern of neo-Marxist critical theory, is not pushed far enough. I wish to unpack this role. The school assists in the creation of informal groups. These groups (the "lads"), in turn, develop a culture that stands in opposition to many of "the official activities of the school" and its ideologies. Finally, the dominating (more middle-class values) culture of the school (represented in Willis's study of the "earoles") ultimately wins out because, obviously, the limitations (see Apple, 1985) of the informal working-class culture overcome the "strength" of the "lads" to act against the school (and, ultimately, against the unequal power relations in a capitalist economy). This grand narrative of social reproduction and inequality implicitly endorses the unalterable and essential hegemony of unequal capitalists social relations. In short, it denies human agency (see Giddens, 1987). A postmodern social analysis seeks to push the edges of marginality to more fully understand the formation of new personal (and as I attempt to demonstrate in Chapter 5, *collective*) identities.

The Emphasis in Postmodern Analysis

Postmodern social analysis, above all, employs a multiple perspective to the understanding of local cultures and the construction of new political and social subjects. As such it fundamentally concerns itself with an interpretivist epistemology and ontology. It remains vehemently antiessentialist (Smith, 1992). It simultaneously embraces the phenomena of multiple realities, the decentering of power and subjectivity, the cultural mediation of dominant social and economic structures, and, finally, the possible transformation of these oppressive material and ideological structures. An example is in order.

In *Learning to Labour*, Paul Willis's social class analysis of the role that working-class culture assumes in the reproduction of inequality ultimately relegates local ("informal" student) culture to a subordinate position vis-à-vis the dominance of capitalist social relations. Rejecting this explanation as a form of metanarration, postmodern analysts would assert that through the use of language and other "articulatory practices" (Gramsci, cited in Smith, 1992, p. 16) local cultures ultimately modify these dominant material and ideological structures. In the following passage, the complexities of the postmodern emphasis on local culture as a potential (historical) source of the mediation of dominant economic and ideological patterns can be illustrated:

> Meaning is not an objectified given but the result of contests between the dominant and subordinate "cultures" of a given society. *These contests are both mediated through the dominant cultural system* and are historically contingent, and as such, are political in nature and hegemonic in scope. (Kelly & Liu, 1993, p. 22; emphasis added).

Although the passage is meant to underscore the intellectual transition in public education from a modernist paradigm to a postmodern one (a focus of Giroux, 1993), the meaning of local cultures and their political potential to modify hegemonic practices is ultimately undermined. The transition remains incomplete.

The processes through which such mediation and potential transformation occur is the focus of postmodern urban ethnography and the concern of Chapters 4 and 5. Suffice it to say here that a postmodern analysis would require, at the very least, a more thorough—dialectical—understanding of both domination and marginality. Everyday practices on the margins of micropower relations are, themselves, inseparable from the praxis of resisting structural domination, traditionally viewed as the central cause of unequal power relations.

An orientation toward multiplicity signals the postmodern quest to give "voice" to marginalized groups. More importantly, such multiplicity in the interpretation of social phenomena celebrates difference. Again I turn to the work of urban theorist Michael Smith (1992):

> Marginal groups are not pure, monolithic, essentialist entities. Rather, different gendered relations, generational, occupational, and local residential experiences, as well as divisions of labor operate within households at all social levels and among all social groups. This means that even within the same "ethnic" household unit the "implosion" of macrostructural social divisions, contradictions, and systems of signification are subject to interpretation by differently situated social actors. (p. 25)

Thus, the postmodern leaning toward difference does not constitute a romantic political naivete; rather, by fostering (through urban ethnographies) the multiple vocular narratives of marginal groups, it allows for practical radical critique through its intellectual abhorrence of patronization. Carol Swain, an African-American scholar who left Duke University because of patronization, put it succinctly: "I think many black scholars would feel stigmatized if they applied for a job at Duke. I think white liberals are among the most racist people I know; they are so patronizing towards blacks" ("Racism in the academy, 1993, p. Y17).

Finally, postmodernism as a method embraces the idea that the past is remade in the present (see Jencks, 1987). With regard to the theoretical formations of personal and ethnic identity, the focus of the next chapter, previously socially constructed identities potentially meld away in "a local present-becoming future" (Clifford, quoted in Smith, 1992, p. 24). In Jencks's (1987) phrase "double coding," the postmodern social analyst looks to history so that past remnants can be "coded" within a new future vision (see also Doll, 1993; Stack, 1993).

A Break with the Past?

In this chapter, I have sketched and analyzed the social context of urban schooling. In particular, I have illustrated how the current crisis in city schooling is situated within the nexus of the political ideologies, public policy, and the legacies of positivism. It is clear from this analysis that it is in the political and economic interests of governmental elites, whether of the liberal or New Right philosophical persuasion, to socially reproduce crises in city schooling to legitimize their interests. Lyndon Johnson exploited the Civil Rights movement to shore up his support for an activist federal role in public education. He successfully mobilized this social movement to launch his attack on poverty. Improving city schooling was an ideologically palatable means to begin that process.

Similarly, Ronald Reagan blamed the public schools as the cause of the declining U.S. position in the global economy to launch the New Federalism. This exportation of the economic crisis to public (mainly, inner-city) schools marked the onset of the conservative restoration. Each of the three "periods," whether of modernist or postmodern orientation, engulfs concrete understandings (definitions) of urban schooling. Each definition carries with it the attendant processes of social construction.

Urban Schooling as Governmental Intervention

In the Great Society, urban schooling was equated with intervention by the federal government. The purposes of intervention were that: (a) Johnson and his circle of policy and social science advisors wanted the federal government to eliminate poverty in the ghettos of America and viewed a strong system of public education in the cities as the primary means to accomplish this task; and (b) The Johnson Administration hoped to use the issue of urban schooling to shore up its political base in the inner city.

The federal government used categorical funding (ESEA, Bilingual Education, Head Start) and a host of advisory commissions to socially construct urban schooling. These attendant processes of social construction furthered the social and political goals mentioned earlier.

Urban Schooling as Free Market Tool

During the period of the New Federalism, the Entrepreneurial Coalition emerged to push forth an ideology of the free market. In the sphere of public education in the cities, schooling was viewed as a tool of free enterprise. The goal of the elites of the New Federalism was to get government off the backs of the people.

Both the elites in the federal government and the private sector use various procedural tools (documented earlier) to advance the values of free enterprise through public education in the cities. These procedures, in turn, gave rise to the reemergence of state government as "education regulator." As I illustrate in the next chapter, the policies and regulations of state government opened new political space for constructing the crisis in urban schooling as a crisis in governance.

Urban Schooling as Ethnic Difference

In the emerging postmodern climate, within the new social space of ethnic identity (Smith, 1992) schools are sites of identity politics. Ethnic difference is both a source of conflict and a means to build community around a celebration of, and respect for, difference. In Chapter 5, I show how many social practices in the school work to keep African Americans (and other ethnic minorities) "stuck in the quagmire of race." At the same time, however, new forms of student resistance and struggle are causes for cautionary optimism for democratic practices in inner-city public schools (see Miron & Lauria, 1995; Mouffe, 1988).

At the same time I explore the viability and the efficacy of the postmodern turn in social analysis and its application for transforming city schools. By *transformation* I mean the cultural mediation of dominant ideological and material structures so that a genuine democratic culture in public schools can take place. This new democratization of city schools is based on Giroux's (1993) premises of border pedagogy, which he summarized in this passage:

> Border pedagogy is attentive to developing a democratic public philosophy that respects the notion of difference as part of a common struggle to extend the quality of public life. It presupposes not merely an acknowledgement of the shifting borders that both undermine and reterritorialize different configurations of culture, power, and knowledge. It also links the notions of schooling and the broader category

of education to a more substantive struggle for a radical democratic society. (p. 28)

My assumption is that Giroux's vision of the the reconfiguration of a radical democratic society through the vehicle of education is not hopelessly utopian. Like the emancipatory possibilities in Michael Smith's characterization of the postmodern method, Giroux's pedagogical discourse rests jointly on the solid ontological ground of multilayered subjects who engulf "both liberation and subjugation" (quoted in Kelly & Liu, 1993, p. 26) and to the political joining of power, knowledge, and language. In subsequent chapters I explore the theoretical concerns of postmodern social analysis with its concrete manifestation in city schools, the terrain of identity politics.

Chapter 3

The Perennial Quest for Ideological Control of Big-City Schooling

A major argument of this book is that the current crisis in city schooling is part and parcel of the situated character of big-city schools—their social context. I argue repeatedly throughout the text that inner-city schools sit at the nexus of two forces—global and local. On the one hand, the emerging global economy has caused profound changes—social, demographic, economic, cultural, and political—on the quality of life in the inner city (Wilson, 1987). The worldwide economic restructuring of cities, in turn, have left schools situated in the most distressed neighborhoods barely able to cope materially and educationally in comparison to better funded suburban schools (Carnoy, Daley, & Ojeda, 1993; Kozol, 1991). Put plainly, inner-city schools have experienced growing inequality owing to global changes and the migration of limited English-speaking families (Cummins, 1993), whereas private and suburban schools have actually witnessed an increase in per-pupil funding (Hugg & Miron, 1991; Lamorte, 1989).

On the other hand, the multiethnic culture that has arisen simultaneously with the transformation of U.S. urban centers has created a new social space of ethnic awareness and identity (Marcus & Fisher, 1986; Smith, 1992). Although there is considerable debate within the scholarly and research community (see, e.g., Heath & McLaughlin, 1993; Weis & Fine, 1992) as to whether ethnic voice, and growing consciousness, is silenced or "empowered via pedagogical intervention" (Cummins, 1993, p. 105), the material and cultural expressions of ethnicity, whether exhibited through ethnic gangfare or the infusion of arts in the curriculum, are empirically indisputable. The (now minority) ethnic population is rapidly becoming a majority in sheer numbers across urban America.

Many of the arguments I make here are not new. However, scholarship and academic research rarely move between the macrolevels of political economy and the microlevels of lived culture and experience. As I noted in the introduction, this project seeks to make that structural and existential connection explicit. My concern here is to combine the structuralist understanding of the problematic of the new global economy with students' lived cultural experience in city schooling. For it is certainly the case that much critical scholarship, especially during the last decade, has ideologically tied the production of educational reform and innovation to the property interests of entrepreneurial industrialists and corporate stockholders. The consistent emphasis has been on the abstract (often ahistorical) structural relations, rather than on the lived cultural experience of students in city schools.

This chapter focuses on the ideological strategies of the social group I call the Entrepreneurial Coalition. This informal coalition currently provides the moral and intellectual leadership (Gramsci, 1971) for (now global) economic growth. I group these ideological strategies into five categories: school choice, shared governance, school-business partnerships, state regulation/state takeover, and school intervention. Following Popkewitz (1991), the five discrete strategies can be understood as a reemergence of state steering and social regulation over public schooling, specifically city schools. Again, my focus is on making explicit the link between the schooling demands of the new global economy and the new social space of urban ethnicity in which large-city schools presently are socially embedded and historically situated.

THE ENTREPRENEURIAL COALITION AND CONSENSUS BUILDING

The history of education in U.S. cities is replete with references to substantial business influence in school governance. In the early 20th century, business and educational leaders designed a corporate model of schooling in cities to "produce" students desired by the economy and the larger society. Coupled with a school culture dominated by administrative progressives, national elites sought to establish the corporate model of public schooling as a hegemonic ideology (Miron, 1992) and dominant discourse (Bell, 1995). This ideology dominates schooling, in spite of the "centralized fragmentation" of the educational bureaucracy (Tyack, 1993).

Owing primarily to the global fiscal crisis and the subsequent downsizing and restructuring in the corporate culture, a new model of schooling has seeped into the urban context. I argue in this chapter that the values of the entrepreneur, embodied in the corporate cultures of corporations such as 3M (Peters & Waterman, 1984), now underlie current school restructuring activity in large-city school districts. Fundamentally, the idea of bringing school decision making closer to the "customer" (parents and students) forms the bedrock of what I call the ideological strategies of the Entrepreneurial Coalition.

The goal of the Entrepreneurial Coalition is much the same as that of the business and industrial leaders, who successfully won out in the early 20th century over competing educational ideologies and philosophies, such as those of John Dewey, to forge a new societal consensus in urban centers that would more closely align the aims and means of schooling with the global economy. The popular values and goals of the Entrepreneurial Coalition are embedded in the comments of the prominent national urban journalist, Neil Pierce (1993):

> In the resource-scare 90's, there's a critical role for the so-called "reinvention" principals in today's governments—being entrepreneurial, treating citizens like valued customers, involving employees and citizens in setting an organization's mission priorities, delegating authority and then holding managers accountable for results. (p. B5)

I stress that the Entrepreneurial's Coalition drive for consensus building, in particular, ideological control and dominance, is an enduring political struggle (see Whelan, Young &

Lauria, 1994). It involves intellectual and moral leadership (Abercombie, Hill, & Turner, 1980) and compromise, and the outcome is always in doubt. The outcome of the new consensus building depends on local history and culture, regime type, and the strength of countervailing local social movements (see Stone, 1989).

Who, exactly, is this new Entrepreneurial Coalition? Led by corporate, education, and political elites in major urban centers (Miron, 1992), it has formed alliances with civic groups, educational leaders, parents, and community organizers such as Robert Moses, a former civil rights leader from Mississippi, who is leading a national mathematics movement (the *Algebra Project*; see Jetter, 1993) to place mathematics and science teaching and learning front and center on the nation's education agenda for poor and minority students in the inner city. Above all, it is a new social movement that has sought to target the goal of the national reform movement in education to redefine public education in inner-city, public schools (see Apple, 1993). Its spokespersons have included Owen Butler, former chairman of Procter & Gamble, who as head of the Committee for Economic Development led the efforts to hold teachers accountable for an educated worker capable of erasing the declining levels of economic productivity (see Cuban, 1994). It is also loosely organized by national corporate groups such as the Committee for Economic Development (CED) and the Business Roundtable, which were concerned with the "rising tide of mediocrity" in the nation's public schools (National Commission on Excellence in Education, 1983, p. 6).

The Entrepreneurial Coalition quickly emerged in major U.S. cities, where school performance and student achievement were widely perceived by Chamber of Commerce groups and others as hindering any economic redevelopment goals. The group embraces the spirit of enterprise and the values of the entrepreneur. It believes that the answer to social problems lies outside of government. Only the free market can provide the financial incentives necessary for government (public schools) to accomplish excellence. Its informal members range from the American Federation of Teachers (whose president, Albert Shanker, is a big promoter of Goals 2000) to the Committee for Economic Development,[1] who has embarked on a public campaign to redirect

---

[1] The Committee for Economic Development (CED) is a national organization of Fortune 100 companies chief executive officers. The group has published several influential policy reports, including *Investing in Our Children*.

teaching and learning in U.S. public schools (see Committee for Economic Development; 1995; Shanker, 1995).

In the literature on urban redevelopment, Whelan et al. (1994), Swanstrom (1985, 1988), Stone (1989), and others have, respectively, characterized these business and industry groups as the "growth machine" and the "corporate regime." The idea is that business groups serve as a catalyst for economic redevelopment strategies in urban centers, and that elites in business and industry mobilize local community support for these initiatives (Fainstein & Fainstein, 1983). Business leaders are largely successful in realizing their economic and political goals because they are able to garner the intervention of state and local governments, which often enter into partnership (see later discussion) agreements with business and industry. These partnership strategies effectively assume the risk management of capital, thereby allowing the accumulation process to resume smoothly and organically (Marcuse, 1981).

On the urban educational front, business interests do not typify a monolithic regime or machine. The coalition it has organized with education, labor, and the nonprofit sectors does not constitute a conspiracy for vouchers. Rather, within the sphere of public schooling, business assumes an institutional mission to politically empower (see later discussion) parents, students, and the community. From this perspective, empowerment functions to undermine the authority and control of education professionals. The role that the Entrepreneurial Coalition assumes in matters such as urban school governance, therefore, is that of a convener of community-based, quasi-democratic processes such as school district decentralization, site-based management, and school choice (see Elmore, 1993; see also Carnoy, 1993). By cloaking populist reform movements as democratic processes, the Entrepreneurial Coalition is able to win over new converts for its vision of the broad aims of public education. In the fiscally and socially distressed inner city, this means equating the ends of education with employable skills in an emerging integrated global economy.

This new coalition has successfully exploited the crisis of legitimacy of city school governance. Ironically, contemporary governance arrangements have their roots in the culture of the managers of virtue. Business and educational elites promoted the practice of administrative discretion in the older U.S. cities in the late 19th and early 20th centuries. Then, the educational leaders in cities sought to mold the public schools in the image of the corporation, in which the institutional icon "of rapid consolidation of corporate capitalism and concentration of wealth among urban elites" was born (Tyack & Hansot, 1982, p. 6). As I discussed in Chapter 1, the current focus on reforms of educational governance makes local school boards politically vulnerable to the pressures exerted by the Entrepreneurial Coalition, who, ironically, embraces the values which in large measure gave rise to the governance crisis in the first place.

I call this phenomena the "new politics of community," and I describe its effects later. A *potential* significant political result is the emergence of ideologically palatable control over inner-city schooling in the form of school choice and empowerment. I empirically examine this control vis-à-vis students' identity politics in two distinct school cultures in Chapter 5.

THE IDEOLOGICAL STRATEGIES OF THE ENTREPRENEURIAL COALITION

This discussion begins with an analysis of the intellectual and political means that the Entrepreneurial Coalition employs in city schools to accomplish consensus building and to vie for ideological dominance. I previously identified five ideological strategies the Entrepreneurial Coalition has employed in an age of official knowledge (see Apple, 1993; see also Miron & St. John, 1994): school choice, shared governance, school partnerships, state regulation/state takeover, and school intervention.

School Choice

The New Right has employed school choice as its most ideologically controversial policy proposal. Indeed, it is difficult to argue with educational reform groups from both authoritarian populist camps (Hall, cited in Apple, 1993, p. 4) and well-intended liberal educational researchers and activists as to the common-sense appeal of choice proposals. In Milwaukee, for example, journalists have documented how inner-city African-American parents have successfully lobbied the legislature to implement a voucher proposal that provides direct funding to families for their schools of choice, public or private (see Fine, 1993). Viewed on television, these parents present articulate cases for the *state* financing of *private* inner-city schools tuition. To paraphrase one parent: This is not about destroying the public schools. We just can't afford to wait for the system to improve. (I note that these private schools in Milwaukee purport to serve the needs of the *local* African-American community and do not, therefore, appear to be motivated by racial and religious prejudice so typical of the all-white, Christian "academies" during the desegregation era in the South.)

We need to take a more critical look at the origins of these schools in Milwaukee, and similar ones elsewhere (see Fine, 1993). When viewed within a critical perspective, it soon becomes apparent that it, in the Milwaukee and Minnesota cases (see Bredo, 1989; Mazzoni, 1987; Nathan, 1990), the state legislatures have assumed regulatory control over inner-city schooling through the popular appeal of choice. A coalition of entrepreneurs, corporate executives, and state policy analysts and researchers in the Academy and within the Beltway think tanks such as the Brookings Institution has won consensus both from elite business groups and from subordinate parents' groups. This coalition has advanced the policy goal of increased state regulation and control under the guise of the palatable banner of individual choice, the hallmark of American democracy and liberal political philosophy.

I dissect this argument further. The concepts of the possessive individual and authoritarian populism, both of which a host of diverse critical theorists have advanced, will prove helpful in furthering the theoretical and cultural connections between school choice and the requirements of the global economy.

The Possessive Individual and the Politics of Choice

As Apple (1985), Popkewitz (1991), and others have noted, individuals, not groups, purchase goods and services in a capitalist economy. For capital accumulation to proceed, consumerism—the norms of perpetual buying—is not only an economic principle, but "buying power" is a revered social practice among all social-economic groups. Although the free market (and mass advertising) dictates that shopping is an individual, private exercise of economic choice, the ideology of possessive individualism "tend[s] to permeate all of our experience, sets of social relations, and expectations" (Apple, 1985, p. 122). The social outcome is that consumerism stimulates more than simply compulsive shopping. Following Anthony Giddens's (1987) theory of structuration, possessive individualism both organizes *individual* economic behavior to purchase goods and services and culturally reproduces the system of institutional *patterns* of consumption (the market economy). Capitalist social relations are therefore reproduced through the choices of human agents.

Giddens's theory of structuration argues that these broader patterns (capitalism) of social relations both affect, and are affected by, other institutional systems, specifically the schools. Apple (1988b) makes this complex issue in relation to public schooling clear:

> By stimulating an ideology of possessive individualism, the economy "creates" a crisis in the school. The [inner city] school, which under current financial and ideological conditions, cannot meet the stimulated needs of competing individual *and* interest groups, loses its legitimacy. The state, in order to maintain its own legitimacy, hence, must respond in a way that both continues to expand capitalist social relations and an individualistic market at one and the same time. (p. 122; emphasis in original)

The effects of the ethos of possessive individualism, then, reach much further than the economy and the schools. When viewed within this framework, the crisis in inner-city schools makes poor families susceptible to ambitious politicians, who are eager to serve their constituents, but who may not comprehend the unintended long-term consequences of choice (see Fine, 1993). For the Milwaukee parents I described earlier it gives them a genuine feeling of change. It aligns them with elites in the conservative restoration and the Entrepreneurial Coalition. These elites both seek to make social the production goals of a global economy and restructured cities (Miron, 1992; Whitt, 1982) and dream of restoring the nostalgic vision of the two-parent nuclear U.S. family, proving that it is the *state* (government schools), not the failures of corporate policies and practices, that is responsible for low academic achievement among inner-city students.

By denying the social (ideological) roots of the calls for choice in public education, the Entrepreneurial Coalition can decree the failures of city schooling as *failures of government*. It is this crisis of legitimacy that the politics of authoritarian populism seeks to both remedy and exacerbate.

The Politics of Authoritarian Populism in City Schooling

The close connections between the state and the economy in the Entrepreneurial Coalition's pursuit of school choice have profoundly affected the practice of democracy in the United States. National spokespersons among both neoconservative and neoliberal groups (the distinctions are often blurred as the public policies currently promulgated in the Republican-dominated Congress demonstrate), such as the Committee for Economic Development, the Business Roundtable, and the Coalition on Educational Alternatives, have succeeded in exploiting the legitimation crisis of the state. In the inner city parents, schools, classroom teachers, and the central office bureaucracy have all been blamed for poor school and student achievement levels. School choice policies, especially when the state appropriates funding for poor public school parents to choose among private and parochial school alternatives, is viscerally appealing in a societal climate that is increasingly perceived as fostering "descendant" levels of social deviancy (Moynihan, 1993).

As Apple (1993) observed, the ultimate effect of the policies and strategies of authoritarian populism is a manufactured consensus among both dominant and subordinant (parent) groups for the goals of the economic and political elites I described earlier. In the situated restructuring of inner-city schooling in the school districts of Chicago, Milwaukee, and New Orleans, for example, policies such as the decentralization of budgeting become embedded in the discursive practices of school-based management/shared decision making (see Miron & St. John, 1994). The clarion calls for school choice, then, extend beyond the options of exiting (Hirschman, 1970) public schools and institutionalize entire systems of state regulation (masked through polices such as school vouchers, board waivers, and school incentive programs). As I will show, state regulation of public (inner city) schooling also helps foster local social control, as the Entrepreneurial Coalition is able to garner state administrative and policy support for site-based management and the like. In a restructured city economy, now more fully integrated into the global economy, nothing could be more pleasing to entrepreneurs and corporate executives.

Popkewitz's (1991) historical analysis of the origins of educational reform emphasizes the reemergence of state regulation of public schooling. My project on the social construction of the crisis in city schooling sheds light on a qualitatively different phenomena: the emergence of social regulation of inner-city schooling as both medium and outcome of the integration of the global political economy (Morales & Bonilla, 1993). The second ideological strategy of the new Entrepreneurial Coalition, shared governance, illustrates how the social relations embedded in entrepreneurism work to undermine the espoused values of democracy in city schooling.

Shared Governance

As I argued in Chapter 1, elite groups in the corporate, political, educational, and nonprofit sectors view the reform of educational governance (specifically the reform of local school boards) as one concrete area in which they can make a substantial impact over the outcomes of public education. This issue is significant for more than simply academic reasons. Governance reform—elite groups and citizen coalitions alike have variously defined the process as decentralization, school-based management, and local school board accountability—has proved to be an activist rallying cry in many large urban school districts. The (often genuine) expression of concern underlying legislative, programmatic, and electoral reforms in cities like Chicago, New Orleans, and New York cannot, and should not, be summarily dismissed as insignificant (see Miron & Brooks, 1993).

The political question specifically facing the Entrepreneurial Coalition, however, is the means to actually implement school governance reform on a day-to-day basis. Here, entrepreneurs look to the lessons from corporate downsizing and restructuring as models for public education in the city. During the global fiscal crisis, corporations have laid off many mid-management personnel, automated business services, and, in general, brought decision-making authority closer to the bottom line of customer satisfaction. Shared governance exports the strategic responses of the corporation (cf. 3M) to the global fiscal crisis to the social arena of city public schooling. The entrepreneurial spirit, so revered in Fortune 100 companies and multinational corporations, now appears to pervade school-level governance as local community councils, school governance boards, and advisory committees struggle to wrestle decision-making authority away from one educational bureaucrat—the principal—and place it in the hands of a (as yet amorphously defined) community or shared governance group.

I caution that school personnel do not robotically succumb to the logic of capital as expressed through the ideologies of shared governance. For school insiders, shared governance potentially takes on a life of its own and mediates the powerful pull from the Entrepreneurial Coalition to simply "cave in" to the needs of the global economy and the world system of capitalist social relations (see Chilcote & Edelstein, 1983). Obviously, the school's institutional processes are much more complicated than that.

However, by redefining the contours of the educational discourse and sets of discursive practices in entire school communities, not simply the school building itself, corporate and business elites locally influence the full spectrum of the educational conversation. Embedded within the fiscal crisis of the state and the city (O'Connor, 1971; Smith, 1992) are the *surface* structures of educational issues such as an educated workforce that masks the deep (Giddens, 1987; Levi-Strauss, 1968; Miron & Elliott, 1990) relationships between the practice of school-level shared governance and the speed and extent to which an increasingly integrated global economy requires educated graduates. All these macrostructural and micropolitical issues are quite complicated; in the actual day-to-day pressures of implementation within the school community, little time is available for reflection on the competing, and perhaps conflicting, goals, such as critical literacy and multiculturalism. I expand on this point next.

Contradictory Practices of Shared Governance

Entrepreneurial ideology aims to remove the bureaucratic layers from school politics and bring decision making closer to the educational marketplace. By decentralizing governance, corporate and industrial elites in the inner city expect to satisfy the market demands of whom they perceive are its two primary educational consumers—students and parents. Their support of school governance reform thus carries the twin ideological banners of democracy and the free market (for our purposes, possessive individualism and authoritarian populism). However, by removing themselves from representation in most school-site governance decisions, as an analysis of secondary material reveals later, these ideals are far from being realized in the daily institutional practices in the school.

The Impediments to Implementation

Wong (1992) conducted a vast review of the scholarly and empirical research on shared governance in large urban school districts, such as Chicago, New York, Salt Lake City, and Miami: "By the 1990s, virtually all major urban districts have some form of shared governance where parents and community representatives participate in the decision-making structure at the school site" (p. 13). Although governance arrangements vary across large urban school districts, business elites as a political bloc have universally supported school-level parental empowerment, which they perceive is an expected outcome of shared governance.

I draw three generalizations from these findings. First, the empirical evidence suggests that in the inner-city ethnic minorities do not necessarily exercise their political rights when given the option, as in the case of the decentralization experiments in the New York City school system during the 1970s illustrates. Although the studies do not distinguish between district-level decentralization and shared governance at the school level, the overall observation about the variance in ethnic minority participation in elections generally is worth noting. The point is clear: Simply providing the means to practice *procedural* democratic governance, mainly in the form of school board elections, does not guarantee *substantive* democratic practices. (I have more to say about the discursive practices embedded in the new politics of community at the end of this chapter.)

Second, the teachers' unions pose institutional and political limits on parents' authority in school personnel matters. Here the research picture is much cloudier as the context for the escalation of conflict over teachers' firings in the Ocean-Hill Brownsville district in New York in the late 1960s and the battle over decentralization in Detroit between 1969 and 1982 was mired in racial politics. I return to the theoretical and normative issues of race and racial politics in inner-city schools in more detail in Chapters 4 and 5; at this point I simply note the empirical research that points to the competing values of parents' rights versus teachers' rights in the politics of shared governance (Mercanto, 1970; Ravitch, 1974; Campbell et al., 1985, cited in Wong, 1992).

Third, and most significant for my purposes here, the school's contradictory institutional processes constrain parental participation in shared governance. In Salt Lake City, for instance, a study of decentralized governance in eight schools revealed that the balance of "power" (legal decision-making authority) did not fundamentally alter during implementation (Malen & Ogawa, 1988, cited in Wong, 1992). These studies suggest several institutional constraints worthy of repetition here. First, two decision structures characterized the school partnership between staff and the community—one for the principal and the professional staff, the other for both the staff and the parents.

Obviously, the school's professional staff gained dominance in policy matters as they controlled the formal agenda and maintained its historical organizational control over school information (Peterson, 1979). Second, parents did not possess the discretionary authority over the school budget, participate in personnel decisions related to the selection or dismissal of the principal, and only rarely did they get an opportunity to evaluate teachers. Third, no formal elections determined the composition of the parent committees; rather, the principal sent invitations to those parents whom the principal perceived as sharing similar values. Parents, then, in the Salt Lake City studies assumed the role of facilitating the perpetuation of system norms and values; they had minor impact on substantive school policy.

Finally, a review of the literature on the bold experiment in the Chicago Public Schools to devolve power from the school board to locally elected parent councils sheds light on the effects of mandated (legislative) empowerment (see Lewis & Nakagawa, 1995). Parents comprise a majority representation on the councils. By state law, the local councils have the authority to hire and fire the principals, control the school budget, and propose school improvement ideas. Business and nonprofit organizations have sponsored training in organizational development, budget planning, and evaluation methods. In the first test of council power—the renewal of principal contracts—the councils voted to reappoint 82% of those contracts that were scheduled for review. These statistics imply that simply including a majority of parents on the local councils does not guarantee substantive changes in governance (see Lewis & Nakagawa, 1995).

School-Business Partnerships

In the mid-1980s, the Committee for Economic Development (CED) issued a policy statement that suggested that business assume a dominant role in the national educational reform movement. Owen B. Butler, who was chairman of Procter and Gamble, argued that the role of business was more than an ancillary one; the national business community would assume leadership responsibilities in key school-level operations—financing, curriculum, workforce preparation or training, and the organization and management of schools. Butler captured the business perspective—which set in motion the creation of thousands of school-business partnerships in cities nationwide as the volumes of case studies illustrates (see McGuire, McLaughlin, & Nachtigal, 1986):

> The relationship between economic development and the quality of public school education is recognized as an issue of prime importance by CED. In recent years, CED has become increasingly concerned with the ability of American business to compete in world markets. The Committee's study of productivity trends showed that the decline of educational standards in the United States, despite the existence of many fine schools, is linked to the nation's flagging economic competitiveness. (Butler, in Levine & Trachtman, 1988, p. ix)

In the inner city, school-business partnerships have long been touted by district administrators and corporate executives as a means of both relieving some of the burdensome fiscal stresses on school financing and more closely aligning K-12 educational goals and outcomes with the needs of the economy. The entrepreneurial social classes make a strong case for greater influence over the curriculum, administration, and teaching strategies by stressing the interconnections between an educated workforce and a competitive global economy. I point to the Union Carbide Corporation's endorsement of Outcome-Based Education in St. Charles Parish, Louisiana, as a curriculum and teaching model that will prepare students to learn all phases of the production enterprise.

School-business partnerships (which Levine, 1985, loosely conceptualizes as joint ventures between the public and the private sectors) are commonplace practices in inner-city schools and school districts. Their purposes and activities vary from school to school and across districts, ranging from restoration of school facilities to curriculum intervention (see Miron & Wimpelberg, 1989). Based on the vague principle of collaboration, which implies a two-way communication process and the mutual development of shared goals and objectives (Haynes, 1993), businesses in the inner city have promoted the strategy of partnerships under the reform ideological banner. This ideological strategy of the Entrepreneurial Coalition bridges the dual needs of the financial and human resources requirements of the school and the facilitation of the school-to-work transition for business and industry.

These alliances between corporations and urban, public schools exist at all levels of the educational system: local, state, and federal. For example, using funds earmarked for school reform from a constitutionally protected trust fund, Governor Roemer of Louisiana supported the Cities in Schools project, which sought to provide support services in inner-city middle schools in New Orleans and Shreveport as it has in major cities throughout the country. The program is funded locally through the privately supported Girl Scouts organization. Furthermore, during the Bush Administration, the Job Training and Partnership Act (JTPA) established the Private Industry Councils (PICs) to oversee the distribution of federal dollars to mostly private contractors to provide remedial education and work training and employment to inner-city youth, many of whom lived in public housing developments. Entrepreneurs in urban centers throughout the country such as oil wildcatter Pat Taylor[2] and energy executive James ("Jim Bob") Moffett of New Orleans have touted the PIC and other partnership mechanisms as a means of instilling the values and attitudes of business in undereducated and poor youth in inner-city schools.

In addition to instilling the values of business and industry in minority students, partnerships have had an impact on school governance. Through formal school-business partnership arrangements (Chicago and New Orleans boast the largest number of individual partnerships totaling several thousand), business representatives are now formally involved in the agenda issues of the school at the point of greatest vulnerability—finances and management support. In exchange for small funding and technical expertise, classroom teachers and the principal *may*, in turn, agree to curriculum changes and other substantial school policy reforms. In shared governance, school partnerships then often pit business representatives against parents and teachers, who may serve on school advisory committees (see Miron & St. John, 1994). However, as I discussed earlier, parents in the inner city often lack the financial and organizational wherewithal to influence school policy and practices directly (see Wong, 1992). When the changes in governance advocated by members of the Entrepreneurial Coalition do not materialize, or do not produce the attendant increases in academic achievement, then a final resort is a direct appeal to state government.

---

[2] Pat Taylor is president of Taylor Oil Companies, an independent oil and gas producer in Louisiana. Taylor is founder of "Taylor's Kids," a nationally recognized scholarship program for at-risk students. He has been successful in persuading the state legislature in Louisiana and other states to fund free tuition programs for any high school graduate who meets basic academic requirements and who otherwise could not afford to pay college tuition.

State Regulation/State Takeover

In May 1993, the Education Commissioner for the State of New Jersey hired Rebecca A. Doggett as new auditor general of the Newark public school system. Ms. Doggett's appointment came on the heels of voter resentment in New Jersey for Governor Florio's $2.8 billion tax increase, for which he won legislative approval in 1991. Many of the tax increases Florio earmarked for the improvement of large urban school districts such as Newark and Jersey City, whose large concentration of at-risk students necessitated vastly increased state funding. Taxpayer disenchantment with state government, and urban school districts in particular, grew out of the widespread belief in New Jersey that the government was now broke, largely as a result of spending fortunes on urban schools (Wines, 1993, p. 1).

Doggett hoped to avert a state takeover of the Newark school district, which is authorized under state statue in New Jersey as it is in several other states (Pancrazio, 1992). Ironically, the acute fiscal and achievement problems in Newark accompanied the court remedies prescribed in *Abbot v. Burke*, in which plaintiffs representing poor urban students successfully sued the State of New Jersey in State Supreme Court. The Court found that the:

> inadequacy of urban students' present education measured against their needs is glaring. Whatever the cause, these [poor urban] school districts are failing abysmally, dramatically, and tragically. Poorer students need a special supportive educational effort in order to give them a chance to succeed as citizens and workers. (cited in Hugg & Miron, 1991, p. 964)

Although there is strong historical and legal precedent in the U.S. Constitution authorizing the state, through its Department of Education, to assume responsibility for the operations of an entire school district, it is only during the reform decade of the 1980s that we have seen state government take such dramatic measures. In this context, *takeover* means "that the state temporarily assumes policymaking and administrative leadership for the district" (Pancrazio, 1992, p. 74). The question of whether the State of New Jersey's Auditor General will recommend that the state assume temporary control of finances and administration is part and parcel of other substantive concerns.

In the political context of legislative mandates for additional funding for large urban school districts and increased school district flexibility to meet student needs (see Hugg & Miron, 1991), the issue highlights a fundamental tension in contemporary urban school governance reform: school district decentralization and increased regulation in the form of state mandates and local ideological control.

Decentralization

Tyack (1993) asserts that the current trend toward devolution of decision making from central office to the school level masks a pervasive historical pattern of educational governance—"a steady march from decentralization to centralization" (p. 7). In broader terms, the moves in New Jersey and in several other states (Kentucky and West Virginia) to take over school districts signals the reemergence of state regulation of schooling generally (Popkewitz, 1991) and the reallocation of the authority of urban school boards through state fiscal control (Cronin, 1992; Miron & Wimpelberg, 1992; Shelley, 1994). Thus, the current reform fad to dislodge the control of central bureaucracies of urban schools is fraught with contradictions. The ideological strategies I cited previously—shared governance and school choice—are feasible if (and only if) the narrow outcomes of the specific reform interests of the Entrepreneurial Coalition are in fact met: higher tests scores and the mastery of academic knowledge and dispositional skills embedded in the global economy.

Fond of emulating the business practices of corporate America, educational professionals touted the virtues of efficiency and expertise during the progressive era's push for centralization. These same corporate values are embodied in the current wave of decentralization (Tyack, 1993). In the context of fiscal scarcity, and the "politics of organizational decline" (Crowson & Boyd, 1992: 88) in large-city school districts, it is clear that decentralization will likely produce only marginal effects on classroom practice (Elmore, 1993; Sarason, 1990). Moreover, the unanticipated outcomes of decentralization on inner-city schools and school districts are likely to exacerbate the entrepreneurial call for market-based solutions to urban schooling—privatization. Carnoy (1993) defined *privatization* as the process whereby "individual schools—whether publicly owned and secular, or privately owned and religious—would operate with equal access to *public* resources, and largely independently of public controls, in a free market of educational services" (p. 164; emphasis added).

Following Whitt (1982), I have elsewhere termed this pattern "the privatization of the public interest" (Miron, 1992, p. 281) of which I will have more to say at the end of this chapter. I turn now to the theoretical connections between decentralization and increased regulation over inner-city schooling in the form of ideological control.

Ideological Control Over Inner-City Schooling

Historically, bureaucratization in city school systems has produced an interesting dual phenomena—"tight coupling" of classroom practices (standardization) and "fragmented centralization" of central office decision making. Surveying governance arrangements in the early development of urban schooling, Tyack (1993) wrote that:

> [The] patterns of governance were extremely heterogeneous, not to say chaotic, but instruction was tightly coupled to the course of study established by administrators. Ideological agreement among most citizens concerning the general purpose and nature of schooling encouraged school leaders to organize instruction more efficiently, even where politicians contested over the spoils of office or engaged in ethnocultural disputes. (p. 10)

In the absence of vertically integrated governance arrangements and centralized authority, Tyack forcefully argues that a deeper, longer lasting control permeated institutional school life in the early 20th century. This "invisible hand of ideology" accounts for the remarkably consistent pattern of classroom structure and practices school governance reform advocates must contend with today.

I extend Tyack's argument about the ideological nature of institutional conformity in urban public schooling and claim that the contemporary *source* of this ideological control lies within the values and ideological strategies of the Entrepreneurial Coalition. Furthermore, the interests of entrepreneurial elites are now contested in the cultural war in inner-city schools and classrooms over the control of the content and processes of city schooling. The political "winner" in the struggle over the dominant discourses of community will shape the educational landscape in cities for years to come.

Critical scholarship over the past two decades has persuasively documented the flawed assumptions of neutrality in the political and normative educational enterprise and painstakingly studied the reproduction of educational and social inequality as an outcome of public schooling. This understanding of public schooling, particularly in viewing the curriculum as a political text (Pinar & Bowers, 1992), demands that critical scholars delve into the question of which groups should begin with a preferred access (see Smith, 1974) to the structure of unequal power relations in educational policy and how do these dominant group interests manage to win the consensus of subordinate groups (parents and teachers) for their programs over time? In Chapter 1, I reviewed Michael Apple's (1988a) work on the noninstructional purposes of schooling in the stage of advanced capitalism. Subsequently, a host of historical research on the influence of *private* groups outside of formal public schooling (e.g., the American Book Company, Channel One, see DeVaney, 1994) cements the theoretical ties between the structure of schooling and the wider political economic relations outside of the school and school district.

In U.S. cities, owing to the changes in the global economy (Smith, 1980; Smith & Feagin, 1987), corporate elites have assumed a leadership role in articulating the interconnections between good public schools and economic development (Butler, 1988; Miron, 1992; Swanstrom, 1988). As Gramsci's (1971) theoretical/political work informs critical scholarship and research, dominant groups gain the approval of competing interests, not by force but, rather, by providing moral and intellectual leadership.

I assert that the most significant tool that the Entrepreneurial Coalition in cities has at its disposal is ideational. The power of ideas to *potentially* gain hegemonic influence in advanced capitalist societies—now nationally and globally connected through information technology and the news media—cannot be underestimated in the urban context. Business and industry have appropriated the use of ideological control and influence to win remarkable standardization over the organizational forms in public classrooms, whether rural or urban. These interests are now *vying* for ideological control over governance of inner city schooling; if their ideologically driven strategies of decentralization ultimately prove successful, this control over governance will ultimately lead to hegemonic influence over the aims of *public* (I emphasize, not private) schooling. In the urban context, the "tight coupling" metaphor of ideological control that Tyack borrows from the work of Karl Weick, which is the basis for the institutionalization of the corporate model of classroom organization, may well lead to a rationalized acceptance of the fulfillment of the training needs of employers as a measure of academic success. In a word, an educated student in inner-city schools is an employable worker in a global economy. Apple (1993) makes this complex theoretical argument clear:

> In the process, not only are schools increasingly incorporated into the market governed by the "laws" of supply and demand and by the "ethic" of capital accumulation, but *students themselves become commodities*. They too are bought and sold as "targets of marketing opportunity" to large corporations. (p. 101; emphasis added)

However, I am getting ahead of myself. I need to analyze the final ideological strategy of the Entrepreneurial Coalition to complete my argument. This is the strategy of school intervention.

School Intervention

The most widespread strategy the Entrepreneurial Coalition employs to influence city schooling is intervention. Intervention strategies range from the extreme of private institutions such as Boston University's School of Education assuming temporary leadership over the Chelsea, MA, school district to a school-business partnership's providing after-school tutoring services. In this section, I concentrate on two models—"accelerated schools" and the Comer model—both of which have gained notoriety in federal documents (*America 2000*) and of which hundred of schools have implemented nationally. My purpose in comparing the two approaches is not to evaluate the results of these programs; rather, I critically analyze the extent to which their development and implementation in inner-city schools nationwide has had the unintended consequences of furthering the aims of the Entrepreneurial Coalition.

I begin with an overview of the Accelerated Schools Process (ASP), which Henry Levin and his associates at Stanford University and training centers across the country have designed as an integrated process of school change to bring so-called at risk students into the educational mainstream.

The Accelerated Schools Process

In 1989, after extensively researching approaches to intervention in inner-city schools, the Chevron Companies awarded Stanford University a $1.4 million grant to pilot test the ASP in four urban centers; San Francisco, Los Angeles, New Orleans, and Houston. Borrowing from the historical research conducted at Stanford University on educational reform (Cuban & Tyack, 1990), the designers of the ASP concluded that educational reform in the United States has generally failed because of its piecemeal approach. In the 1950s, for example, curriculum reforms in math and science teaching and learning, driven by the launching of Sputnik, were implemented without changes in governance (Levin, 1988; Popkewitz, 1991). In the 1990s, as I previously illustrated, decentralization and shared governance are the current educational panaceas for the belittled inner-city schools.

The ASP, therefore, mounts a three-pronged attack on the historical problems of the mismatch (Cuban & Tyack, 1990) and cultural distance (Ogbu, 1974) between the home and community resources of poor, ethnic minority, at-risk students in innercity schools and the (largely, White middle class) expectations of conventional schools and school districts. The strategy calls for simultaneous school-level changes in curriculum, teaching, and school governance. Embedded within this model of integrated school change (special education and Chapter one teachers, as well as parents and community members, are brought into the change process as school "cadre" leaders) are three core principles: unity of purpose, building on strengths, and empowerment coupled with responsibility (Hopfenberg & Levin, 1993).

Very briefly, *unity of purpose* refers to the entire school community, including parents and business and neighborhood leaders, pulling together as a team to set a shared vision for the school and to establish goals and objectives. *Building on strengths* refers to using the combined talent of everyone in the school to further the overall mission of bringing at-risk students into the educational mainstream. Finally, *empowerment coupled with responsibility* embraces the philosophy and techniques of school-based management to grant teachers the informal authority to make educational decisions in the best interests of children in exchange for taking additional responsibilities, rather than deferring to the principal or having decisions dictated from above at the central office and by "remote control" from state boards of education (Levin, 1988). I should note that at the heart of ASP is the *Inquiry* method, first promulgated by Dewey, wherein classroom teachers in particular invoke a systematic reflective practice to pose and solve educational problems (Hopfenberg & Levin, 1993; St. John, Miron, & Davidson, 1992). Thus, school leaders employ a dialectical process of looking inward through the inquiry process and looking outward to community resources to realize their shared vision and transform the school to meet student needs (see Miron, 1991).

Stanford University field tested the Accelerated Schools model in the Bay Area in California and later collaborated with public universities in the cities I mentioned earlier to implement the process in a context of fiscal and organizational decline in inner-city schools (see Crowson & Boyd, 1992). Miron and St. John's (1994) research on the implementation of the ASP in the urban context found that the deeper, unresolved racial, financial, and ideological tensions expressed in teachers' strikes, school/community relations between White administrators and African-American teachers and parents, and the notoriously low level of per-pupil funding greatly constrained the process. Not surprisingly, the leadership capacity of administrators, teachers, students, and parents to mediate these constraints largely determined the success or failure of the model in inner-city schools and school districts. One common means to secure additional financial and organizational support, which I will not go into here (see Bogotch, Miron, & Garvin, 1993), was the enlisting of both corporate and political support for unmet school needs, such as wiring for air conditioning.

That certain dimensions of the ASP map the contours of the Entrepreneurial Coalition's ideological strategies are apparent from this brief description of the ASP. Most noticeable is the reliance on school-based management (embodying the principle of empowerment) as one "leg of the triangle" of the school change process. In principle, teachers are free, within the constraints of state and local policy guidelines, to enact pedagogical strategies to meet the achievement needs of at-risk students. In practice, the values of the Entrepreneurial Coalition undermine teacher and parental/community empowerment (see Miron & St. John, 1994). For example, classroom teachers may decide to include alternative assessment practices (student portfolios) rather than rely solely on the gains made on standardized achievement tests. However, to date, these innovations to promote greater equity for minority students have remained dormant (see Haynes, 1993). It is frequently argued by state and local superintendents of education alike that alternate assessment measures lack a well-developed technology and are costly and labor intensive. These barriers are formidable to the implementation of the core philosophical principles and organizational change strategies of the ASP.

ASP has been successful in some schools "situated" within the urban context (Miron & St. John, 1994; St. John et al., 1992). However, the situated character of school restructuring in the inner city makes the conditions for exporting the principles of the ASP highly problematic (see Miron & St. John, 1994). The danger is that a good process on paper will become overroutinized and, ultimately, undermine the benefits for at-risk students the ASP is purportedly designed to serve.

The Comer Model

In 1968, psychologist James Comer of Yale University's Child Study Center introduced into the New Haven Public Schools his School Development Program (SDP) as a model of school improvement to provide a "mechanism at the building level to allow parents, teachers and administrators to, first, understand the needs, and then to collaborate with and help each other address those needs in an integrated, coordinated way" (Comer, 1988, p. 2). His model is grounded in the developmental needs of children and in their relationship issues to parents, other children, the school, and the community. A school organizational and management system designed to comprehensively address these central issues of child development is the basis for school change.

Comer stresses that the SDP differs from other approaches in that it unites the entire school community—students, teachers, business owners, and parents—to work together to coordinate resources and programs to meet the specific goals and objectives of each school. However, the governance and management team consist of all of the adults in the school, typically, the principal, a mental health team member, two teachers selected by their peers, and three parents selected by the parents organization. Apparently, no students serve on the team. Significantly, the school principal is always the leader of the school team (Joyner, 1991).

The purposes of the governance and management team are to establish policy guidelines; plan, implement, and evaluate changes in the curriculum, social climate, and staff development; coordinate school programs and groups; and to assist the parent group in planning an annual social calendar. The governance and management group plans and organizes these school activities to improve the climate of the school (Haynes, Comer & Hamilton-Lee, 1988), raise student achievement, and provide staff development activities to meet school goals and objectives (Haynes et al., 1988). Although the principal is the governance team leader, consensus is the basis for program decisions; the principal should not use the team to "rubber stamp" administrative decision, nor should the team seek to derail the principal's leadership and authority. A guiding principle of "no fault" structures the problem solving processes in the school (Comer, 1985). The problem-solving model leans heavily on community involvement.

Parents comprise the bulk of community involvement in the SDP. They constitute three members of the governance and management team, and they participate in other levels of school activities as well. For example, parents are involved in structured social activities that the parents' organization coordinates; they are also hired to assist teachers in the classrooms as tutors or aides.

Despite the structural emphasis on shared governance, it appears that the Comer model does not alter the fundamental unequal power relations within the school organization. Some researchers have noted that the concept of a professional team does mitigate against the historical isolation and autonomy of school professionals in their interactions with parents (see Crowson, 1992). The principal still remains the formal, final decision maker. Although parents do provide input in a consultative role (Glickman, 1993), their activities seem limited to keeping the social calendar and supporting the functions of the school. Comer's model has helped parents become genuine partners within the school. Empirical research would be needed to ascertain whether there is sufficient organizational space for parents and community members to assume more substantive roles.

SUMMARY

I assert that these ideological strategies result in a new inequality in the educational opportunities and outcomes for racial and ethnic minorities in the inner city. Paradoxically, the new social and academic inequalities provide space for identity politics because students often resist their dominant representation as deviant and at risk of academic failure. The ideological strategies of the Entrepreneurial Coalition would have effects that are confined mainly to schools located in the inner city if a concurrent national movement for curriculum standards were not in place. The following discussion underscores the extent to which the requirements of the global economy pervade the rationality of the educational discourse in rural and suburban districts. However, as I repeatedly have argued, city schools, caught as they are in the nexus of the global economy and a postmodern movement toward multiethnic student identities, bear the greatest organizational and discursive burden of these economic and cultural paradigm shifts. These schools are entangled in what I call the "new politics of community."

THE NEW POLITICS OF COMMUNITY

National Curriculum Goals

In September 1989, at the University of Virginia, President George Bush and the nation's 50 governors jointly issued an agreement (see *The Statement*, 1989, E1). This statement outlined a national vision for public education that emerged from what the White House had billed as a historical occasion: the commitment of the President to facilitate the development of national education goals through the work of the National Governor's Association Education Task Force.

Following the themes of the federal Department of Education's 1983 report, *A Nation at Risk*, the Compact stressed the vital importance of maintaining the U..S.'s competitive position in the world economy. However, the statement went a step further, calling for the formation of a federal-state partnership to steer the development and implementation of national education goals (and, subsequently, a national curriculum). This newly defined intergovernmental collaboration is highlighted in the following statement:

> The President and the nation's Governors agree that a better educated citizenry is the key to the continued growth and prosperity of the United States. Education has historically been, and should remain, a state responsibility and a local function, which works best when there is also strong parental involvement in schools. And, as a nation, we must have an educated work force , second to none, in order to succeed in an increasingly competitive world economy. (p. E1)

Not only are the connections between education and global economic competition tightly drawn in this excerpt from the *Jeffersonian Compact*, but the authors also provide a hint of the community-based strategy for implementing national goals and standards in their emphasis on strong parental involvement.

President Bush's second Secretary of Education, Lamar Alexander (a former governor of Tennessee), launched his administration with *America 2000*, a community-based education strategy that reflected the vision of the President and the nation's governors. The discourses surrounding the implementation strategies of *America 2000* were cast at the rhetorical level. They were designed to employ the language and rhetoric of community empowerment as it simultaneously left out the voices of teachers and parents and neighborhood residents in the formation of goals and the development of alternate reform objectives (see Sizer, 1995).

The Rhetorical Community Discourse of America 2000

It took former President Bush nearly three years to embark on a strategy to involve local communities in the discourse of the national education goals and standards. In August 1991, Secretary Alexander released thousands of copies of *America 2000*, the Department of Education's written "plan to move every community in America toward the National Education Goals adopted by the President and the Governors." Significantly, local communities— in particular, fiscally distressed cities—had no voice in the adoption of the education goals. However, President Bush called on them to "join him in a 'populist' crusade to make America('s)" schools better (Alexander, 1991, p. 1). Furthermore, although the report did not specifically target urban centers, it is clear that the Bush Administration (and its allies in the Entrepreneurial Coalition) would target the nation's inner city schools. They would receive the greatest impact of the implementation of national goals and standards because of their chronic state of fiscal and "organizational decline" (Crowson & Boyd, 1992, pp. 88-91).

Obviously, inner-city schools, unlike their better funded and supported suburban counterparts (Kozol, 1991), posed a threat to the Entrepreneurial Coalition's ambition to improve the labor force. Their perceived weak aggregate performance on standardized tests, inordinately large school dropout rate, and culturally and socially diverse school populations scared many entrepreneurs and business executives. In major U. S. cities, as I show later, groups such as the Chamber of Commerce have subsequently assumed volunteer leadership positions in galvanizing public support for the educational goals set forth in *America 2000*, and its successor during the Clinton Administration, *Goals 2000*.

A cursory analysis of the national education goals reveals that the idealized outcome of this national education strategy is the alignment in the inner-city classrooms with the training and education needs of the global economy and the curriculum and pedagogical practices of city schooling. A synopsis of the national education goals follows.

By the year 2000, the majority of U.S. students will:

1. Begin school ready to learn;
2. Graduate from high school (90%);
3. Leave grades 4, 8, and 12 competent in the core subject areas of English, mathematics, science, history, and geography;
4. Achieve first place in the world in math and science competition;
5. Be literate and possess the skills necessary to compete in a global economy and exercise the rights and responsibilities of citizenship; and
6. Rid themselves of drug abuse and violent behavior in schools. (adopted from *The National Education Goals*, cited in Alexander, 1991, p. 3).

I now compare the achievement rates, school dropout rates, and incidents of drug abuse and violent behavior in the nation's 47 largest school districts. Data provided by the Council of Great City Schools (1992) indicate that, in 1990, the school dropout rate was 39% higher in large urban school districts compared to the national average, 32% of inner-city public school students scored in the bottom quarter on national standardized achievement tests in reading, 27.8% in math. Furthermore, only 5.3% of poor, minority inner-city students met national math standards compared to the national average of 14.9%, or about three times as many. Finally, on the use of illegal drugs, the Council of Great City Schools' data do not report substantial differences, certainly much less than the achievement data, between inner-city students and nonmetropolitan students; 33% illicit drug use compared to 30%.

These data point to the dangers of embarking on a generic community-wide strategy to implemental national education goals and standards in large urban school districts. Without attention to the local social context, priorities and goals may be arbitrarily set and outdated by the time the means are found to realize them. Moreover, the socially constructed character of urban schooling and its common-sense crisis status is graphically illustrated in the data on illicit drug use. It is widely believed that in inner-city schools, violence and undesirable behavior is rampant (Shanker, 1992), and drug use is one of the critical factors associated with these behaviors.

Although the achievement data in math and reading point to school-and system-level problems, a closer look points to the dispelling of the alleged failures of urban schooling. For example, the Council cites a National Assessment of Educational Progress study that shows that, during the period between 1970 and 1989, 9-year-old inner-city students increased their reading achievement by 12.8 points, almost three times the national average of 4.5 points. I believe that a strong case can be made that the unintended targets of the national education goals remain inner city schools and school districts. However, the strategy of mobilizing local communities to adopt, support, and implement the goals and the emerging sets of core curriculum standards without attention to *both* sets of findings (in which educational outcome inequalities remain glaring, *and* in which substantial progress has been made) will ultimately harm the groups this strategy might have benefited—students, teachers, and parents in city schools. The roots of this harm lies in the systematic silencing of voices in the discourses and politics of community and the formulation of national educational goals.

The Silent Voices in the Discourses of National Education Goals

Economic, political, educational, and civic elites—the consensus-building group I call the Entrepreneurial Coalition—formulated the national education goals and are now embarking on their implementation. Like most of the programs of educational reform begun between 1983 (with the publication of *A Nation at Risk*) and the present, not much is likely to change in the technical core areas of teaching and learning, which is the official focus of the Goals Panel. The reason is that those actors most likely to have an effect on achieving the requisite changes in the culture of the school (see Bogotch et al., 1993; Fullan, 1990; Sarason, 1990) have not been consulted by the elites in the Entrepreneurial Coalition. Rather, a community-based strategy, which political elites such as school superintendents and civic group leaders have devised locally, is expected to garner the support of inside members of the school community.

Put simply, the national goals discourse is about the *means* of education, with no conversation about *ends*. Indeed, under the administration of Lamar Alexander, staff for *America 2000* implementation meetings in local communities routinely insisted in involving and showcasing prominent education establishment leaders such as state and local school superintendents, school board members, and, in some cities, occasionally even the mayor. The assumption was that these state and local educational and municipal leaders had already "signed off" on the national goals, and their role was then to convince those at the bottom of the hierarchy to endorse them—and to arrive at a grassroots means of achieving the goals. For example, in Richmond, VA, the leader of the Chamber of Commerce's education committee organized a 125-member steering committee, co-chaired by the wife of the former governor, which with the financial backing of corporations formed the Mets Foundation.

This foundation organized itself into 14 working groups, which in turn focused on specific curriculum issues, school organization, and the like (*Goals 2000 Background Paper*, 1993). The leadership of the steering committee had obviously adopted the national goals, and the discourse of the subsequently organized task forces and forums was on the processes of reaching these goals in the metropolitan Richmond schools. No mention of the roles of students and teachers was contained in the federal Department of Education's May 18, 1993, summary. The text of *America 2000* is ambitious on what the American people can do *for* its public schools: for students, radically improve all 111,000 schools; for teachers and school leaders, establish Governor's Academies with federal seed monies; and for parents, promote school choice. However, the text is conspicuously silent on what the nation can do *with* teachers, students, and parents. The rhetorical strategy, rather, implores the nation to "look beyond our classroom to our communities and families" to assist groups like the Goals 2000 panel to meet their objectives and ambitious timetable (see Department of Education, 1991).

Empowerment and the New Politics of Community

Two related themes run parallel in the ideological strategies employed by the Entrepreneurial Coalition. The first theme is empowerment, the second community. Despite their acute differences, both school intervention and state regulation strategies take as their fundamental theoretical premise the empowerment of parents and community. For example, the hallmarks of both the Comer Model and ASP are quality parental involvement, which fosters the taking of ownership and responsibility for the quality of children's learning. A second hallmark is broadly defined community involvement, in which neighborhood groups, businesses, churches, and social organizations (see Heath & McLaughlin, 1993) help define the goals of inner-city schools and school districts and jointly forge a shared vision of the school with leaders.

Clearly embedded in the rhetoric of *America 2000* and the literature of the National Goals panel is the idea that school change will derive outside of the institutional (building boundaries) of the school. *America 2000* authors and advocates astutely understood the political opportunities germane to the national school restructuring movements by advancing a rhetoric of a grassroots campaign to change schools community by community (Alexander, 1991). What is not clear at this point is in which direction the community strategy of the Entrepreneurial Coalition will take in urban centers. It can lead toward a narrow discourse on the economic vision of the aims of public schooling or toward a more broadly defined, diversely situated "common good" (Raskin, quoted in Apple, 1993). The latter alternative vision embraces the values and needs of local communities in the conceptualization of economic development and economic growth (see First & Miron, 1991; also Miron, 1992).

THE SOCIAL PRODUCTION OF KNOWLEDGE IN THE CITY

Thomas Popkewitz (1991) has persuasively argued that the history of educational reform is best understood in the context of social regulation generally and the reemergence of state steering over public schooling in the 1980s and 1990s particularly. Although Popkewitz (1991) focuses on "the *regional* ways in which power affects and produces social relations" (p. 3; emphasis added), my concern is with the specific *local* means in which social relations affect and (re)produce knowledge in city schools and their local communities. In cities, the state's administrative regulation over public schooling, opening as it has new social and political spaces of community and identity (see Chapters 4 and

5), is decoupled from the social regulation (and control) over knowledge, potentially controlled by the Entrepreneurial Coalition. I must continually emphasize *potentially controlled* because the struggle for ideational consensus in the city is continuously being waged.

The Entrepreneurial Coalition takes its educational goals, which are to align the outcomes of city schooling with the training needs of a global economy, as social givens. However, the Coalition looks not to educational professionals to achieve these goals, but rather to the local community. The local communities in the inner city, as fiscally distressed as they are, have formed partnerships and other institutional arrangements with business and industry.

Parents, also contradictorily positioned (but politically aligned) with business groups and other members of the Coalition, are now stationed as partners within the educational trusteeship of the reinvented governance scheme in urban centers. The impulse is strong for parents, school administrators, and teachers to uncritically accept the corporate model of city schooling in a global economy—to "produce" the skilled workforce that will (ostensibly) enhance job creation for impoverished students and their families. Knowledge production and acquisition in this context is no longer a positive function of the culture of "technocratic rationality" (Giroux, cited in Feinberg, 1982, p. 110); it is locally embedded in social relations, which inexorably link knowledge with power. Specifically, the knowledge that some inner-city students come to acquire is *knowledge about employability and economic survival in a context of local and global fiscal crisis.*

Other competing forms of curriculum and its content, such as critical literacy, are in danger of being viewed as "interesting, but a luxury." Regardless of which direction this competition between alternate visions of public schooling in the city ultimately assumes, it is clear from the analysis and illustrations in this chapter that the social contours of knowledge in city schools now map the (dis)courses of the social action educators and parents are likely to take. By uncritically bringing the "other" into the educational mainstream via the new politics of community, the Entrepreneurial Coalition may in fact make invisible the differences that enrich the shared heritages of African-Americans, Latinos, and other ethnic groups in city schools.

CONCLUSION

Admittedly, it is a struggle to remain optimistic about the prospects of the values of local communities setting the parameters for the discourses over the aims of public city schooling. Critical scholarship on the discourses embedded in the cultural politics of the school (Apple, 1993) and on the political economy of the state (Poulantzas, 1978; Smith, 1980) underscore the *contested* terrain of cultural struggle in the civic arena of public schooling in the competition for hegemony. However, the Entrepreneurial Coalition in cities has a jump start. It has astutely exploited the legitimation crisis of the state (Habermas, 1975; Young, 1988), in particular, the governance of public schooling. The recent victory of the Republican Party in Congressional elections underscores the perception that the values and political ideologies of the Entrepreneurial Coalition have won out. The calls for the reinvention of government and government schools are illustrations of its successes in the battle to define the discourse in the public and civic arenas.

The battle is not yet over however. Two political outcomes are possible. On the one hand, parents have seemingly won important symbolic battles to alter governance arrangements in cities such as Chicago, New Orleans, and Cleveland (National League of Cities, 1993). A critical look at these victories reveals that business leaders, working through supportive (but financially dependent) nonprofit organizations have at times underwritten these grassroots campaigns to change the composition of local school boards (Miron & Brooks, 1992). The payoff is expected to be the loosening of the unwieldy grip of the central office bureaucracy over school-level policies and practice through decentralization (see Hannaway & Carnoy, 1993). The ideological rallying call purports that such maneuvers will help put children first (Excellence in Education Committee, 1992). Perhaps unintentionally, though, such tactics will intensify the pressures for privatization and school vouchers (Carnoy, 1993; Elmore, 1993).

A second possible outcome is a direct result of the political space opened by the new politics of community. Parents and other community members do indeed embrace the values of the Entrepreneurial Coalition, but are able to allow their (primarily non economic) interests to prevail. Parents hold the key. Also, the family and extended family plays a role in the transformation of the economic development values of the Entrepreneurial Coalition to those of the local community (see First & Miron, 1991). As I discuss in Chapter 5, how this process plays out in the values that inner-city high school students uphold is quite rich and complex.

Parents, as part of both the school and broader community, can greatly influence the direction of the school. As *inside* stakeholders (see Crowson, 1992), they, with adequate support and training, can focus the policies, leadership styles, and instructional practices of inner-city schools on the moral purposes of helping students learn, aiding their communities in the process (see Foster, 1989; Maxcy, 1991; Miron, 1995; Miron & Elliott, 1990). As *outside* stakeholders, parents can also serve as powerful advocates for the potential resolution of deep-rooted historical problems, such as racism and the inequitable distribution of financial, cultural, and human resources. To the extent that parents and their cohorts in the local and broader social community are aware of the dominant discourses that potentially help foster hegemonic control employed by entrepreneurial elites, their (now awakened) consciousness and strong voices potentially can transform these tendencies. Thus, they may help initiate new direction away from the discursive practices of possessive individualism and authoritarian populism, toward a genuine embracing of local community values.

Time will tell. My interpretative analysis of student voices vis-a-vis their identity politics in Chapter 5 will partly reveal the relative influence these dominant corporate discourses and values carry in the day-to-day lives of students. Through a postmodern focus on student voices and lived cultural experiences, critical theorists can bring the abstract theory and practice of urban school reform into the everyday living in schools. Perhaps then can we avoid the (seemingly perpetual) social reproduction of crises in urban schooling.

Chapter 4

Postmodernism and the Politics of Urban Pedagogy

In Chapter 2, I traced the patterns of social reproduction of crises in urban schooling by locating these crises in their historical and social contexts. I demonstrated how the political ideologies and public policies of the Great Society and the New Federalism defined the discourses in urban schooling, shifting its public image from actions to be taken in behalf of a more just society to its current focus as a drain on the domestic economy.

I also explored the tenets and general orientation of a postmodern social analysis. Specifically, I outlined the postmodern stress on the understanding of the everyday, the meaning of marginality, its opposition to the modernist assumptions of a unitary self and determinancy, and the possibilities of local cultures modifying material and ideological structures of domination. In this chapter, I expand the project of postmodern social analysis to focus on what Henry Giroux (1993) and others have called "rewriting the politics of identity and difference." In particular, I analyze how the new social space of ethnicity in the global context of the cities is played out in the pedagogy of city schools. This process is, obviously, quite complex and ultimately optimistic. However, in the hopes of avoiding some of the romantic pitfalls associated with radical pedagogy and democracy, I am careful to highlight the thorny problems of pervasive racism, the ideological constraints on schools and teachers, and the lingering conceptual traps of a modernist paradigm. For, despite the optimism that postmodern social analysis exudes for altering oppressive practices of domination, the fact remains that public education, particularly in the inner city, remains entrenched in a modernist paradigm, which sees reason, scientific principles, and technology as alleviating much of the suffering currently experienced in distressed schools.

I begin this exploration by dealing head on with how modernist assumptions shape our understanding of ethnic identity. I specify what I mean by "modernist assumptions." Following Anthony Giddens's (1982) reading of Habermas, modernism embraces both the methods of knowing and the constitution of knowledge itself that are based on technical rationality. In the realm of personal identity and subjectivity, modernism gives rise to an autonomous self, whose actions are rationally motivated in pursuit of "technical interests" (see Habermas, 1970).

My concern in this and subsequent chapters is with the conceptualization of an ethnic identity and the identity politics that inner-city schools both give rise to and resist. My contention is that the underlying conception of identity embraces the philosophy of consciousness (Biesta, 1994), which views the self as autonomous and isolated. I argue that this view has devastating consequences for inner-city students as both their ethnic differences and commonalities bear little relevance for the social practices in the classroom and in the school. I begin with the prevalent, common-sense understanding of ethnic identity.

THE MODERNIST VIEW OF ETHNIC IDENTITY

Ethnic Identity as Self-concept

The prevailing view of ethnic identity is that it is a psychologically fixed product of acculturation and descent (Smith, 1992). Ethnic identity is thought to be an unalterable dimension of self-concept. Spindler and Spindler (1994) characterize this view of self-concept as students' sense of their "enduring self." Members of the same ethnic group are believed to share a similar "set of characteristics, including cultural values, traditions, and behaviors in common. . . ." These characteristics are transmitted through socialization processes, as well as heredity" (Ocampo, Bernal, & Knight, 1993, p. 15). Clearly, the modernist assumption of a fixed, unitary self is an explicit component of the definition quoted here. Because ethnic identity and ethnic group membership are in part genetically transmitted, no room is left for the concept of identities located in multiple discourses, which might serve a multicultural student population in the city. In particular, the concept of *hybridity* (Behdad, quoted in McCarthy & Crichlow, 1993), which some critically oriented postmodern theorists have advanced, is the dynamic shaping the formation of subaltern identity (Grossberg, 1993) and subordinate subjectivity (see Mouffe, 1988).

The modernist perspective of ethnic identity emphasizes its function as an important component of self-concept. Its focus is psychological, its goal self-realization through a "natural" process of socialization. What is important in the formation of ethnic groups is *personal* knowledge about one's own ethnic group and awareness of the individual self as a member of an ethnic group. As Bernal and Knight's (1993b) conceptual model asserts, "Knowledge about other ethnic groups, other than necessary to define one's own group, is not viewed as part of ethnic identity" (p. 33). In a word, no identity politics is possible within this conceptualization.

The first assumption of the modernist view of ethnic identity is acculturation, defined simply as the process of adapting oneself to the broader social surroundings. Knight (1993) argues that when minority persons come into contact with the dominant group, acculturation occurs" (p. 222). Here, ethnic identity is tied to unequal power relations because it consistently is the ethnic minorities who must adapt to the dominant (i.e., white, male?) culture. Within this framework, then, ethnic identity is in fact predetermined by the dominant culture. The processes of socialization mean that ethnic minorities give up at least parts of their identity as they adopt to the values and norms of the dominant group. Knight (1993) is clear on this point in the case of Mexican Americans. He wrote: "The Mexican American family, particularly if there is a long history in the United States, is adapting to the dominant culture, and as a consequence, *its ethnic identity also changes*" (p. 222; emphasis added).

The second assumption is that schools are somehow forced to play an assimilation role and abandon the values and praxis of pluralism. Even within this perspective, however, the schools as socializing agents and sites of pedagogical struggle (Gore, 1993) have a choice to make as they function to reproduce or modify dominant cultural patterns. These "nonfamilial socialization agents" such as the school or community-based organization may, alternatively, strengthen an ethnic orientation or enhance the dominant cultural patterns (Knight, 1993). I explore how the school and other agencies may develop ethnic orientations—hence, promoting collective ethnic identities—at the conclusion of this chapter.

In order to acquire the capacity for social action (knowledge and agency), school professionals need to come to grips with the third assumption of the modernist paradigm—the European model of ethnicity. Schools need to embrace what Cornell West (1993a) and others deem the postcolonial perspective. It then becomes possible to forge a strategy of respect for difference when difference is valued as a resource, not something to be subsumed, and obliterated under the umbrella of multiculturalism.

The European Immigrant Model

The naturally progressive view of ethnic acculturation stems from the experience of White immigrants from Western Europe in the early 20th century. Omi and Winant (1986) labeled this model of ethnicity *the immigrant analogy*. They argue that:

> The origins of the concepts of "ethnicity" and "ethnic group" in the U.S., then, lay outside the experience of those identified . . . as *racial* minorities: Afro Americans, Latin Americans, Native Americans and Asian Americans (blacks, browns, reds, and yellows). The continuity of experience embodied in the application of the terms of ethnicity theory to both groups—to European immigrants and racial minorities—was not established. (p. 17; emphasis in the original)

With the publication of *An American Dilemma*, ethnicity theorist Gunnar Myrdal challenged the dominant biological view of racism. Myrdal took an assimilationist position on black disenfranchisement.[1] As early as 1944, Myrdal asserted that Black inequality, segregation, and prejudice had undermined the U.S.

---

[1]Myrdal's position implied that Blacks would eventually gain full entry into the fabric of U.S. society.

goals of democracy, equality, and justice. America would eventuality have to resolve this contradiction by extending the values of the American Creed to Blacks. Myrdal's optimism of racial equality and the incorporation of Blacks into the fabric of American society was based on the European model of assimilation.

The United States had absorbed the European immigrants, awarded them their individual rights, and witnessed their arrival as full Americans. Mirroring the modernist paradigm of the unitary self and the natural progressive movement of history, Myrdal (1944, p. 16) "firmly believed that black assimilation was an ineluctable imperative" that presented the nation with the clear choice to prove to the entire world that Blacks could be integrated into modern democracy.

Assimilation, therefore, became viewed as a natural and inevitable response to the contradictions of racism. Perilously close to the blame-the-victim syndrome implied in Lewis's culture of poverty thesis, Myrdal implied that so-called pathological dimension in Black culture must be cured by the promises of assimilation (Omi & Winant, 1986).

The social construction of ethnic identity became historically linked with the experience of (White) Europeans, whom despite nativist hostility and discrimination largely were able to take advantage of economic and social opportunities in the United States. The same dynamics do not hold true for native Blacks, immigrant Hispanics from Latin America, and other racially defined minorities For these minority groups, the modernists framework defined their identities, not in ethnic terms, but in categories of race (people of color).

The Pervasiveness of Race

The social construction of racially defined identities for people of color dampens the optimistic view of postmodern social analysis. For racial minorities, the postmodern orientation toward *multiple identities* does not bode well for the historical experience of racism, especially for Blacks, in this country. However, the school and other nonfamilial agencies have a strong role to play, as I explore at the end of this chapter and in subsequent chapters. I share Mouffe's (1988) perspective that "identity is something forged in discourse and hence reformed in political struggle" (quoted in Smith, 1992, p. 503). Before entertaining this postmodern possibility of forging a new identity politics, however, we must (at least cursorily) come to grips with the pervasiveness of race in forging new (or reformed) identities for blacks and other people of color.

Omi and Winant argue that the ethnicity school of personal identity wrongly borrowed from the European model of assimilation to make the case for the eventual incorporation of Blacks into mainstream U.S. society. As such, the (mostly Western) European perspective neglected race as a separate category of socially constructed identity (see West, 1993a): "A qualitatively different historical experience" shaped the identities of racially defined minorities—slavery, colonization, and in the case of Native Americans, virtual extirpation." We have also seen how the assumptions embedded in the assimilationists' view of Myrdal and others embraced a deficit model of culture, tending to blame blacks and others for their supposed cultural pathology, thereby deflecting "attention away from the ubiquity of racial meanings and dynamics" (Myrdal, 1944, p. 21).

The implications for the politics of identity are that race is socially reduced to a component of ethnic identity (see Ocampo, et al., 1993). Subsuming racial categories under the conceptual umbrella of ethnicity fosters the mistaken view that Blacks and other racial minorities are culturally deficient because they are unable to replicate the successful model of assimilation of European White immigrants. The identities of White European immigrants (e.g., the Italians and the Irish) are *ethnically* defined, whereas the identities of blacks and other people of color are predetermined *racially*. The racial politics of identity for Blacks in particular poses dilemmas for schools to foster a multicultural curriculum that assumes that ethnic identity is a shared cultural heritage. For most classroom teachers and other educators, Blacks belong to a race not an ethnic group.

Blacks remain stuck in the quagmire of modernism. The assumptions of a unitary, universal, fixed self continue to haunt Black Americans, especially because, on the one hand, the general population refuses to acknowledge racism as an explanation for economic and social inequality among Blacks (Bridges, 1993; Wilson, 1987). Paradoxically, on the other hand, Black identity is constructed racially and as such is subordinate to the ethnic immigration model, which was based on the White experience. The racially constructed identity of Blacks masks the historical unequal power relations that White ethnic groups exploited to assimilate into U.S. society, grabbing along the way the benefits that incorporation would bring. The assumption of "structural assimilation" is quite unwarranted with respect to racial minorities, whose distinctiveness from the white majority is often not appreciably altered by adoption of the norms and values of the white majority. It would in fact be just as plausible to assume that in the case of racial minorities *"common differences" consists in relatively permanent racial difference and non incorporation.* (Omi & Winant, 1986, p. 22; emphasis added)

Modern ethnicity writers, thus, have historically not been interested in the differences within the Black community. There is a sole, universal difference that marks the Black experience—color. Unlike Italian Americans, and arguably even Latin Americans (see Smith, 1992), Blacks are racially identified with the genetic transmission of skin color. Their cultural differences as African Americans have been historically excluded in the identity politics of race and ethnicity in this country. The following reporter's account of the story of Greg Osborn, an African American of Creole descent, well illustrates the frustration many Blacks experience as having difference universally defined in racial terms:

> The difference between black and white has always been abundantly clear to Greg Osborn. Growing up in Los Angeles, Osborn, 26, would often be presumed to be white. Other times, people would be puzzled and ask if he was white or black. "Neither" was always his answer. "I'm a Creole." It is an answer that has not always satisfied. White people often are confused, uncomfortable with the notion of someone who will not choose black or white. Black people often accuse him of betraying his race, of thinking he's better than them because of his light skin and white ancestry. Osborn is a cousin to Jack Belsom as well. The two of them share a white ancestor dating back to the earliest years of the Louisiana colony in the late 17th and early 18th centuries. But unlike Belsom, who has lived all his life as a white man . . . Osborn spent 19 years trying to live as a Creole, taking haven in the definition that he thought allowed him to live in any world he wished. Neither white, nor black. A mix of both, yet unlike either. Osborn thought he could stay on the fence, not choose. . . . Today, white people who have African ancestry still are confronted with the racism that makes them view that ancestry as tainted, that gives it the power to obliterate other ethnicities, other colors. And so they do not embrace it as part of themselves. (*New Orleans Times-Picayne*, 1993)

Much of the criticism of theories of ethnicity currently points to the pervasiveness of racial categories. The identity of ethnic minorities (people of color) is defined in universal terms based on the modern view of the self. In order to move beyond such stereotypes (ethnic groups are confined to a White, Western European origin), it is imperative to recast identity politics. Theoretical moves such as the new social space of ethnic identity can then assume practical import in inner-city classrooms. What is ultimately left out of a modernist (and many postmodern) social analysis is any notion of hybridity (McCarthy, 1988). In the next section I develop this notion further.

RECASTING THE POLITICS OF ETHNIC IDENTITY

Toward a Notion of Collective Identity

Students' lived culture is fertile soil for the fomenting of identity politics over the struggle of who students are in the classroom. As the composition of student demographics undergoes rapid change in many large urban school districts, owing to the infusion of new ethnic groups, students' personal identities become problematic. Indeed, the urban classroom is transformed into a site of the formation of collective (social) identity. The classroom becomes the terrain of "identity politics" (see Grossberg, 1993; see also Aronowitz, 1994). For example, immigrant groups and students of multiple ethnic origins (e.g., Chicanos) collide with mainstream U.S. culture (Spindler & Spindler, 1994), spawning the formation of the "subaltern identity" (see Grossberg, 1993). The formation of subaltern identities is a dialectical process that both derives from minority students subordinate positions as well as student culture (see Lauria, Miron, & Dashner, 1994).

Researchers in bilingual/bicultural education (Baca & Cervantes, 1989; Fishman, 1976; Paulston, 1980) as well as English-as-a-second-language (Cummins, 1993) have well understood the phenomena of cultural and linguistic "switching." Shifting from native language (L1) to English (L2) or between dialects for students whose native language is English reveals a capacity for students to shift not only codes of language (sometimes within the same class period), but such cultural dexterity, in which language plays a significant role, signals a capacity to switch identities. This shifting is part of students' coping strategies when their "enduring" self is threatened (Spindler & Spindler, 1994). This capacity is theoretically heightened when identity is viewed as relational and in the process of formation (Smith, 1992).

As I illustrate in the next chapter, students resist their representations as disadvantaged minorities when viewed through the conceptual eyes of the dominant culture. When thrust into elite schools, as Herr and Anderson's (1993) research illuminates, token ethnic minority students often cast off old identities at school, only to reassume them at home or in the neighborhood. It is clear that students assume a variety of identities in school, but the site of cultural and identity politics extends far beyond the inner-city school (see Bondi, 1993). As students gain a sense of their own ethnic heritage, thereby becoming an active participant in their individual and collective identity formation, knowledge and awareness of *others'* ethnicity renegotiates their entry into the terrain of identity politics. Biesta (1994) calls this transition in pedagogical relations the development of "practical inter subjectivity" (see Chapter 6). The political implications for student resistance and agency for large populations of ethnic minorities such as African Americans and Latinos/Latinas will become evident in the qualitative analysis of student voice in the next chapter.

I argue here using the previous analysis of ethnic identity that dominant power relations embedded in racial formations have largely prevented Blacks from making affirmative gains in cultural/identity politics. Moreover, the governing psychologically based definition of ethnic identity as a component of self-concept has reproduced modernist assumptions of a unitary, autonomous self. Henry Giroux's (1992) insights into how modernism shaped an individual, atomistic politics of identity are worth noting at length:

> The modernist construction of the human subject . . . often ignored how individuals were constructed within complex, multilayered, and contradictory social formations. At the same time, the autonomous self became the most important unit of analysis in understanding human agency, freedom, and politics. Anchored in the notion of a static and unified identity, the conceptions of subjectivity and freedom were organized around the theory of a free and independent individual. Within this ideological matrix, the freedom and autonomy characteristics of the self contained subject became the ideological referent for defining choice as the measure of freedom in the capitalist marketplace. In this

> version of modernism, the logic of the marketplace narrowly defined the parameters for both human agency and the larger sphere of democracy itself. . . . Missing from this discourse was any analysis of those social and political forces that constructed individual and collective identities across and within different economic, cultural, and social spheres. (p. 206)

Modernist theorists conceptualized identity in purely psychological terms. Ethnicity was also atomized within the free, unitary self as "an individual's membership in a group sharing a common ancestral heritage" (Buriel & Cardoza, 1993, p. 197). However, we must be cautious about the postmodern possibilities of forging a new politics of ethnic identity in city schools. Such social realities as the concept of individual, autonomous identity do not disappear simply because radical theorists, bent on achieving a deepening experience of democracy, declare the onset of a postmodern age. However, as I have illustrated in the historical development of the social context of urban schooling, ideologies (and public policies) *do* change. The postmodern argument is that "discourse shapes the world." I agree with this contention and suggest that the place to begin forging a new cultural politics of ethnic identity is with new language and new ideas. The first of these is the concept of identity as process.

Ethnic Identity as Social Process

Ethnic identity is not a commodity that is formed naturally as a by-product of descent, culture, and genetic transmission. Rather, like other social realities, ethnic identity is socially constructed and reformed owing to historical conditions (Smith, 1992). Ethnic identity is, itself, part and parcel of a *social formation*, a process that is not fixed in time and that can change over time. In the present context of city schooling in particular, the reconstitution of demographics with a majority ethnic population in major U.S. cities potentially marks a period of the development of new ethnic identities. Schools can make use of the new social space of ethnic identity and strategically shape a sense of their individual and collective self (such a deliberate move on the school's behalf requires use of moral leadership, according to Maxcy, 1994). Doing so assists students in what Philip Wexler believes is their most important labor—identity work. He asserts that:

> Students work in school. Their most central activity is the work of "becoming somebody." To become somebody means to establish a credible identity in the specific context of school work conditions and exigencies. The most salient of these conditions are: organizational ideals and demands; and specific cultural channels of peer-defined status. (quoted in Herr & Anderson, 1993, p. 16)

Although Wexler focuses on a social class analysis of public schooling, he does make note of the "cultural channels," which I assert circulate both inside and outside of school. It is the site of cultural politics in the city school, the arena in which the contests for unitary versus collective identity formation is waged, where this important part of student's work can be nurtured.

The central point about understanding ethnic identity as *social process* is that the process is *relational*. That is, there is no personal ethnic identity apart from a relationship to other (ethnic and nonethnic) identities (see Hall, 1991). Furthermore, the processes of identity formation within the social context of ethnicity (defined here as discursive practice of one's own and others collective ethnic identities) is inseparable from the broader social relations of power and material and ideological structures. In the words of Michael Smith (1992):

> Ethnic consciousness [is] a relational construct made possible through articulatory practices. Ethnicity is socially produced largely through group-level interactions. These establish the ethnic identity of a group by specifying its relations with other groups. Ethnic identity is shaped by contested rhetorical explanations of inter-group similarities and differences. (p. 24)

Without the discourse into other ethnic groups, there can be no consciousness of ethnicity as a *collective* lived cultural experience for students in inner-city schools. More to the point: If African-American students, historically predefined by racial categories, are unaware of the cultural legacies of theirs and other ethnic groups (e.g., Latinos), then they may continue to view themselves as "Blacks." The rapidly changing demographics in city schools thus presents both new cultural opportunities to forge identity politics and institutional barriers (racial and social) to realizing such a new praxis in the hopes of further democratizing public schooling (see Giroux, 1993; see also Britzman, 1993). The problematic issue is the processes by which both teachers and students can develop the capacity to engage in discursive practices such as communicative action.

Embracing Ethnicity

A postmodern politics of ethnic identity embraces consciousness of other groups. It also calls for social action through a constant reflexive monitoring of the intentions, motivations, and reasons that propel groups into action (Giddens, 1984). *Action* here means deliberately forging a strategy of equivalence (Mouffe, 1988). The process of collective ethnic identity formation therefore moves substantially beyond the notions of the autonomous modern self to embrace the recognition of *ethnicity* as a contested cultural terrain whose borders city schools can redraw. This reboundarying assumes considerable degree of conflict over values and the shared sense of common purpose (Ball, 1987; Olsen, 1994). Within this framework, conflict is elevated to a normative status.

The current popular movement to incorporate multicultural curricula and cultural diversity in urban school districts rests on the conservative assumption of what Kobena Mercer calls "imaginary unities" (cited in Giroux, 1993, p. 310). The goal of most multicultural curricula and cultural diversity initiatives is to celebrate difference under the banner of cultural harmony (see West, 1993a). There is no politics of identity and difference within this scenario, no "contested cultural terrain" that the schools, through struggle, confidently embrace. By denying cultural conflict, these school reform initiatives unintentionally deny ethnic minority students the opportunity to draw on collective identities within the sociality of ethnicity.

Borrowing on Giroux's notion of border pedagogy, I explore the implications in this and subsequent chapters of the deliberate politicizing (through cultural conflict) by schools and other institutions for the formation of ethnic identity for students. The purposeful use of conflict resolution techniques moves beyond the utilitarian notions of fostering individual identity by improving students' self-concept and self-esteem. The concern here is with the building of *collective* identity, therefore restoring a sense of community, springing from a respect for difference that does not relegate the culture of ethnic minorities to the status of the "other" (Fordham, 1983; hooks, 1993; Ogbu, 1988).

The entrenched social reality is that ethnicity is experienced primarily by White individuals and groups. In cities such as New Orleans, Atlanta, Detroit, and other heavily populated Black urban centers, the stories of Greg Osborn I recounted earlier are all too common. Inner-city Black students are shaped primarily by race, with class and gender categories playing important intersecting roles. For example, low-income Black male youth who live in public housing developments live their lives in racial fear: fear of crime from other Black youth, and fear of harassment and intimidation from White citizens and police officers. Before postmodern social analysis can inform political practice, the constitution of subjectivity at the intersection of race, class, and gender in the context of inner-city schools must be firmly confronted.

Let me be more specific. The dynamics of racial formation have shaped the constitution of subjectivity for racial/ethnic minorities by the essential trait of skin color: the darker the skin, the greater the subordination (see McCarthy & Crichlow, 1993). I have more to say about the implications for the altering of practice to realize this theoretic ideal of the confrontation by Whites of the social construction of human subjectivity through racial, ethnic, gender, and class categories of identity (Foster, 1993; West, 1993a) toward the conclusion of this chapter.

Given the pervasiveness of race in the formation of individual identity for Blacks and other racial minorities, ethnicity must be not only imagined but deliberately fostered in the innercity classroom. Inside the school as sites (and as I will argue later, increasingly outside of the school building) of cultural production and contestation, it is possible to take seriously the insight that "the real is not a pregiven state that reproduces itself by means of the political but rather is political production itself" (Delany, quoted in Britzman, 1993, p. 25) and, further, that:

> Such categories as "the real," the "authentic", and "identity" are prescriptive and inscriptive, not descriptive. The point, then, is to consider—and not without argument [conflict]—how these constructions regulate, position, and valorize particular versions of identity and at what cost.

Embracing ethnicity, then, means two concrete things. One is to imagine how ethnic identities were constructed for particular groups of people, for example, Blacks, Hispanics, and Whites, in a local social formation and, second, to *critically reimagine* how such ethnic identities can be redefined as embracing the praxis of drawing from collective ethnic identities in the new social space of the city. Only through a recasting of the politics of ethnic identity as a form of the cultural politics of the school and of the classroom is this conceivable within the dominant paradigm of modernism. The postmodern cultural imagination can become real only through a genuine debate and appraisal of the modern social structures of race, social class, and ideology.[2]

From Ethnicity to New Political Subjects

A relational definition of ethnic identity not only focuses conceptual attention on ethnic identity as social process, but it also sheds light on the constitution of new political subjects (roles).[3] The binary categories of the project of the Enlightenment—structure versus agency, the individual's recognition of universal reason versus the awareness of collective political actors and their material self-interest—potentially erode. Ultimately, whether employing Marxist or liberal theories of the political subject, this bifurcation of subjectivity "offers a reductionist view of the relationship between consciousness, agency, and social change" (Smith, 1992, p. 500). The implication for urban schooling (and for a theory of urban pedagogy, which I discuss later) is that educational (social) change in inner-city schools derives from students' total experience of their own ethnic identities, their discursive consciousness of ethnicity (Giddens, 1984) in relation to their own group, and their awareness of differences within other ethnic groups. Put simply, in the new global context of city schooling, students can mobilize for democratic educational change to the extent that they give equal value to erasing injustices and inequality for all ethnic groups in the multiethnic urban school. On these complex matters regarding the interconnecting of democracy, education, and social relations, it is worth noting Chantal Mouffe's comments at length. Mouffe asserts that:

> If the task of radical democracy is indeed to deepen the democratic revolution and to link together diverse democratic struggles, such a task requires the creation of new

---

[2] I agree with Spencer Maxcy's observation that "this (may) be a task of philosophy or philosophy of research" (personal communication). However, my vision of the role of urban schools embraces the idea of social action. Public schools would then take on the abstract task of initiating public debate on the productive and reproductive dimensions of these social structures.

[3] For a different perspective on the relationships between human agency and institutional structures, see Nicos Mouzelis (1992).

[political] subject-positions that would allow the common articulation, for example of antiracism, antisexism, and anticapitalism. These struggles do not spontaneously converge, and in order to establish democratic equivalences, a new "common sense" is necessary which would transform the identity of different groups so that the demands of each group could be articulated with those of others according to the principle of democratic equivalence. *For it is not a matter of establishing a mere alliance between given interests but, of actually modifying the very identity of those forces.* . . . It is only under these circumstances that struggles against power become truly democratic. (cited in Giroux, 1991, p. 147; emphasis added)

In the idiosyncratic vernacular of postmodern social analysis, the political subject is *decentered*. This means that in an age of multiple identities, there are no clear roles that political subjects may assume in their quest for the deepening of democracy. Classroom teachers, for example, both labor under oppressive conditions of state regulation and, as discussed in Chapter 3, may join with parents under the ideological space of empowerment in the struggle to make public schooling in the city more responsive to, and more reflective, of local community needs and values. Also, students under a more democratic educational system may pressure school boards, principals, and central office administrators for greater control over the curriculum and their own learning. Elsewhere, I have illustrated both the prospects and limitations of discursive practices in contemporary school reform to use power to pursue moral ends (Miron, 1991; Miron & Elliott, 1994). These ends derive from the shared values of local communities and the conflict over values embedded in the practice of radical democracy in urban public schooling.

The point for the radical democratization of city schooling, then, is that classroom teachers must jointly with their ethnic minority students (see Biesta, 1994) enter the discourse of the politics of education as new political subjects. Exercising their power morally to authorize and create deep democratic space for their students in their own classrooms (see Giroux, 1993), classroom teachers can engage students in the cultural politics over the struggle for collective ethnic identity and difference. By extension, students potentially reconstitute themselves as political/learning subjects, capable of questioning, resisting, and transforming dominating forms of discourse such as national curriculum goals.

It is vitally important, therefore, for both the theory and practice of the constitution of new political subjectivity in inner-city schools to hold foremost the idea of the school and classroom as a site of cultural/identity politics. Historically, classroom teachers and other education professionals at the school site viewed the curriculum as depoliticized texts (see Pinar & Bowers, 1992). Indeed, because of the manipulative ideologies that divorced education from politics, classroom teachers engaged in procedural democracy (election of school board candidates and, in the classroom, equal treatment for all racial groups) mainly through the auspices of the teachers' unions, and then only begrudgingly. The idea that their own sites of practice may also be considered (and valued) as political is a foreign idea to most classroom teachers. Postmodern social analysis, however, offers the possibility that classroom teachers, like Socrates, may become teachers of the body politics as well. Practicing their craft as transformative intellectuals (Foster, 1986; Giroux, 1983), classroom teachers (and other caring professionals; see Goldner, 1993; Noddings, 1984, 1994) may engage their students to undo racism, deconstruct the ethnocentrism of Western Civilization, and embrace the feminist agenda of liberation for all from the terrors of patriarchy. Following the postmodern social analysis of Henry Giroux, I explore the underlying values and philosophical tenets of this view of radical democracy in the praxis of the urban classroom in the next section.

A THEORY OF URBAN PEDAGOGY

In *Border Crossings: Cultural Workers and the Politics of Education* (1993) Henry Giroux proposes a theory of pedagogy to realize the ideal of deep, radical democracy in the school and other public spheres.[4] I stress here that my reliance on Giroux's metaphor of *border crossings* and his development of *border pedagogy* as a postmodern praxis for the deepening of democracy in the

---

[4]My appropriation of Giroux's work to the current crisis in urban education acknowledges the controversial nature of his writings. By "controversial," I mean several things. First is the highly abstract (and occasionally jargonized) use of language, which Giroux (1993) himself acknowledges and for which he makes no apologies. The second controversy (lodged by several neo-Marxists) points to broader concerns over the putatively nonpolitical orientation of postmodern analysis and analysts. The third controversy speaks to the attack from a strand of feminist writers and activists who view Giroux's and colleagues such

Politics of Urban Pedagogy 117

urban public school classroom is based on the richness and intensity of the writing. It is my belief that Giroux's work is in dual need of empirical evidence (see Chapter 5) and critique (see Chapter 6). I intend to make his writing more accessible to practitioners and theorists in urban education. Giroux's capacity to develop a theoretical project and vision that entertains an idea about what democracy can mean in the public school classroom is, in my judgment, rare in radical scholarship and in dire need of appropriation in the context of city schooling.[5] All too often, as I tried to establish in Chapter 2, the discourse of crisis surrounding the social context of public education in the city has wrongly focused educators' attention away from the problems and prospects of the social production of knowledge to the virtually impossible task of providing technological panaceas to fix schools and students.

Situating Power/Knowledge in City Classrooms

Giroux is careful to credit radical, critical scholarship of the past two decades. He does not stop there, however. Giroux extends the influence of critical theory to propose counterhegemonic strategies to the conservative Reagan and Bush Administrations. Cast mainly in functionalist categories, much critical scholarship of the 1970s and 1980s broke the mythological split between public schooling and inequality; poor quality schools, as Bowles and Gintis argued in *Schooling and Capitalist America* (1976), "produced passive workers who would adjust to the imperatives of the capitalist order" (quoted in Giroux, 1993, p. 151). This understanding contrasted markedly with the hegemonic ideology of public schooling as fostering upward economic and social mobility for the masses of poor and minority students. However, Giroux (1993) argues that much of the radical, critical scholarship "exhausted itself in its ability to take up power *dialectically*

---

as Peter McLaren's theoretical writings and political practice as steeped in relations of patriarchy. Although there certainly exists elements of male (and White) dominance in this network, I simply point out that Giroux's project is to synthesize feminism, postmodernism, and modernism (see Giroux, 1991, esp. pp. 1-60, 100-119). I reject the unexamined relations of patriarchy in the writings cited here. In fact, as George Noblit has indicated (personal communication), my project approaches feminism in my quest to turn upside down the hierarchical organization of the school and classroom.

[5]The radical scholarship of Jennifer Gore (1993) is a notable exception.

[productively] or to consider what schools could do to apply power productively" (p. 151; emphasis added; see also Foster, 1986, 1989; Miron & Elliott, 1994). Following Foucault (1977), I assert that power is everywhere and is inextricably tied to knowledge. Students can exercise power, and the move by principals and teachers to embrace their voices builds on what I term the "moral exercise of power" (Miron & Elliott, 1994). Pervasive throughout students' lived cultural experience in inner city classrooms is the use of power to resist representations by the dominant culture and to forge an identity politics in the struggle over their personal and collective identities (see Chapter 5).

In the context of public education in city schools, I argued in the previous sections that classroom teachers could, as transformative intellectuals, foster students' new ethnic identity and awareness of others' ethnicity. In turn, this knowledge would create new political student subjects who would act on Mouffe's concept of democratic *equivalence* by resisting racism, sexism, homophobia, and ethnocentrism in their schools and local communities. Giroux's concept of border pedagogy embraces the notion that classroom teachers' use of power can both oppress and liberate students. In the increasingly ethnic majority urban school districts across the country, schools as sites of cultural/identity politics can foster the possibility of multiple student identities, wherein schools can celebrate difference while searching for community. More concretely, Giroux (1993) argues that a new postmodern cultural politics in the classroom should move "beyond identifying [specific] interests . . . to ask how these interests function. How do they produce particular ways of life?" (p. 153). For example, students would confront the ideologies and discursive practices of the new Entrepreneurial Coalition, which in cities like New Orleans help reproduce classism and racism by segmenting middle-class African Americans, Asian Americans, and Latinos in magnet schools from ethnic groups from lower socioeconomic classes in traditional neighborhood schools (see Dashner, 1992; Miron & Lauria, 1995).

Understanding, through pedagogy, how students construct meaning rather than simply how students receive it through reified knowledge (Everhart, 1983) is central to linking power and knowledge in the classroom. Although it is certainly true that racism pervades inner-city schools, classrooms, and local communities, many Black and White students resist racism as well. In New Orleans, for example, students at a magnet high school, well known for its large minority student population, formed a club whose specific intent was to celebrate the multicultural influences that students from different ethnic groups brought with them to school each day (Miron & Lauria, 1995). At the University of New Orleans, faculty in the Department of Curriculum and Instruction are searching for ways to incorporate *A World of Difference*, an antibias curriculum project of the Anti Defamation League, a national Jewish organization dedicated to fighting prejudice and racism against all oppressed people.

By incorporating curricula that lay bare the colonizing legacies of Western Europe, Giroux (1993) argues that educators and other cultural workers[6] can take "seriously the identities of subordinate cultures" (p. 154). Schooling for ethnic minorities in city schools can then assume a counterhegemonic role as a site of cultural politics. I extend Giroux's case and argue that *only* to the extent that public school teachers in the city are fully capable of understanding how students construct meaning can schools in the city be transformed from technical arenas of instruction to sites for cultural praxis and liberation.

In this regard, Giroux makes the following specific points: First, there exists material structures that constrain the production of meaning and knowledge in the classroom. Textbook companies, school-business partnerships, state government, courses in free enterprise, all limit the discourses on students' construction of meaning. In the context of the crisis in urban schooling, these material and companion ideological strategies of the Entrepreneurial Coalition (which I analyzed in Chapter 3) are especially problematic, as meaning can be subsumed under the experience of individual student choice. Institutionalizing the latter under the discourses of the Entrepreneurial Coalition, obviously, would make the possibilities for culturally based politics in city schools and classrooms problematic indeed.

Second is the issue of the production of texts (which includes both formal textbooks and less formal instructional materials such as films and videos). Giroux is concerned with the processes through which the production of educational texts in the wider society both shape and provide spaces for the construction of meaning in the classroom (see DeVaney, 1994). Texts in their various forms provide powerful discourses that produce the ideologies that students carry with them in schools. As students engage in the dialectical process of receiving and creating meaning through their lived cultural experiences, such ideologies (like

---

[6]Giroux and other postmodern writers (e.g., Cornel West) include as cultural workers artists, intellectuals, and educators.

competition, individualism, or diversity) help locate their social position in history and equip them with power (conceived as self-knowledge) to modify these positions through new discourses. I take an empirical look at the student construction of meaning through language and other mechanisms in the next chapter.

The third point concerns the possibilities of communities. A theory of border pedagogy in the urban context necessitates that classroom teachers take students out into local communities to examine how cultural articulations (see Smith, 1992) and local ideologies "accumulate historical weight" for students (Giroux, 1993, p. 154). In addition to the ideologies that students carry with them into their schools and classrooms, also of vital interest to Giroux are the processes whereby historical, social, and political conditions foster lived experience for students initially. Racism, for example, in the inner city vastly determines the social identities of students from racially defined categories, for example, Blacks and Native Americans. Precisely pinpointing how racism helps constitute human subjectivity for students in segregated school decades following *Brown v. Board of Education Topeka, Kansas* is prerequisite for the construction of meaning in the cities' multiethnic/multicultural classrooms throughout America.

Embracing the Value of Radical Democracy in City Public Schools

As illustrated in Chapter 3, the current decentralization of large urban school districts in the form of school-based management and choice is unlikely to lead to democratic practices in the classroom. Giroux argues that schools should be conceived as democratic public spheres. Conservative ideological movements have successfully exploited the crisis of authority in American society and called for the redefinition of government. In public education, the concept of *public* schools is equated with *government-sponsored* schools. Hence, the negative characteristics associated with a bloated governmental bureaucracy—inefficiency, riddled with patronage and corruption, and organizationally driven, rather than client oriented—are pinned on public schools, not altogether wrongly.

Giroux's dream is to radically redefine the public sphere in education by making explicit the institutional and cultural links between schooling and the reconstruction of public life. This is one of many border crossings he implores teachers and other cultural workers to take up the courage to fulfill the goal of the deepening of democracy in the broader society, the foremost ideal of critical pedagogy (see McLaren, 1994). Teachers and administrators are presently located vast social distances from the cultural and epistemological border that Giroux wishes to traverse. The conditions of widespread poverty, single-parent families, chronically underfunded schools, and a historically unresponsive professional bureaucracy bent on maintaining the contours of the one best system (see Tyack, 1974) make for a social context that makes incremental reform difficult (see Miron & St. John, 1994) and deep democracy nearly impossible to attain.

Radical democratic practice in the urban classroom is nearly impossible, simply because there is no value of democracy undergirding professional activity, neither in the discourse of reform nor the politics of organizational maintenance (see Schlechty, 1990). This pessimism is predicated on the modernist assumption that educators will find neither the will nor the courage to take seriously Giroux's (1993) admonition that "schools and teachers need to gain a vision of why they're doing what they're doing" and to place "the notion of authority" within "an ethical and political referent" (p. 154). However, the opening of the new politics of community developed in the previous chapter allows for the possibility that even beleaguered innercity schools can engage in the cultural struggle for democracy in the classroom. Whether the intensity of this engagement is radically or incrementally designed is an empirical question. I attempt to make some empirically grounded connections among the forging of democracy, identity politics, and student resistance in the next chapter.

Educators in the city cannot be expected to muster the courage to take up this struggle alone. Based on the common principles of difference, equality, justice, and personal and community freedom, educators can join forces with artists and other cultural workers, such as those in the KOS (Kids of Survival) project in the Bronx. In this manner political coalitions based on Mouffes's (1988) concept of democratic equivalence can be established with the intent "to reclaim progressive notions of the *public* in public schooling so that education can become a real public service just as one might say that the arts need to be taken up pedagogically in the same ways" (Giroux, 1993, p. 155; emphasis in original). It goes without saying that no government mandate such as school choice can further the goal of deepening democracy in public schools.

The theory of border pedagogy makes imperative the centrality of language in equipping classroom teachers and others with the vocabulary to redraw the boundaries of the public schools. Classroom teachers can then engage in communicative action (Habermas, 1970) to insert a critical concept of democracy. In this sense, Giroux argues that discourse is the praxis of border pedagogy. Finding the appropriate methods and techniques to teach students in the inner city the effects of racism is not only misplaced. Worse, such technism undermines the global project of formulating a critical educational vision and imagination. By focusing on the discourses of methodology, the language of classroom teachers becomes depoliticized. Negotiating the transition from instructional technicians to cultural pedagogical workers implies redefining teachers roles as public intellectuals (see J. Anderson, 1993; Foster, 1986). In the context of the city, wherein a decidedly antiintellectual milieu prevails, this means that school-business partners must come to realize the value of a redefined teacher role. As I discuss at the conclusion of this chapter, this is not easy.

Authorizing Student Voices

As critics of critical pedagogy and postmodernism[7] have argued, the unequal power relations between teachers and students in the classroom may work to disempower, rather than morally empower, students (see Ellsworth, 1989). In inner-city schools the increasing public health hazard of violence and the absence of a strong democratic tradition makes for the potential abuse of power by police, teachers, and school administrators (see Troyna & Hatcher, 1991; see also Curcio & First, 1993). Giroux, however, distinguishes between *authoritarianism* and *authority*. Educators cannot disavow authority relations in the classroom; to do so would be immoral. The concept of authoritarianism in the classroom derives from the banking notion of education that Paulo Freire first criticized (see also Illich, 1971). That is, this view assumes that teachers simply *transmit* knowledge from one authoritative source (teachers or textbooks) to a passive, unreflective student. As Biesta (1994) theorizes, this pedagogy wrongly assumes an asymmetrical relationship between teacher and learner.

---

[7] I do not enter into that debate here because, first of all, I obviously do not share that position, and it has been taken up competently elsewhere (see Liston, 1990; see also Harvey, 1992; Graham, 1992).

The multiplicity of identities and subjectivities embedded within the paradigm of postmodernism creates intellectual room for *student* production of knowledge. Within this framework teachers can instill in their classrooms the conditions wherein students can engage in both the critique and production of knowledge. For example, students in distressed neighborhoods in the city can make use of oral histories to interrogate how the ideologies of economic growth helped legitimize the dislocation and removal of poor Black families during the construction of interstate highways. By exercising authority, not romantically denying its institutional presence, teachers can overcome Bakhtin's warning that institutions function to silence certain voices "before they even become vocalized in the public domain" (in Herr & Anderson, 1993, p 13). Schools can affirmatively engage in the student production of knowledge. Their historical role of transmitting and distributing the knowledge and values of other cultures can (and should) be overcome. As I illustrate with the example of the oral histories of Greg Osborn and Victor (see later), the processes to accomplish that in the social conditions of the city are historically ripe.

Giroux is quick to point out that it is not enough to uncritically give voice to student experiences. The critical reflection of students' own lived cultural experiences is potentially a powerful tool for the forging of a border pedagogy in the city. The concrete interrogation of the processes by which hegemonic ideologies and socially constructed realities such as racial and ethnic identities shape their understanding of their histories is a marker that begins the process of border crossing. What I mean to say is that student empowerment through the cultural struggle to find voice in the classroom should not focus on the sometimes cathartic process of storytelling (although this could indeed be cathartic for some oppressed students); rather, the politics of finding voice in the classroom is not separate from the politics of difference: Both struggles are inherently *social* and *political*. They are designed primarily with the long-term aim of critical pedagogy of the deepening of democratic practice in the wider society. In the short run, these sites of cultural politics are meant to achieve student understanding of how social relations are constituted so that they can be ultimately transformed via resistance and the mediations of student culture. Such lofty goals must, of course, be built out of a theory of pedagogy and new political communities that seek to unify while embracing and celebrating difference.

BORDER PEDAGOGY AND THE POLITICS OF DIFFERENCE

My overriding purpose is to examine the crisis in urban schooling by situating it at the nexus of the global economy and the new social space of urban ethnicity. Conceptualizing the postmodern category of difference is paramount. In particular, developing a theory of urban pedagogy that helps teachers and students deconstruct the social determinants of race and ethnicity in city schooling marks a border crossing from the schools as transmitters of knowledge to schools as active producers of knowledge for the mutual benefits of students and local communities. Breaking down the barriers of *artificial* (socially constructed) difference, then, enables the cultural politics of genuine difference based on achieving the principles of justice, freedom, and equality for students occupying varying historical locations to commence. Giroux organized his understanding of the concept of difference into the categories of conservative, liberal, and radical.

Difference as Social Deviance

As Giroux observes, conservative ideological forces such as the New Right have invoked the notion of difference to justify social relations of racism, male dominance, and classism. Invoking the supposed natural laws of science and culture, New Right groups have justified these unequal power relations by equating the category of difference with the idea of deviance. Giroux (1993) argues that:

> In many instances, difference functions as a marker of power to name, label, and exclude particular groups while simultaneously being legitimated within a reactionary discourse (e.g., racism) and politics of public life, i.e, nationalism patriotism, and "democracy." What needs to be noted here is that there is more at stake than the production of particular ideologies based on negative definitions of identity. When defined and used in the interest of inequality and repression, difference is "enacted in violence" against its own citizens as much as against foreigners. (p. 171)

The effect of this conceptualization of difference is well illustrated with the history of bilingual education in this country. Prior to the enactment of bilingual education, speakers of languages other than English were prohibited from receiving instruction in their native tongues because foreign languages were viewed as linguistic handicaps in the United States (see Fishman, 1976). I hasten to point out that even within the broad social context of the global economy, calls for English-only legislation are not abating. There seems to be an even greater reluctance on behalf of classroom teachers in inner-city schools to build on the rich oral language traditions of African-American students as a pedagogical bridge to acquiring standard English. Although temporarily ignoring the ethnocentric bias of conventional curricula in underfunded inner-city classrooms, I simply point out how material and ideological structures greatly constrain the opportunities for teachers to employ alternate views of difference with their multiethnic student clientele.

The Liberal Ambivalence with Race

Liberals are ambivalent in their attitudes on race. An ideologically palatable position holds that tolerance for racial differences should co-exist within a framework of cultural diversity. Under that vague conceptual umbrella, liberals place the construct of race in a generic, universal category of diversity as one example of endless possibilities within the varied cultures in the United States. Giroux agrees with Rothenberg's argument that a major difficulty with this perspective is that, by refusing to ascribe any independent status to the category of race as a central factor in the construction of the social formation in this country "it redefines race in a way that denies the history of racism in the United States and, thus, denies white responsibility for the present and past oppression and exploitation of people of color" (cited in Giroux, 1993, p. 171; see also West, 1993b). The modernist's unproven assumption of the natural progressive movement of history, as witnessed by a societal denial of the viscousness of racism under the rubric of an unspecified difference, undergirds liberal ideology and unintentionally reproduces unequal power relations hidden in race (see Giddens, 1984). The implication for city schools is ironic. By celebrating cultural diversity, for example, through specifically designated African-American awareness weeks, I argue that *both* Whites and Blacks are attributed responsibility for the pernicious effects of race on poor Blacks, Hispanics, Asians, and Native Americans.

Giroux asserts that the liberal ambivalence with racism is also evident in the widespread attempts at cultural assimilation.

By treating racial inequality in culturally deficit terms, students' lived cultural experiences of history and language get relegated to the invisible category of the *other*. I contend that no cultural narratives can be produced within a model of race that views Blacks and other minorities as having cultural deficits because they were not able to fully integrate their culture into the dominant U.S. culture as White European immigrant groups seemingly accomplished. The ironic realization is that the ideology of assimilation continues as educators and other professionals continue to plead that education can lead the way out of poverty (Frazier, 1993).

Radical Conceptions of Difference

A critical postmodern analysis of racial and other categories of difference points to the multilayered and fractured construction of individual identities. As I have illustrated, ethnic identity is socially constructed and can be reformed in discourse and political struggle. Racial identities, too, are unstable and have shifted according to the drifts of political winds. Once defined by the U.S. Census Bureau by race, Hispanics are now identified by ethnic categories as Central American, Mexican American, Cuban, and the like.

Giroux takes issue with the radical, postmodern notion that identities are shaped in discourse through language use and the content of what students are allowed to voice in the classroom. By stressing the indeterminacy of the self, Giroux argues that little space is available for human agency. In my judgment this conclusion on agency is wrong (see Chapter 5). He observes: "In effect subjectivity becomes an effect of language, and human agency disappears into the discredited terrain of human will" (p. 172).[8] I agree with the position taken by Anthony Giddens (1982, 1984) that social theory must always leave theoretic space for human agency. My concern here is to show how social context and discursive practices in urban schooling construct individual and collective identities. I assert that discursive practices such as schooling both shape and allow space for agency.

In the social context of urban schooling, it is clear that much pedagogical practice rests on the assumption that ethnic dialects interfere in the goal of assimilation for minority stu-

---

[8]I believe that Giroux is wrong on this point. This perspective on human agency undermines his assertion that personal identity is always "relational" and a product of sociality (see Giroux, 1991, 1992).

dents. Many students of multiple cultural backgrounds, for example, immigrants and Mexican-American students in border towns and states, are therefore silenced or forced to make a choice of survival, rejecting one of their multiple identities (the ethnic one) in favor of assimilation. Clearly, individual identities are woven in discourse, privileging specific use of language and silencing other uses. Herr and Anderson's (1993) oral history of Victor, the first Hispanic admitted into a private, affluent high school in a southwest city is telling:

> I really don't see myself as a Hispanic person. We were talking about this in the car this morning with Ariel and he said that when you go to this school it's like going to Candyland. . . . You know, hypothetically speaking there's no drugs, there's isn't any alcohol. . . . It's Candyland. . . . You go and you're sheltered. . . . I really don't label myself as the typical Hispanic person; I kind of label myself as the typical Anglo Hispanic person. . . . I kind of look at myself as kind of an Anglo person in some ways. The way I speak sometimes, I really don't have a strong accent and Black people have some strong accents, you know the way the way they pronounce the words and Vietnamese and Asian people and all that—you know I really don't, if you look at it, I'm Hispanic, you know my blood, my color, my background, but right now I'm turning into an Anglo. (p. 14)

Giroux makes the same criticism of certain postmodern conceptions of the differences within social groups as he levies against the disappearance of a theory of human agency. In particular, he controversially attacks a strand of feminist discourse for its version of identity politics because of its often unstated assumption that one's social location (i.e., gender) determines political stance and ideologies. This unreflective embrace of "the authority of experience" ignores the way that personal identity is often taken up in multilayered and contradictory fashion. Because personal identity is potentially always shifting, Giroux argues that it cannot be an unproblematic basis of political practice. A relatively straightforward example is the divisions within the Latin community in Miami, in which Cubans are often ideologically pitted against Central Americans from countries like El Salvador and Nicaragua as well as the Caribbean immigrants from Haiti and elsewhere. In these instances, one's shared cultural background does not universally determine a political position vis-à-vis U.S. imperialism.

ANTIBIAS PEDAGOGY AS CULTURAL POLITICS

The foregoing review of both traditional and radical conceptions of difference makes clear that Giroux views significant social struggles such as resisting racism as part of the broader politics of the deepening of democratic practices. For if a hierarchy of oppression exists in progressive social movements, one that privileges dominant relations of any kind (whether of race, gender, or class categories), the hopes for forging a common purpose in education and other cultural spheres remain dim. Giroux relentlessly calls for a mode of resistance that keeps foremost in mind the philosophical principles of freedom, equality, and justice. Forging an antibias pedagogy, then, in the inner city and in other urban contexts characterized by the divisiveness of racial, political, and ethnic cleavages (as well as growing economic and social inequalities) poses a genuine test of the utopian dream of a radical democracy.

Giroux continues to insist that forging the deepening of democracy must begin with a radical pedagogical practice. After all, racism, like other forms of social biases, are both taught and learned. Within this perspective, pedagogy is not separate from politics; indeed, it constitutes a form of cultural politics within the schools and inside of the classrooms. By insisting that teachers especially reject all forms of totalizing narratives under the guise of universal reason, it is conceivable that public school educators can join with other public servants such as artists and activists within the academy to forge a "wider struggle for democratic public life and critical citizenship" (Giroux, 1991, p. 245). In the remainder of this section I map out how an antibias pedagogy might wield potential for achieving the radical goals of critical pedagogy. I continually emphasize the situatedness of urban education, schools caught up in the midst of extremely complex circumstances and harsh material life. Many students in the inner city, large percentages of whom live below the poverty line, confront dangers on walks to and from school, and generally face the pernicious effects of racism every day of their lives in the form of dilapidated public housing, underfunded and rigidly organized schools, and a legacy of slavery and colonization. These unintended consequences of social reproduction (see Giddens, 1984) are institutionalized in the discursive practices of schools, despite decades of legislation and affirmative action programs.

First, a critical literacy must be formed that places at the center of social analysis the unequal power relations that systematically work against people of color. In this way, illiteracy among racial/ethnic minorities is not viewed as a technical problem of a lack of reading and writing skills, but rather works to sustain high levels of poverty among poor Blacks, Hispanics, and Native Americans. Paulo Freire recognized this phenomena early on in his attempts to teach peasants critical literacy in Brazil using the process of conscientization and the construction of generative themes. Grounding literacy pedagogy in the circumstances of oppression constructed meaning for the poor in Brazil, linking the formal learning of language with resistance to bias and oppression. As Freire (1973) well describes in *Pedagogy of the Oppressed*, Brazilian peasants saw relevance and value in literacy skills, in part out of their collaboration with their adult teachers, and in part out of the common struggle against poverty.

In the same manner, critical literacy and antibias pedagogy can be coupled by the reading of various texts (books, print media, advertising) that both create conditions for the reproduction of racial inequality and offer students the opportunity to move beyond racism by writing their own texts. Giroux offers the example of Black students conducting oral histories to examine which voices are silent and which are privileged in conventional history books.

Such a critical literacy in the context of city schooling can reconfigure the concept of ethnicity as a means for students and teachers to exercise power through the cultural politics of the school. The construction of new subject identities (political roles; see Mouzelis, 1992) within a multiethnic milieu redefines the negative labeling of race as a means to maintain White, middle-class hegemony. Blacks can become collective political agents. They may form alliances with other ethnic-racial groups to struggle against undemocratic schools.

Second, an antibias pedagogy as part of a theory of urban pedagogy must be more than a postmodern exercise in deconstruction. Both teachers and students of color need to understand in their bodies and souls—not only in their head—how racial "narratives are taken up as part of an investment of feeling, pleasure, and desire" (Giroux, 1991, p. 249). For it is certainly true, despite contemporary racial political rhetoric, that some racial social groups benefit from the discourse of racism. For example, Black and Hispanic elected officials wield enormous power as part of caretaker regimes (see Stone, 1989; see also Reed, 1988) in the urban centers of the United States. By doling out patronage in the form of government jobs and contracts, these politicians (and the neighborhood groups that support them) reproduce the legacy of racism that prevented racial minorities from entering public service. In other words, when well-financed corporate political action committees line up to offer financial support for Black school board candidates or mayoral prospects for the expressed purpose of controlling public policies (see Miron & Brooks, 1993), the jobs and material rewards that these officials ultimately dole out to loyal constituents may ultimately sustain White, corporate hegemony in urban schooling. In short, an antiracist pedagogy must begin with the discomforting realization that, perhaps unwittingly, racial identities for Blacks and other people of color are difficult to shed. Ironically, there is sometimes both satisfaction and grief in the lived cultural experiences of racism.

Finally, embracing a broader cultural politics of democratic practice in the urban classroom, antibias pedagogy gives voice to racial minorities that extends beyond individual accounts of racism. It is equally important to weave individual narrative accounts within the relational properties of racism. Clearly, racism as hegemonic ideology serves the material interests of specific groups (e.g., White, middle-class male professionals) and therefore works against democratic principles of equity, justice, and fairness. Classroom teachers in the city, of all racial groups, must attend to how they might unintentionally subscribe to racist ideologies and practices. Only then can they begin to view the issue as rooted in a culture that reproduces the *structural* causes of racism as they decry individual transgressions of the oppression of racial-ethnic minorities (Giroux, 1991).

I offer the following illustration drawn from my own teaching to underscore both the complexities and the passions involved in formulating an antibias pedagogy. In 1989, I asked White and Black students at Loyola University of New Orleans to investigate whether specific institutional practices within the social relations of fraternity and sorority life reproduced racial segregation on the campus.

Loyola University in New Orleans is a Catholic university governed predominantly by the Jesuit Order. It is well known in Catholic circles for its programs in civil rights, specifically the Institute for Human Relations, which has consistently advocated in behalf of Black prisoners on death row. Jesuit priest, and Loyola faculty member, Dan Berrigan, and other less-known activists priests/scholars have vehemently protested U.S. policies in El Salvador, Nicaragua, and other Third World nations. They have also campaigned for other human rights causes such as world hunger and homelessness. In short, Loyola is well known among activists for its liberal practices to combat racism and other forms of human suffering.

I taught an undergraduate elective course entitled *Culture and Learning* to a class of 40 students, of whom approximately 10 were Black and 30 White. I assigned them the task of investigating why there existed separate Black and White sororities and fraternities on campus. Did selection or recruitment practices formally or informally prohibit Black or White students from joining these institutions? Did the university by-laws governing the charters of student organizations encourage the formation of distinctly racial social groups?

I learned that the formal policies and procedures of the university and student-run organizations did not prohibit Black students from joining White social organizations, nor White students from joining Black social organizations. Indeed, the universal finding of all of the research groups I had helped the students to organize was that racially organized fraternities and sororities were the result of freedom of choice of the students themselves. Indeed, there was Black representation on the Panhellenic Council, the university governing board of fraternity and sorority life. However, Black students ran their own organizations and, with a few exceptions, White organizations had exclusive White membership (I recall an instance or two in which a White fraternity had a Black in its membership).

When I opened the final class meeting to discussion as to why the university would allow students to form separate social organizations for Whites and Blacks, given the long history of advocacy for civil and human rights, the answer I received was that "both Whites and Blacks wanted it that way." Shockingly, I learned from my mostly middle-class Black students that, as a social group, they distanced themselves from low-income Blacks in the inner-city neighborhoods and public housing developments in New Orleans. "Those students aren't 'black'" they informed the White students (and myself) in the class. I believe that the substantive point that the middle-class African-American students were trying to make to the White students enrolled in *Culture and Learning* was that the Black fraternity and sorority members were proud of their organizations. What had become the Black stereotype in New Orleans, as in many cities, was Black identity as the deviant underclass. For Black students in my class, then, being Black at Loyola University meant being a member of the middle class, just as middle class as the White students. I am reminded of Herr and Anderson's oral history of Victor (cited earlier) who really did not see himself as Hispanic.

Had I explored the boundaries of racism in the context of the university, indeed had I crossed the cultural border of voluntary racist practices, I would have encouraged both Black and White students to examine not only the accommodating culture of racism within social life at the university. I would also have tried to open a dialogue to examine how race, identity, class, and gender categories shaped racial identity for both middle-class Black students at Loyola University in New Orleans and lower socioeconomic Black groups. In hindsight, I would have pointed out that, in both cases, racial identities are *socially constructed* by White, middle-class experience. The White students in my class, however, remained virtually free of racial identification. That is, whereas Black middle-class students were quick to inform their white classmates that poor Blacks living in public housing were not really Black, the practice of holding up Black social organizations as models of middle-class student life—capable of competing with White organizations—was unintentionally reproduced. The modernist conception of racial identity pervades the constitution of subjectivity in the pedagogical illustration I cited.

From my recollection of the class discussion of seven years ago, the cultural category of ethnicity was not part of the discourse. Indeed, when I look back over it from a postmodern perspective, my organizing of the research project, and subsequent class discussions, unconsciously took up the social construction of race—exclusively for Black students. Owing to my genuine concern with the incongruence between liberal ideologies of the Jesuits and the clear social segregation of student life by race, I set out to explore the causes of racial segregation. Ironically, the class discussions focused on the relationships between culture and learning; yet I raised no questions of Black or White ethnic culture. Nor did my students ask any questions about ethnicity. Anecdotally, it seemed that all social celebrations of Black student life were defined in race and class terms. The contribution of African-American culture to the vitality of the social organizations, the university, and to the larger New Orleans community was conspicuously absent.

THE BOUNDARIES OF THE URBAN SCHOOL

This brief account of my introduction to antibias pedagogy highlights the difficulty of border crossing in any concrete pedagogical situation. This difficulty holds special relevance when the cultural and pedagogical borders literally fence in an inner-city school, thus making real the construct of social isolation (see Garvin, 1994; Wilson, 1987). Giroux is correct in his observation that educators must deliberately create alliances with other cultural workers if the goal of the deepening of democracy is to begin to take root in the city classroom. Schools situated in the inner city have historically been undemocratic places. Research and intervention in the implementation of the Accelerated Schools Process (ASP) in urban school districts (see Miron & St. John, 1994, St. John et al., 1992) found that the traditions within some predominantly lower socioeconomic African-American populated schools often relied on corporal punishment and verbal abuse of Black students to enforce formal and informal school discipline policies. Such a blatant coercive climate of disciplinary power (Foucault, 1977) in some of the poor African-American school communities does not bode well for antibias pedagogy or critical pedagogy of any form.[9]

When schools were better funded and national policies were more favorable to the alleviation of human suffering in the urban ghettoes, the larger struggle for civil rights helped teachers share a common vision and purpose. However, the present social and economic conditions in these schools make fighting crime (the random violent destruction of human life) the prime concern. It will be difficult to wage the struggle for the deepening of democracy in public schools in which metal detectors, safety, and drug trafficking are daily obsessions with parents, administrators, and the general public. It is not an exaggeration to state that, in many schools in the inner city (and increasingly even in rural and some suburban school districts), the high school campus resembles a modern police state.[10] Under these social conditions, it is perhaps unrealistic to expect teachers and students alone to concern themselves with the crisis of democracy. It may come to pass that the place to begin this ambitious undertaking is outside of the formal boundaries of the urban school.

---

[9]By no means am I suggesting that only African-American populated schools resort to these coercive tactics to discipline students. I have also witnessed practices in rural White schools, in which parents gave written permission to the principal to use a wooden paddle to administer discipline. In these cases, the students, together with their parents, were willing participants in these practices. Indeed, the students found them preferable to enduring detentions after school or on Saturdays.

[10]In a recent report on the NBC Nightly News entitled "Society Under Siege," a national survey conducted for the network found that 75% of students said that school violence is a problem. Other news reports

Eventually, the institution of public schooling may have to be reconfigured in the inner city (see Miron, 1995). The circumstances of economic and social hardship may pose too difficult a set of institutional barriers to redirect pedagogical practice to a cultural politics. I suggest that we borrow images and metaphors from the performing arts. I briefly outline these at the conclusion of this book in the hopes of creating educational/cultural alliances with artists who practice an ethnic tradition. These include jazz (Wynton Marsalis) and sculpture (John Scott), among others. Around the country students are linking up with arts programs as a means of forging personal and ethnic identity (see Ball & Heath, 1993). As I have argued in this chapter, the place to begin in the context of the changing demographics of city schools is with students' sense of their own ethnic identity and the collective celebration of difference through an appreciation of the multiple possibilities of forging ethnic and social identities. I propose a reconceptualized vision of urban schooling following the analysis of student narratives of their awareness of their and others' ethnicity, which schools can deliberately foster or institutionally hinder.

More immediately, in Chapter 5, I seek to let the voices of ethnic minority students in city schools speak for themselves. Although I do not believe in removing one's moral politics from the representation of student's lived experiences and personal/social identities, my aim is to use the medium of student voices and qualitative research to both combat the school's historical silencing of student narratives and to temper my own passion for affirmative ethnicity (see Paulston, 1980). What I hope to achieve in these student narratives is a concrete portrait of student culture, in particular, of how students' understanding of their own lived experiences in the school and classroom is part and parcel of what Wexler (1988, cited in Herr & Anderson, 1993) characterizes as identity work. I partially establish that there exists in the school (conceptualized as a social organization) a hidden cultural politics that fosters an accommodation (Everhart, 1983; see also Gilligan, 1993) of student ethnic identity to the dominant culture of the school and wider society. At the same time student culture resists this tendency to accommodate.

---

have pointed to the high incidence of students carrying weapons to campus. It has become customary for students to find hordes of extra police and security on campus in cities like Los Angeles, New York, Washington, DC, and New Orleans, where school and neighborhood violence is perceived as rampant.

Chapter 5

Postmodernism, Identity Politics, and Student Resistance

In Chapter 4, I embraced the method of postmodern social analysis to theorize on identity formation and the social construction of ethic identity in inner-city schools (see also Miron & Lauria, 1995). I argued in Chapter 4 that the "new social space of urban ethnicity" is not only a theoretical concept worth debating in the context of urban pedagogy, but it is also one that necessitates careful empirical investigation. This is my aim in this chapter—to thoroughly examine the creative deployment of the inner-city schools as sites of "identity politics" (Giroux, 1993; Grossberg, 1993).

    A secondary aim is to theorize on the interrelationships between the social and relational constitution of racial-ethnic identity and the potential practice of radical, deep democracy (Aronowitz, 1994; Giroux, 1991). Although I take issue with Beyer and Liston's (1992) claims that postmodernism engulfs a morally bankrupt politics/praxis, I endorse the call for an empirical assessment of its possibilities for transformative educational practices such as radical democracy in schools.

Specifically, I describe the results of a qualitative study of two inner-city high schools located in the southeastern United States. One school, a citywide school with high admission standards, admits exclusively African-American, lower to middle-class population; the other school enrolls an ethnically and racially diverse population of students from a lower socioeconomic neighborhood. Using the framework of identity politics (Aronowitz, 1994; Giroux, 1992; Grossberg, 1993), I describe how students' ethnic identity becomes a means of resistance *and* accommodation to both schools' formal and hidden curricula and instructional practices. The broad theoretical problem I explore through structured qualitative interviews is how *student's lived culture* (as expressed through language and other "circuits of communication"; Smith 1992) modified the formal and/or *hidden* curriculum and pedagogy in the two subject schools whose students reflect different class backgrounds (Anyon, 1980). More abstractly, I document in this chapter the efficacy of Marcus and Fisher's assertion that "culture mediates all human perceptions of nature" (quoted in Smith, 1992, p. 5).

STUDENT RESISTANCE AND IDENTITY POLITICS

Despite a vast literature on resistance theory (e.g., Everhart, 1983; Fine, 1989, 1992; Gilligan, 1993; Giroux, 1983; Willis, 1977), there exists few empirical studies on student culture. Perhaps more grossly overlooked, given the multiethnic student population in the inner city, is the terrain of *identity politics* (Giroux, 1992; Grossberg, 1993).

The approach here is a refusal to adhere to the notions of identity as constituting an autonomous, unitary self. Thus, human agency is not grounded in notions of the philosophy of consciousness (see Biesta, 1994). As I illustrate in this chapter, identity—ethnic identity especially—is socially constructed and embedded in social political relationships and discursive practices such as inner-city schooling (Smith, 1992). Within schools power is decentered and present everywhere. Subjectivity is, dialectically, both a product and determinant of power relations. Human agency, the capacity to pursue alternative courses of action, stands as a paradoxical by-product of unequal power relations, forever contested at the level of micropolitics of the school and its sets of dominant discourses.

Human Agency and Structural Relations

Links among identity politics, human agency, and structural relations are dialectical and problematic. On the one hand, a critical postmodern view shares much common theoretical ground with critical social theory. Deep structural relations, such as the world political economy (Miron & Elliott, 1994), constrain the oppositional strategies that actors may execute locally. This view is consistent with many strands of postmodern and poststructural thought (Foucault, 1977; Giratelli, 1993).

Human agency is tied to discourse and discursive practices. As such, it is inherently social and not solely dependent on abstract, ahistorical *structures*, whether deep or surface. Like agency, identity is relational, constantly reformulated and acting on organizations and the larger institutions such as the school and family in which it is situated. The important point is that people, acting socially in history and creating meaning through culture, *forge* structures. Structures constitute sets of complex organizational, ideological, political, and economic relationships, not commodified products. Human agents, acting collectively, may redefine them. However constraining, structural relations of any kind do not "tell people what to do." They also do not last forever.

The state's regulation of K-12 schooling and higher education is a case in point. Regulatory authority and supervisory functions affect and constrain the strategic choices of administrators, educators, students, and staff. However, the state's existing regulations, statutes, policies, curriculum standards, and administrative procedures are not uniformly received. Depending on the historical patterns of accommodation or resistance, and the balance of power, faculty and staff differ in the amount of professional leeway in complying with these forms of disciplinary order (Doll, 1993; Foucault, 1977; Stack, 1993). Quite obviously, tenured university faculty enjoy considerable freedom to occasionally ignore these means of social control.

I am not suggesting that such resistance necessarily benefits faculty or students. Clearly, when curriculum standards and textbooks are inadequate to meet the educational needs of a diverse student clientele, actively disregarding the state's bureaucratic wishes is morally necessary. At other times, state intervention, whether through regulation, legislation, or court order, may be fully justified.

As postmodernism weaves its theoretical path onto the terrains of research and scholarship in micropolitics, there is renewed interest in studying resistance. Although there are some promising developments in the conceptualization of resistance in the cultural sphere of schooling (Gilligan, 1993), scholars are understandably skeptical about the appropriation of a concept that remains bridled. As Everhart (1983) claims:

> I have come to believe that much student "resistance", rather than constituting an active revolt against the perceived unfairness or lack of significant regard which the school structures generates, merely is an escape from its anxieties. It gives the impression of power while ignoring the conditions under which relative powerlessness exist. (p. 250)

My fundamental assumptions about the nature of student resistance, as an organized ideological expression of power, differs sharply from Everhart's perspective. My understanding begins from the ground of student everyday life and from the poststructural tenet that power is decentered and everywhere. Indeed, within this framework students are not powerless. Investigating the conditions that foster organized expressions of power, and the circumstances that students exploit to engage in political, collective forms of resistance, therefore, warrants my serious attention as a researcher. Inner-city schools are uniquely situated to study this phenomenon as changing demographics and global and national migration continue to reconstruct schools as host sites of identity politics.

In writing this chapter, I have two aims. The first is to investigate the sites of inner-city schools, where contests over identity are waged. The second aim is to theorize on the relationship between the current status of democratic practices in inner-city schooling and what Michael Smith (1992) suggests is the new social space of urban ethnicity. I begin with an overview of my conceptualization of student resistance in the context of what Grossberg (1993), Giroux (1991), and others call *identity politics*.

Student Resistance as Collective Expressions of Power

The theory of student resistance I developed here sets out to establish the relationships among school culture, student resistance, and human agency. I briefly expand on the starting point—the expression of power in the everyday life of student culture.

Following the theoretical scholarship of Giroux and Grossberg on postmodernism and identity politics, and my notion of collective ethnic identities, I view identity relationally. As indicated in previous work, I refuse "to adhere to the notions of student identity as constituting a fixed, unitary self" (Lauria, Miron, & Dashner, 1994, p. 2). Students assume a multiplicity of roles in the school: compliant student, class clown (McLaren, 1989), bearers of racial pride. Identity is relational and socially constructed rather than fixed and essential (see also Mouffe, 1988). According to Smith (1992):

> [In] postmodern social analysis, the subject is decentered precisely because there are no clear cut roles waiting for subjects to occupy in pursuit of their historical mission. Rather, there are a multiplicity of roles that people (e.g., inner city students) come to play in history. These produce a 'self' experienced not as a single, completed identity, but as multiple, incomplete, and partial identities, formed in historically specific relation to the different social spaces people inhabit over time. Viewed in this light, the constitution of personal identity is best understood as necessarily *historicizing* the subject in all his or her spatial particularities and temporal contradictions. (p. 501)

Moreover, in the social context of inner-city schools, the multiethnic student population and the intersection of race, class, and gender make it likely that students will forge new identities or reshape existing ones.

As Smith (1992) noted, identities, and ethnic identities in particular, are constantly formed and reformed in the changing discourse of contemporary life in cities. Within the organization of schooling, the construction of school violence and underachievement, and the historical mismatch of school, home, and community resources (Tyack, 1993), inner-city students are deemed at risk of failure or dropping out of school altogether. However, at the level of lived cultural experience, students constantly challenge these images of who they are as students. In short, they resist them, both individually and collectively.

My contention is that the ability to engage in collective, ideologically organized forms of resistance arises out of students' capacity for human agency. Students in the inner city wage struggles for both personal and collective identity formation. Furthermore, their identity politics is tied to broader socialpolitical relations, for example, racial-ethnic formations. To the extent that minority, inner-city students acquire discursive awareness (see Giddens, 1987) of their and others' ethnic identities, students gain the most significant form of power in the context of public schooling: self-knowledge and knowledge of social identity. Simply stated, students may resist the formal and hidden curriculum of the school because acts of resistance are embedded in identity formation and identity politics in the inner city. These acts of resistance constitute important dimensions of students' "identity work" (see Wexler, 1988).

Schools in the inner city, therefore, play a significant role as sites of identity politics. I do not wish to romanticize this possibility, however. There is too much utopian work being undertaken on radical democracy and emancipatory pedagogical practices already (see, e.g., Aronowitz, 1994; Giroux, 1991). What I aim to do here is to investigate the struggles for personal and collective identity formation and the attendant politics of student resistance. I characterize this resistance as ideologically organized expressions of power. Although I begin with the theoretical and oppositional assumptions that such struggles are forged daily, I do not take them for granted. But first I need to explicate my framework for studying such phenomena: identity politics.

Human Agency and The Micropolitics of the School and Classroom

In part, poststructuralism is concerned with the contest over power at the everyday level of organizational life, that is, with *micropolitics* (Ball, 1987; Blaise, 1992). As such, it implicitly embraces Clegg's (1989) and Foucault's (1972) notion that power within the organization is always an outcome, not a given, and that within the cultural sphere of public education, power is inseparable from knowledge. Thus, political coalitions in the school struggle for various forms of control with the school administration. Teachers and principals may vie over the distribution of resources (Bolman & Deal, 1991), ideological control, and hence meaning (Anderson, 1992), and the content and form of the curriculum (Apple, 1990; Ball, 1987). Frequently, the school administrator, acting as a "manager of meaning and non-events," glosses over these conflicts over power by compromise, the nonintrusive use of symbols, and an ideological concern with meeting students' needs (Anderson, 1992). Under this scenario, the likelihood for the active, organized forms of student resistance (Gilligan, 1993), which may lead to substantive change in the school and classroom, is undermined.

As the critical scholarship and research of the aforementioned work by Apple, Gilligan, Giroux, Fine, Willis, and Everhart has pointed out, however, there is political space both within the school's practices and teachers' pedagogical methods to foster considerable forms of student resistance. One of the keys to facilitating student challenges to the formal and informal culture of the school is the school leader's active engagement of conflict (Ball, 1987; Olsen, 1994). I do not review the literature on the relationships in social organizations between conflict and change. My assumption is that the documented presence of student resistance is an indicator that school administrators and teachers are surrounded by conflict. How school leaders embrace conflict (e.g. between teachers and students) will shape whether conflict escalates into violence (see Miron & Lauria, 1995).

Student Agency and Resistance

Agency, or the capacity to identify and implement alternatives, is most readily evidenced in schools by the presence of student resistance. Unfortunately, despite a vast literature on resistance theory, very few empirical studies exist on the processes and forms of resistance that may derive from what I call *student culture*. In particular, as Herr and Anderson (1993) contend, "Few researchers have systematically probed the subjective experience of school life as disclosed by the students themselves" (p. 2). Perhaps more grossly overlooked is the postmodern terrain of identity politics, specifically ethnic identity.

Student identity has followed a particularly rigid definition limited to self-esteem (Ocampo et al., 1993). Student resistance is confined to individualized expressions of nonconformity, creativity, or just acting out. In the caricatures of Michael Apple, Robert Everhart, Peter McLaren, and others, student culture and resistance remain politically and relatively unorganized. I intend to illustrate how much more is going on in the school and classroom in the form of student collective (ideologically organized) forms of resistance that flow from the categories of micropolitics and collective student identities.

THE STRUGGLE FOR RACIAL-ETHNIC IDENTITY IN THE URBAN CONTEXT

Lawrence Grossberg (1993) has argued persuasively that identities have no "essential origins." Cultural heritage as a marker of ethnic identity (Longstreet, 1987) in the inner city is only one factor in who students are—today—in their lived cultural experience in inner-city schools. As argued earlier students may assume, and do assume, a multiplicity of roles in the daily conduct of school activities. As seen in the following discussions, being African-American in one school setting (the citywide school) is a vastly different qualitative experience than that found in a different setting (the neighborhood school). Students' experiences of their own (and others) ethnicity, then, differs. On the one hand, they may view themselves as Americans, African-Americans, or Creole. These comprise only a few of the possibilities.

In inner-city schools the struggle over students' identity is indeed a political one. Ethnic minorities resist both the attempts at minimizing their differences as minorities (Lauria, Miron, & Dashner, 1994) and the stereotyping that is often associated with a specific social class. For example, African-American students in the neighborhood school I interviewed from lower socioeconomic backgrounds complained that teachers and administrators expected them to perform badly in school. CH, an African-American male from the neighborhood school, put it this way:

> CH: Like today say Mr. W. what ditto paper I'm missing? Could you tell me? Find out for yourself. . . . I'm doing my work now. . . . Like yesterday I made an A on my paper and everybody else made B's, he looked at me like I was cheating. Here take that paper. Take that paper. He tries to embarrass you for no reason.

Identity Politics and Racial Formation

The concept of identity politics grew out of the fragmentation of the political agenda of the radical left. As such, it was spawned by a host of autonomous social movements such as ACT-UP, whose remarkable fight for legalization of drugs to combat the AIDS virus "forced the scientific and medical establishments, including the Food and Drug Administration, the National institute of Health, and the United States Congress, to take seriously the movement's demands for more funds for AIDS research" (Aronowitz, 1994, p. 49). Locally, in cities like New Orleans, social movements such as All Congregations Together (a coalition of dozens of churches) have forced local governments to become more aggressively involved in the fight against violent crime in distressed communities such as public housing developments. Although the residents of public housing are nearly exclusively African-American and poor (Garvin, 1994), the coalition is biracial, comprised of both White and African-American ministers and parishoners. Underlying their successful political struggle against inert governmental bureaucracies is the recognition that being African-American and poor is not synonymous with being a criminal.

Identity politics arose as a result of what Aronowitz (1994, p. 49) described as "autonomous movements." However, for African-Americans, identity politics remains embedded in the historical development of their racial formation (Omi & Winant, 1986, 1993). In cities in the Deep South, racial politics have played a significant role in shaping political regimes and the formation of public policies (see Cook & Lauria, 1995; Reed, 1988; Stone, 1989; Whelan et al., 1994). Put simply, in cases in which African-Americans have garnered considerable political power (such as in the cities of Atlanta, New Orleans, and Dallas), the legacy of the Civil Rights Movement has left a sense of entitlement, both to property rights and person rights (Apple, 1993). As I illustrate later, this legacy powerfully shapes the sense of personal identity for subaltern groups in the inner city and provides a sense of historical and cultural connection that the neighborhood school seemed bent on undermining.

The relational dimensions of identity paradoxically shape the social space within schools. Previous critical ethnography of school culture and what Wexler (1988) calls identity work has focused on the material forces that set structural limits on student resistance and the cultural expressions of power (e.g., Everhart, 1983; Herr & Anderson, 1993; Willis, 1977). However, none of these studies included African-American populations.

There is a paradox here. Whereas lower socioeconomic African-Americans may indeed struggle against their representation as at-risk students, other, more middle-class students' families have won important political concessions tied to the ascendancy of political power for African-American, middle-class professionals and politicians (Reed, 1988). For middle-class African-Americans, their personal and social identities redraw cultural and social boundaries, distancing them from the African-

American underclass. In either case, both social groups resist the identity labeling of the abstract racial category of *Black*. Middle-class African-Americans aspire to be just as successful—socially and economically—as middle-class Whites (Miron, 1995; Wilson, 1992). On the other hand, poor African-Americans in inner-city schools struggle to find their identities within the zombie land of the "border" (Anzaldua, 1987), where from their standpoint (the margin) they have not arrived as socialized insiders, facing the center. They do not see beyond the outside.

I illustrate these theoretical nuances in the analyses of two different African-American student cultures. It is these differences within the cultural life of the students, and the schools in which they are differently situated, that account for the struggle for and the achievement of ethnic-racial identity.

Deepening Democracy in Inner City Public Schools

Radical critical theorists such as Deborah Britzman (1993), Henry Giroux (1993), and Peter McLaren (1994) have long sought to test out the possibilities of forging deep democracy in the cultural and social space of public schools. Indeed, much of the collective theoretical scholarship of the previous 10 years has focused on the emancipatory and liberatory (see Freire, 1973) practices of critical pedagogy. In particular, Giroux's undying belief in the achievability of the utopian ideals of democracy within the contradictory structure of authority relations in the classroom has inspired practitioners to develop and implement a critical theory of education in the everyday world of teaching and learning (see Chapter 4). Kelly and Liu (1993) observe that "inherent in this view is a belief in the power of education to enlighten individuals concerning the benefits of and the need for a radical democracy" in public schools and classrooms (p. 22).

Arguably, critical theorists and practitioners face enormous challenges in employing the authority of classroom teachers to transform the historically authoritarian public classrooms into sites of deep, radical democracy. As I previously asserted, very few studies of resistance proceed from the vantage point of the students themselves. My suspicion is that democracy in the social context of violence, poverty, and fiscal crisis is a luxury few inner-city teachers perceive they can afford. Lest utopian ideals sink into the oblivion of theoretical fantasy, however, it is imperative for critical researchers to assess the validity of these ostensibly utopian claims (see Liston, 1990).

RESEARCH DESIGN

In this chapter I describe the results of a comparative case study (Yin, 1989) of two inner-city high schools located in the southeastern United States. One school, a citywide school with relatively high admission standards, has a student population that is 100% African-American, with the majority from lower middle-class backgrounds (60% on free lunch program); the other school enrolls a neighborhood comprised of a racially and ethnically diverse population of students (79% African-American, 15% White, 6% Asian-American and Latino-American) from a lower socioeconomic background (67% on free lunch program). I used in-depth structured interviews and participant observation methods to document the phenomena of student culture through the perspective of identity politics (see Grossberg, 1993). I obtained access to each of the schools and all of the students from the school principal. The principals consented to the goals of the research and accepted the rationale for my selection of their schools: the investigation of student culture in distinct neighborhood schools, and schools that drew their enrollment across district boundaries.

In each school I interviewed two categories of students. The first group were academically successful (these students all had an A or B grade point average). I did not expect to find much resistance to school values and curriculum from within this group. The second group were deemed relatively academically unsuccessful (these students all had a C or D grade point average). It is within this group that I expected to be able to document student resistance. Each group was comprised of 6 students each, a total of 24 students for both schools. No students who had failed a course during the previous year participated in the study, as I felt that these students were no longer *resisting* the school's academic structure, but for one reason or another simply had given up. I also excluded students who had failed the LEAP test so as not to confuse a student's lack of ability to succeed academically as a sign of resistance. Thus, in Hirschman's (1970) terminology, I excluded those students who chose to exit (failed or dropped out) as opposed to *voicing* resistance or maintaining *loyalty* to school values.

I also gathered the following data from the students' files: grade point average, nature of curriculum chosen, LEAP and CAT[1] test scores, race, gender, income (via lunch program participa-

---

[1] The California Achievement Test (CAT) is a norm-referenced objective test given to all freshmen by the Orleans Parish School Board. Students are tested in English, social studies, reading, science, and

tion), cultural/arts program participation, prior school, transfer school, and year in school. These data were used in interpreting the in-depth interviews and to eliminate student interviews that I suspected were unreliable. That is to say, if a student falsified information in the interview, I eliminated them and their interview for analysis purposes.

Finally, I conducted exit interviews with the principals of the two schools. These interviews had three goals: first, to determine the extent of actual business-school partnership activities occurring at the respective schools; second, to get a handle on school policy concerning values transmitted in the curriculum and pedagogy; and third, to determine if I had inadvertently interviewed any students with extreme disciplinary or behavioral problems. These interviews were not analyzed directly, but rather used as background information for my interpretations of the student interviews. This analysis was facilitated by the use of The Ethnograph (Version 4.0), a qualitative textual analysis program.

Because this was exploratory research, my expectations were rather crude. First, I expected to find different types of resistance between the two schools and a greater amount of resistance in the neighborhood school. Second, I expected to find different types of resistance based on academic performance and a greater amount of resistance in the less academically successful students. Finally, I expected the student culture of the neighborhood school to be characterized by ethnic conflict.

At this point a note of caution is in order. I am not making statistical generalizations from these small sample sizes, especially because I am interested in subsamples (school, class, gender, and race). I am not following a sampling theory process of validating insight; rather, I am attempting to theoretically interpret the data and to develop theoretical abstractions (see Yin, 1989, for a clear discussion of this distinction). In the presentation of the results, I do at times use percentages, but only to indicate comparative presence or absence and direction of difference of particular findings by class, gender, and school. It should be noted that, because of the small sample size, a single student respondent can represent anywhere from 4% to 8% of the sample.

---

mathematics. Scores are reported relative to national percentages. The CAT scores are used primarily as a tool for Honors Program Placement. The Louisiana Educational Assessment Program (LEAP) is a high school exit exam.

THE ENTREPRENEURIAL COALITION'S DRIVE FOR IDEOLOGICAL HEGEMONY IN LOUISIANA

The Social Context of Identity Politics

I argued earlier that students' identity formation and identity politics are tied to broader social-political relations outside of the classroom. In this section I sketch out the broader social context of identity politics in urban, public schooling. This broader social context concerns the formation of a loosely organized group I have termed the Entrepreneurial Coalition. In brief, this coalition has sought to impose corporate and entrepreneurial values throughout large urban school districts in the country. In short, it has sought ideological control over city schooling by attempting to gain consensus over the aims of public schools: economic competitiveness in the global economy. As I illustrate in this chapter, however, this drive for ideological hegemony has not only proved marginally successful, but it also remained largely irrelevant to students' identity politics in inner-city schools and classrooms that I have investigated (see Miron & Lauria, 1995; Anfara, 1995).

In the early 1980s, a loosely organized coalition of business, industrial, civic, public interest, and education groups launched a major campaign in Louisiana, as they did throughout the country, following the publication of *A Nation at Risk*, to overhaul the state system of public education (see Chapter 3). The coalition's goal was to secure ideological support from New Right supporters of the Reagan Administration to institutionalize what Michael Apple (1993), among others, called the *conservative restoration*. Ostensibly, New Right critics such as former Secretary of Education William Bennet pointed to the decline of education standards and performance of public school students throughout the country as a cause of the steep decline in the U.S. economy. The conservative and liberal groups widely believed that low academic performance, especially among high school students and graduates, largely accounted for the loss of economic competitiveness of the United States in the emerging global market. In Louisiana, the first concrete effects of the Entrepreneurial Coalition was the revision of the high school curriculum, commonly referred to as *Bulletin 741*, or the *Louisiana Handbook for School Administrators*.

State Educational Policy

The Louisiana State Board of Elementary and Secondary Education created the Louisiana Handbook for School Administrators (The Handbook) to develop understandable, uniform, and flexible guidelines in the administration of, among other things, secondary instructional programs. The Handbook sets minimal standards for the curriculum, establishes ideal class sizes and teacher-pupil ratios, and dictates attendance norms. To secure approval to operate a school in the State of Louisiana, a school (public or private) must demonstrate its capacity to adhere to the standards set forth in the Handbook. Of particular interest are the differences in academic subjects required and offered, the changes in particular course requirements, and the changes in other policies relating to the required curriculum in the 1990 versus the 1977 Handbook. It is apparent that changes in the Handbook reflected differences among factions of the Entrepreneurial Coalition. For example, the 1990 requirements for student graduation rose a full 3 Carnegie units. Many educational reform reports of the early 1980s called for this increase in academic requirements. The State of Louisiana was no exception. The aim of the reports was partly to link educational practices with the needs of industry and corporations in the United States. The Entrepreneurial Coalition was linked to groups that had an economic and social stake in long-term accumulation of capital, and these educational reports have blamed the educational system with the failure to prepare young people for the demands of the new marketplace. It is precisely this motivation by capital and entrepreneurial rhetoric that is partly responsible for the changes in the high school curriculum requirements in the Handbooks. Galvanizing public attention and support for the new high school curriculum helped unify the loose coalition's political activity in Louisiana.

In addition to the increase in overall required academic units, the number of electives decreased by 1 1/2 units. The increase in required units rose a total of 4 1/2 units without additional funding to implement the new requirements. Of the five subject areas listed in the 1977 document, four increased by one unit each: English, Math, Social Studies, and Science; business groups successfully lobbied the legislature to require 1/2 unit in Free Enterprise and Computer Literacy. Business groups spearheaded the belief of the Entrepreneurial Coalition that simply requiring more time-on-task on the basic skills would improve student achievement (Stack, 1995).

These additions illustrated ideological coherence, further strengthening the ascendancy in Louisiana of business and industry in particular. For example, in New Orleans the Business Task Force, affiliated with the Chamber of Commerce and the Louisiana Association for Business and Industry, lobbied heavily for the Computer Literacy and Free Enterprise units. More significantly, school administrators and teachers welcomed them (see Miron & Lauria, 1995).

By increasing the requirements for the core subject areas and decreasing the number of available units to select, the curriculum has been narrowed with fewer options to deviate from the core curriculum. The Entrepreneurial Coalition argued that U.S. students were behind their counterparts as evidenced by low scores on norm-referenced tests. In the more flexible curriculum students were spending time learning other, less useful knowledge (see Apple, 1993).

For instance, not only have the curriculum requirements for Math and Science increased, but specific types of knowledge within the two disciplines are emphasized. School counselors place more emphasis on statistics courses than calculus. Competency, or at least minimal scientific and technical knowledge, is what is required of a technical workforce facing stiff competition. The Entrepreneurial Coalition's logic was such that if the United States was going to reposition itself in the world economy, then the workforce must be retrained for this leadership to occur.

The transformation of the Handbook and changes in the social studies program goals and objectives were part of an intense education reform movement. Over the last 10 years the published curriculum has not only changed, but the goals and learner outcomes were redirected. The stated goals brought out in the social studies guides shifted from an emphasis on social understanding and skills to an emphasis on intellectual skills, values, and attitudes.

School-Business Partnerships

The Entrepreneurial Coalition's political and educational activities were aimed at the local and the state level. In Orleans Parish and surrounding parishes, the most visible aspect of their education efforts was the creation and promotion of Business Partnerships with individual schools in the metropolitan area. These partnerships were designed to provide a mechanism for businesses and the public schools to work closer together such that schools could learn how to better prepare their students for the ever-changing workplace and so that businesses could assist schools in that training.

In general, my research shows that City High students were more informed about what a school business partner is (75%-17%) and the name of their particular business partner (83%-12%) than were Neighborhood High students (Miron & Lauria, 1995). Although they concurred with Neighborhood High students that they personally did not benefit from the partnership (75%-75%), they disagreed with the Neighborhood High perception that the business partnership was not such a good idea (66%-45%) (see Lauria, Miron, & Dashner, 1994).

These relationships held even when income and academic performance (grade point average) were taken into account. In other words, the distributions of student responses were similar, regardless of whether isolated groups of middle-income, low-income, A-B, or C-D students were evaluated. When gender effects were evaluated, it was found that the distributions still held except for two factors: first, the males were more likely to know what the purpose of a business partner was (55%-31%) and the name of the particular business partner (64%-36%); second, females at Neighborhood High were more favorable to the idea of a school-business partnership than were the males at Neighborhood High (57%-25%). Gender differences help explain the above-mentioned 50-50 split in the low-income and C-D students' perception of the value of school-business partnerships as with the four favorable responses: three are female, and of the four unfavorable responses, three are male.

It is clear that, at the level of state education policy, the Entrepreneurial Coalition has had considerable impact in Louisiana, as it has also enjoyed throughout the country. The group was responsible for prescribing additional requirements in the core curriculum. Anecdotal evidence provided by school boards throughout the country has spoken to disproportionate negative effects of high school graduation rates on minority students. However, state education policy is only tangentially connected to students' lived cultural experience (see Weick, 1976). I know of no studies that have attempted to document the effects of such widespread influence and power on the day-to-day lives of inner-city students in school and in the classroom. Whatever studies exist certainly do not address the issue from the perspectives of student resistance and identity politics (see Grossberg, 1993). In the balance of this chapter, I qualitatively address these questions using structured interviews.

STUDENT CULTURE

In summary, two very distinct *student cultures* existed at the two schools I studied. Although I found evidence of student resistance within both schools, the differential nature and potential consequences of that resistance in each school are theoretically significant. The presentation of the student data and the interpretations that follow are organized to highlight the general finding that student culture between schools has the most interpretive value in accounting for the social phenomena of student resistance. Although in the neighborhood school there was evidence of widespread resistance to the formal, and hidden, curriculum, a startling revelation was that of the students interviewed in both schools; *all* expressed a desire to complete high school. In the neighborhood school, some underachieving students voiced a further desire to attend college. I try to account for this paradox of both resistance to schooling and acquiescence to the dominant belief in the value of education in the presentation of the data and its interpretation that follows.

In particular, as I suggested earlier, the values and ideology of corporations (see Miron, 1992) had little substantial impact on student culture. State education policy, too, had marginal effects on students' everyday life. I found evidence of both explicit, collective forms of student resistance and "tacit resistance" (see Anfara, 1995). The social relations of class, gender, and race all seem subordinate theoretical categories in students' identity politics. Although gender relations clearly shaped identity politics in the microcontext of student culture, it is the culture of the school as shaped by and reflective of student life that holds most interpretive value.

Everyday Life

What it is like to be a student in their school? From the responses to this question I gleaned the students' perception of the school's quality, reputation, and climate. I expected to find significant differences in students' perception of quality and reputation between the two schools. The intensity of these differences, based on responses to this question, and how this intensity conforms with much of the analysis that follows, is illuminating and theoretically "substantive" (see Waters, 1994). Because there was very little variance in student responses within schools, an analysis of gender, race, performance, or class was not helpful. Among the few positive statements concerning everyday life at Neighborhood High, there are strong hints of problems in the school climate:

> KV: Well, to be a student here at Neighborhood High it feels good to me because I like to participate in going to games, football games and stuff like that. And a lot of people don't really have a lot of school spirit 'n that, but I do. And I feel like Neighborhood High is a good school, and I like going here. It's good. You talk to your friends during lunch, going class to class, and very friendly around here. Me, I - I try to . . . I think that see. . . . I'm thinking this teacher isn't controlling her class, so how am I going to learn. How are we going to get a education if this teacher can't control her class and teach it. Other classes' teachers are more strict and they have control over their students. The class is quiet. The teacher has time to teach, and the students don't disturb. Well, one thing about teachers—I think they should have teachers . . . they have teachers that don't know how to control the class. And I think they should have teachers . . . teachers should not have to worry about students being bad, so I think they have . . . the students that are bad in class and stuff like disrupt class, I think those students should be put out, and let the students that want to learn, want to listen and get a good education do what they have to do.
>
> TH: Umm, you know a lot of people. It's fun, but I guess for new people, it's, you know, kind of boring. You don't know anybody. But if you know a lot of people, it's fun because you have a lot of people to talk to. People are nice around here. I enjoy talking to them. It's fun. Going to class, it's enjoyable. You see all the—your friends walking down the hall, you know, you clown back and forth, but administration kind of, you know, they have their ways sometimes. But I think they mean well.
>
> AH: Alright, its fun. It's challenging. It's a lot of peer pressure, but you know, if you do what you have to do, everything will fall in place the way you want it to. Well, I like my classes. I don't have any problems with any of my teachers. I enjoy the classes. Lunch, it's okay. I mean if you go to your classes and do what you're supposed to do, everything will be okay.

Negative comments were more typical. Early on in the interviews at Neighborhood High, the cloud of silence surrounding racial conflict and school violence began to lift:

AB: It's—it's not—it's not all that good to me because at Neighborhood High like for the past three years I've been here it's—it's changed. Well, Neighborhood High, it's okay. I like it, you know, but it's just some of the things that go on at this school that I don't understand and the teachers' attitudes and stuff. Like for instance, I can sit up here and I can ask you, 'well how do you do this certain problem?' And the teacher—the teacher, 'well I just went over that—went over that with you', you know. And I be like, 'well, you know, I didn't understand so that's why I am asking you. Y'all act like y'all dumb', you know. They wouldn't say it like directly towards me. They'll say it out in general, but I know they really mean it towards me. I say about out of all seven of my classes, I'd say I have like three to four teachers that have attitudes.

CH: I hate being at school. School sucks! Teachers come here for life and instead of all that stupid stuff. Nothing because it's boring back here just come to school in the morning, eat breakfast and wait till the bell to ring. The best thing I do is eat—go to lunch.

S: I think the African-American students are treated fairly by the administration. I mean, that if they do something wrong, they'll just have to suffer the consequences. African-American students treat Asian-American students very differently. I mean they would make fun of them you know because of the language that they talk. . . . and cause they can't speak English, other students would talk to them about that. And I'm like saying, well there's no need to do that because if you came from another country and you couldn't speak fluent English either, you wouldn't want anybody doing that to you (the other African-American students) don't seem to care.

KH: Alright, it's alright though to attend Neighborhood High but it's just that it's no activities that they give, you know like they use to give. And it's like it's getting boring to me. I just don't like it any no more. But I don't have no other school to go, so I come here. Yeah, and you know, it's like . . . it's alright. It just that I got to come do what I have to do in order to get out of school.

C: Some teachers have favoritism to (umm) their favorite student, but it ain't no racial. Yeah, she thinks i'm a hoodlum. She thinks every black male she see that dress like me . . . you know have something that's you know in style that black people wear, she consider them a hoodlum or gang member. . . . A lot of teachers say that though. I hear them say that.

> SG: The halls are always congested cause there are students who like to stand in the hallways and talk instead of going straight to class and then when I get in class, sometimes it gets boring from sitting in the class day after day talking about sometimes the same thing maybe like a week or so. And just about in every class, you're going to always have at least two or three students who's gonna make a comment about everything and disturb the class, but otherwise, I think it's fine.

The lack of a caring atmosphere pervades everyday life at the school. Suspension of student activities seems to be aimed at containing student behavior. The exit interviews with the principal suggested that he felt that suspending student assemblies would stop the fighting.

At City High, the students I interviewed had overall positive feelings about the school. They also took pains to point out the absence of school fights. Ironically, too, the students at City High voiced an interest in acquiring cultural knowledge of their ethnic background as African-Americans. This desire was curious given the fact that the school is 100% African-American. It has a tradition of instilling African-American history and a sense of racial pride in its student body. This latent awareness of their own ethnicity, however, must—in a single racial-ethnic group school that comprised the enrollment at City High—come at the expense of other racial-ethnic group identity, such as the Latinos, Vietnamese, and Filipinos awareness at Neighborhood High:

> JM: It's fun, exciting. You get involved with a lot of community activities. You are looked upon as as specially being a young black male myself, you get a lot of prestige and a lot of pushing from your teachers and the principal, and I really enjoy that especially from the principal. And it's just—it's love sort of here, and it really helps a whole lot of children. It really does.
>
> DC: Actually, it's pretty fun. You know we learn a lot. You know feel safer here than we do I guess at any other high school. And I guess we learn more since they have so many cultural things. We learn more about ourselves.
>
> TS: In general being a student here is mainly is excelling in your academics, being involved in a lot of activities. Also, it's really . . . being a student here is like you have a bond with everybody else. You get to at least know a lot of . . . you meet a lot of people here, and you get exposed to a lot of

different things here. Everybody . . . it's—it's—it's sort of a family. We have a family environment here, but everybody guess you would say everybody do.

Students at City High exude a sense of pride, especially racial and academic pride. They feel *honored* to be a student there. The emphasis on academic excellence at City High, and the vastly different student perceptions of how teachers treat them, contrasts starkly with the lack of school pride at Neighborhood High. Students at City High feel chosen, privileged, or honored to attend school. Students must pass an entrance examination to be admitted into City High; there are no entrance requirements at Hood High. The students at Neighborhood High feel stuck *back here*. An interesting embedded finding in these responses is that students rarely mentioned the schools' academic work when they commented on what it was like to be a student at Neighborhood High. References to academic work were nearly always mentioned in the City High students' accounts of everyday life. In general, students at Neighborhood High discussed academic work as *busy work* (in a related finding, see Everhart, 1983). The next section takes a closer look at school work/busy work as central to this study of student cultures and student resistance in inner-city public schools.

School Work

There existed significant differences in what students meant by "work." These differences pointed to broader relationships toward learning. At City High these responses were typical:

CH: Well to be a student, it's—it's a lot of hard work, but after you get the hang of it, you know it's fairly easy if you do all your work and everything. Umm Well, a lot of studying. You have to study, and once you study and catch up and like once you know the work, then you can go on ahead of the rest of the students, and then it would be easier for you. So, you know, when the teacher explains it, then you already know it and you know just get it like that.

TS: I try very hard because at City High, you know, there's a lot of people who make very good grades, and you want to be just like those people. And I know I find myself up some nights to three or four in the morning just studying, studying, studying, you know working this material in my head.

At Neighborhood High the responses were more geared to what it took to simply pass, rather than to strive for "excellence." As is evident, a few of the students blamed the teachers for lowering academic standards and expectations:

> AH: I mean like I might go home and study. Well with me I don't know how to study. I just listen to the teacher. If I catch it, I catch it. I know a boy that's graduating right now that can't read. And you know, they not helping him by you know letting him go. It's gone be hard for him to get a job. He's not going to be able to take care of himself.
>
> KV: I try hard. It's that when you're in the classroom and you have a lot of students around you trying to do your work and stuff like that. You got people talking, talking louder and you try to do your work, and it's hard to concentrate. Homework—homework and study, I like—I try to do my homework while I'm in school that way after school, I don't have to worry doing it. I try cause a "C" not hard for me to get. It's just that . . . a "C" not hard for me to get, so I try.
>
> DAVID(interviewer): So, you telling me that you try to get "A's," take books home, do your homework and you study?
>
> KH: No, I don't do all that.
>
> DAVID: So, what you get out of the class, you know, you can pass just by coming? Is that a fair assessment?
>
> KH: I pass just by coming.
>
> DAVID: Uh huh, what about learning that stuff in class?
>
> MM: No.
>
> DAVID: Does that bother you?
>
> MM: Not really, maybe because it's an elective.
>
> NB: I mean you don't even have to study for her test. She would ask us essay questions. She wouldn't even read over the answer you give her. She'll just check and see if I have it right, and if it's not right, she'll just check and see if I have all the questions answered, and she would give us points for that. Yeah, because I just sit there.. You know they just stuck me with . . . they gave me all kinds of classes, and I don't really need them.

Within the school climate of Neighborhood High, there are subtle differences within groups as to how each group approached busy work. Most of the students understood its irrelevance to learning, resigned themselves to "do what they have to do" to pass and earn their diplomas.

SCHOOL CLIMATE AS ORDERED SOCIAL RELATIONS IN THE CLASSROOM

The two schools, one with a neighborhood and the other with a citywide enrollment, fostered distinct social relations in the classroom. Through their contrasting pedagogical practices, the two sets of teachers deliberately organized different sets of social relations. In City High, the all African-American school, students respected, trusted, and supported each other; the teachers generally cared for their students. Each social group worked to achieve the spirit of academic excellence and social mobility for Blacks. In Neighborhood High, the ambience of intense social and racial conflict was present. Students not only competed with one another, but often actually physically fought with each other. Teachers furthered the conflict through their power over the grade and over the diploma. Here the hidden curriculum worked to academically and socially discriminate students (e.g., Asians are expected to achieve greater academic success than Blacks; Whites are generally given more slack during low individual performances and behaviors). This was reflected in the sections analyzing the sets of social relations discussed later.

On Caring

Students at City High felt strong support from their teachers; the teachers were there to help them intellectually, professionally, and personally. The difference was that in this inner-city high school teachers were *doing something*. They were actively engaged in helping students to learn, to become self-reliant, and to prepare to assume one of the select slots among the city's social and economic elites. The City High students only complained about minor issues. For instance, they felt that it was unjust to suspend a student for chewing gum, blamed teachers for wanting assignments turned in on time and making them keep their shirts tucked in during class.

> WT: I think coming here is like a reward as far as the teachers and the administrators and stuff because they really try to help you. I really haven't. . . . I've had some teachers but not as many as I have here who are interested in me learning.
>
> JD: The teachers, they are—they are very helpful because if I have a problem, they are not only our teachers, but they

are also a friend and a counselor towards us. They'll help us during class if I need help. That's—that's like the major thing. If I need help during class, they'll take time out during their class period and pull you on the side and talk to you and not too many teachers can offer that. And if I—if the teachers can't help us, I also have the vice- principal, the principal or our counselors to talk to. And it's just—it's love sort of here, and it really helps a whole lot of children. It really does.

TS: Umm, basically it's a sort of bond between the teacher, and the teacher helps you, you know, develop ideas. And also when you learn to develop ideas, it helps you to develop yourself in a way.

By contrast, pervasive lack of caring becomes a central issue with the Neighborhood High students. At Neighborhood High the students generally insisted that the teachers and administrators treated the different segments of the racial population fairly. That is, an informal belief among the school administration—equal opportunity for all races—is transformed by their students as their "habitus" (Bourdieu, 1977). The administrative practice of treating all racial groups the same—without discernable difference by the students—subtly bred resentment.

CH: Good is good and fair is a li'l under good. All right the difference between good and fair. Good, you just, they don't watch you, you know, but fair is like they got to watch you and make sure you don't do nothing, like they do me, you know. Some of the teachers back here, they don't know me. See some of them could act bad just because they might see me, you know I have got golds in my mouth, you know different things. You know they gone expect bad of me, you know.

Specifically, some students mentioned that teachers expected White and Asian students to be smarter than the African-American students. I observed that this attitude led to subtle differences in academic expectations and discipline in the classroom.

SI: From what I know, yeah, besides . . . like some teachers may think that well, if that person is white, well they are better than the rest, you know the rest of them in classrooms. And you know, another person makes the higher grade than them, they say, "well she probably . . . or that person had a bad day or something like that. Yeah, something is wrong, you know for that day. You know they won't like put them down or announce their grade out, you know in front of anything. They'll just keep it to themselves and come talk to that student.

TH: Now, there's some teachers that won't, you know, it doesn't matter, but there are some teachers that treat blacks differently. You know, if a white person comes in late to class, you know they won't tell them anything. But then a black person comes late to class, they get fussed at. That's not a lot but about 10% of the teachers.

Many of the African-American students interviewed felt that their teachers simply did not care about them. As previously noted, the administrative ideological practice was equal treatment for all racial groups. However, some of the African-American students at Neighborhood High clearly suffered from the stigma of the social construction of racial-ethnic identity (see Miron & Lauria, 1995). For example, they felt victimized by the expectation that Vietnamese students were "smarter":

NB: Yeah, they expect more from the Vietnamese kids that always be smarter and stuff. And they don't really, really . . . I mean it's like the Vietnamese is always smarter, and they never expect a black student to be smarter than a Vietnamese, you know. They always automatically think that we're dumb.

AH: I know a boy that's graduating right now that can't read. And you know, they not helping him by you know letting him go. It's gone be hard for him to get a job. He's not going to be able to take care of himself. I mean I feel like they only care about themselves because if they cared about the students, they wouldn't put up with half the stuff that they do with them. They would let them know, you know they have a big world out there. You have to do what you have to do. And you know if it takes for them to sit down and talk to the students and tell them how hard it is, well let them do that, you know. I don't know. I guess they only look out for themselves.

KV: Teachers . . . I'm—I'm . . . teachers treat me pretty well. It's just the way they teach. They don't teach you. They don't talk to you. They just like to give you work and get you out they're—get you out their way, so they can do their stuff on their own, and they just give you work, sit you down, make you do work in the book and they don't teach you.

Some Neighborhood High students mentioned that the teachers would threaten them with failure. This possibility was never mentioned in the City High interviews and as can be seen by earlier discussions, the students felt an injustice.

> MM: It's just like . . . I don't know. It's not all the students fault. Sometimes, it's the teachers fault back here cause different teachers do different things back here. Some teachers don't give a care what you do. Teachers back here have favorites either they like you or they don't. They like you, you really—you really—you really—you really have advantage. If they don't like you, they're going to make it hard for you, but they can't fail you. But some will. Some—some will tell you, if you know, 'you better, you know, do what I say or I can fail you. And there's nothing you can do about, and there's no way you can prove it. It's your words against mine. Some teachers back here make you aware of back here, what they want done back here. They won't help you.

MM's narrative illustrates students' perception of the authoritarian character of the school. Students felt stuck back here, but nonetheless managed to pass their academic subjects, even graduate .

On Trust

The perceived lack of caring at Neighborhood High, and the contrasting perception among City High Students that their teachers were counselors and friends, have both psychological and social consequences. If the students at Neighborhood High did not feel that teachers cared for them, then mistrust ensued. The chasm between students and teachers heightened. The school administration became more isolated from the everyday activities of the school and more removed from the nascent conflict.

At City High, care fostered trust. Accordingly, trust evolved into positive communication. The students, teachers, and administration all felt that unique family "bond." The student culture was embedded in the school's traditions, its history, and its social relations to the city. As potential sites of "radical cultural politics," inner-city school construction of students' social identities are inseparable from the social and spatial relations of the city (Soja & Hooper, 1993, pp. 23-30). In contrast, students at Neighborhood High did not trust their teachers. They complained that information the students shared in confidence with teachers provided fuel for gossip that students overheard coming from the teachers' lounge:

> AB: Yeah, cause they do have their li'l conversations about certain students. Like—like you said sometimes ya' know, they'll have teachers that hear your conversation. Then they'll start their own conversation about the subject—about the certain person you were talking about or whatever. So, they have they own li'l attitudes toward certain students. No, I don't really know if they if they would treat them differently, but I think that kind of, you know, affect them in some—some way cause that's not showing a good example. You know, you shouldn't sit up there and if you're supposed to be an adult and supposed to be mature, you shouldn't you know have . . . it's not your business, you shouldn't sit up there and talk about anyone or anyone else's business if they wasn't talking to you. Now, if they talking to you, that should be among you and that person. But as far as going around saying something else to another teacher or you know another administrator, that's not right. So, that's kind of like showing a bad example in life too.
>
> DG: Yeah, Mrs. P. ask you questions. I can't believe. That's like I said you have to watch what you do because in this li'l area right here—this English section—they watch you. And they get in their li'l groups and they will talk, and you know, I know it just don't stay right there. It goes on and on, and everybody . . . that don't . . . a person that doesn't even know you looking at ya, "Oh, I heard about her" And you don't know. . . . You might not be that type of person that they say.
>
> MM: They would . . . I mean some teachers would talk about you. That's the way teachers are. They're like little kids. They'll sit there and talk about you in front of your face. Because I found out that you know . . . I used to do that. Some things happen on the weekend. You do want to bring it to school and tell the teacher if you know you feel you can talk to them. And I used to feel like that, but you know, you tell the teacher something to them. And you said this is between you and me. But then really it's not. You find out that it's not, you know. They would—they would discuss it with other teachers that they're friends with, and the teacher would come ask you about it wanting to get all in your business. It get back. And if it's something bad.

Once again, at City High, the most consistent response was that the teacher/administrator would be helpful:

> JD: They probably talk to you at school, then you know when they get home, they might call your parents to see what's wrong. Like I say, you know, they'll try to help you.
>
> DC: Yeah, I'm sure they'll help. It's just something, just a habit.
>
> CT: But then . . . like some teachers if you having problems, they'll talk to you and offer you help on the side and stuff or you can come in the morning or after school for tutoring or whatever.
>
> JW: Well, most of the administrators at this school, they would try to give us their opinion on the subject in the way they was brought up.

It is clear that the students at Neighborhood High were much more cautious or wary about the implications of their behavior in front of the teachers. They felt that they could not trust teachers because teachers gossiped about them. They did not feel that the teachers actually cared about them or would keep their best interest in mind. Teachers' gossip provided further evidence of a lack of caring about the students private affairs. At City High, the students were much more comfortable that their teachers had their best interests in mind.

On Respect and School Violence

The positive school climate at City High was also apparent in the students' social relationships among themselves, the types of student cliques that formed, and the general lack of escalation of student conflict (fights). None of the respondents mentioned student conflicts as a problem, and one even volunteered that unlike other schools, at City High, there were no fights:

> JD: You know I say it's from . . . so far this year, you know they really don't have you know fights like other schools and things. They rather just talk their problems out with each other.

The types of cliques that formed at City High were overwhelmingly (8 of 12 respondents) school related extracurricular clubs (Spanish Club, National Honor Society, Band, Big Brother, etc.) or sports groups (football, baseball, cheerleaders, majorettes, etc.) followed by religious groups (2), and grade in school, or old friends (1 each):

> JD: Not really, you know they don't bring like groups off the streets to this school, you know. The only groups they bring here is like the band, football team and stuff like that. That's all.
>
> DC: Well, just extracurricular clubs and all types of sport activities, that's about it.
>
> WT: I have Future Business Leaders of America. I have the choir. I have the Art Club. I have the National Honor Society. I have Alpha Theta. That's a Math club. Oh, yeah. (laughs) I have dance groups. I have the modern dance, the Eaglets. They perform . . . cheerleaders, majorette, tracks, sports (ah) baseball, softball.

The general feeling one gets from the interviews is that the students respect each other for being African-Americans *and* performing well enough to get into City High. They feel they are in it "together"—to beat society's odds against them as African-Americans. In contrast to their counterparts at Neighborhood High, and most neighborhood-based high schools in the city, these African-American students succeeded. Moreover, the male high school students overcame the overwhelming odds in which male students had equal chances of getting arrested as graduating from school (see Garibaldi, 1988):

> WT: We treat each other with respect because I mean everyone else tends to . . . society you know they tend look down upon us because we are black, so we treat each other with respect because, I don't know, it's like a family.
>
> JM: Ah, for the greater majority, it's respect, but there are a select few who don't take that Afro-American pride as seriously as they ought to.
>
> CH: Well mostly I stay to myself, but when I do be talking to other people, you know, they respect me . . .
>
> TS: Everybody . . . it's—it's—it's sort of a family. I have a family environment here, but everybody . . . I guess you would say everybody does belong to a group here. It's either . . . there's that kind of bond.

Thus, the general school climate is one of mutual respect and cooperation to learn the socially acceptable behaviors, attitudes, and skills to succeed in the wider society. Trust is clearly linked to race and the atmosphere of Black pride.

Again, the sullen atmosphere at Neighborhood High is mirrored in the student relationships among themselves, the types of cliques that form, and the frequency of the escalation of student verbal conflicts into physical fights. In sharp contrast to City High, the types of cliques most often mentioned at Neighborhood High were based on race, neighborhood, sports; only one student mentioned an academic-oriented group:

> AH: Okay, it's like they might have Japanese be with Japanese. Blacks be with blacks. Whites be with whites. I guess it all depends upon your race. I mean you'll very seldom see a black and white person together.
>
> CH: It's not really a name for the groups, but they just got certain people that hang with each other like some people that grew up around each or some people that stay in the same area like . . . Christopher Homes [a public housing development]. . . . They—some people all stay together. They're some of them from. . . . Some people stay together that's in the Cut-off [a nearby rural community] or some people together as just friends that grew up together. Ah, Chinese people or Vietnamese or Japanese or Ninja or whatever you want call it.
>
> DG: Yeah, because if they get into a fight and somebody from the Cut-off coming from home—somebody couldn't get home, get jumped. They'll all jump in even though they not involved, you know help each other.

Students consistently mentioned problems of student conflict when asked what "everyday life" was like at Neighborhood High. The conflicts are intragroup conflicts, either racial or neighborhood-based gang violence. The reporting of racial conflict and violence runs counter to the perception that racism did not exist in Neighborhood High. As I argue later, students' identity politics is tied to broader social relations outside of the school. Students' sense of who they are is shaped in the classroom and in the places they live (Bondi, 1993):

> KV: Well, gang fights mostly . . . fight them and stuff like that. And people come . . . and they come back want to fight you, and they want to shoot you and stuff like that.

> DG: Uh huh, that's what I think most of the fights are territorial like the Cut-off against Christopher Holmes. You know it don't be over something real like you know "you hit my li'l sister." Nothing like that.
>
> AB: They was fighting like crazy. I think it was like the Hispanics and the Japanese or something like that . . .against Japanese because of this li'l certain person or you know the situation that was going on whatever. They treat them, you know, they'll go to fighting and everything. And the Hispanics would be against the Japanese, and the Japanese would be.
>
> MM: They get called Ching Chongs and make fun of their language, you know. They do all that, and they curse you out in their language. They'll let you know they're cursing you out.
>
> SI: It's more difficult, I think because of all the fights and the things they're having . . . have like assembly. They don't hold them any more, and the reasons is they have fights too much.

Unlike the socially cooperative/academically competitive atmosphere at City High, the overall school climate at Neighborhood High breeds tense social competition that often escalates into physical conflict. I found evidence of social reproduction (lower social class Blacks are responsible for crime). However, in their narratives there is also evidence that there strongly exists the potential for student-driven political opposition to social reproduction:

> AH: I guess it's all about the way you present yourself. If you go up to another student with a bad attitude, and that lady will come back toward you with a bad attitude. They might . . . some of them . . . okay, for instance, you're Asian. I'm American, right. I might come to you with a nice attitude or try to meet you to be friendly. And another student might come along and just pass you up because they could care less what you're doing. I guess it's alright. I think more the black males, they would pick on the white students and the black females whatever.
>
> NB: I think that the Vietnamese and the white groups think that we're like hard and things . . . and dumb. They think all I listen to is rap. They stereotype us, you know all of us or either in jail mainly the males, black males. They think they wind up in jail or in a gang or something or do drugs, sell drugs on the street. Just because a black person will have

money or something or dress real nice, they automatically think that they sell drugs or something. They can't come from a nice family or whatever.

SI: Well, they get teased on that, and there's like when they're taking the ESL classes, well there's ESL problems from the time they get here and most of their 12th-grade year. But when it's time for graduation ceremonies to be handled, they move up into the Val or Salutatorian spot, and then they don't take regular classes. And most of the other students are upset about that cause if you're taking ESL, how are you going to get above someone who's been in other classes. Oh, I . . . well, I don't know if they're hard or not. But if a student is taking ESL and they're in that class for what almost four or three and a half years, and then they could come up and just move into a higher spot than someone whose worked really hard for it, I think that's wrong. Because if you work . . . if you're in ESL and you can't and you're not . . . if you don't understand, how are you going to be able to do it, you know.

These narratives illustrate that students at Neighborhood High want to succeed academically. They resent the apparent academic disconnection in their school. They resist their representation as underachieving, violence-prone Blacks. Although clearly there are fights and violence exists, there is also a push toward high school graduation. Even many of the underachieving students desire to compete for entrance into college.

INTERPRETING STUDENT RESISTANCE

In broad terms, the significant qualitative difference between student culture in the two urban high schools I studied lay in their relative degree of "connectedness" to the wider society. In the neighborhood school, the students described the location of their school as residing "back here." They frequently viewed their major goal of attaining a high school diploma as a vehicle to connect with the "outside." I expected a much greater extent of student resistance to obtaining a diploma and thereby graduating from high school, than I found. Virtually *no* student expressed disinterest in graduating from high school, owing either to a lack of meaningful employment opportunities (the school district is situated within a largely service and tourist economy) or better earnings through the underground economy of drug trafficking.

Rather, students in the neighborhood school resisted the classroom teachers' standard practice of assigning busy work as a means of controlling student behavior. One Neighborhood High student summarized this perspective simply:

> KH: Well, mainly my number one goal right now is completing high school and getting my diploma. And I feel that's very important because without your diploma, there's nothing you can do. After my diploma, I plan on attending a vocational school in electrical engineering, get my degree in that and get a job in engineering. As for my goals, no I don't think it [the curriculum] has really helped me, but in other aspects of life I think they [courses] do. . . . I feel like some teachers really don't know how to teach the students, just try to, you know give work. You know they don't teach the students what they're doing, just give them work to do to keep them busy.

This teacher attitude is echoed by a female student, who said:

> AB: I feel like this, if you're a teacher and I don't understand something, you are supposed to help me. And that's what you are here for. . . . [Like] you'll ask the teachers a question and the teacher, you know, just make a bad comment towards you or whatever or call you out your name and stuff. And they shouldn't do that here. [If I ask you] how do you do this certain problem and the teacher says, "Well, I just went over that—went over that with you." And I be like. "Well you know, I didn't understand so that's why I am asking you. "Y'all act like you are dumb," you know. They [the teachers] wouldn't say it like directly towards me. They'll say it out in general but I know they really mean it towards me.

In City High, most of the students I interviewed felt very connected to their local communities and to the wider society. They also felt that teachers were there to teach and to help students. Resistance to the formal curriculum and pedagogical practices were much less prevalent. One student voiced these relationships and the role her school plays in fostering them:

> WT: You know those kinds of classes that I take, they [teachers] make you watch the news or they'll ask you to watch it, and it becomes interesting because this is things

that are happening around you daily. You need to be informed about these things, some yeah, that's the way that they [teachers] do it. You know they get us involved with it. We're part of society. I make up that statistic, so you know they let us see that. . . . We treat each other with respect because I mean everyone else tends to . . . society, you know, tends to look down upon us because we're black. [The school] is like a family . . . and its like they [teachers] educate us. We are black. They educate us about where we've been, where our ancestors have been at.

Although she voiced contentment with her teachers, practice of injecting a sense of racial pride, other students resist the elitism that results from this practice:

JM: Well [here] they [teachers] encourage going to the top of the line college, Howard, Yale, Oxford, places like that. If you don't apply to a college they call you in the office. "Why haven't you applied for a college? You need to do that." Things of that nature. They keep you in school a lot instead of allowing you to leave, especially juniors and seniors who have already met the requirements for graduation. They [the administration] keep you in school the whole period to get you more "well-rounded," as they say to meet that successful goal [of getting accepted into an elite university]. The administration, they make sure that I have the top of the line. . . . The school should have a balance in teaching so much about success because you [the students] have to keep in mind where I came from and, personally, I don't think all the financial success means a lot. And I have millions of illustrations of that persons who are well known and have lots of money. They kill themselves. . . . I think, instead, that they [the administration and teachers] should allow each person to decide what he wants to do. If you want to be a garbage man, be the best you can be at that. Whereas [at this school] I [the administration] want you to be the executive of this building. I want you to be the "head" of this. The "head" doesn't mean anything. In the majority of cases, the head is not the one who comes out with the fantastic plans anyway, so that's what I think about that.

I need to make clear that, even within this complex analysis, the more glaring differences arise between schools, not within schools. Thus, it appears that student culture is a much more powerful construct in explaining these differences than academic performance, class background, or gender socialization. I find empirical support for Marcus and Fischer's theoretical argument that "culture mediates all human perceptions of nature" (cited in Smith, 1992, p. 5). The ideological structure of many large urban school districts is such that low-income, African-American families do not value public education. The students I interviewed at Neighborhood High clearly did not subscribe to that position. Indeed, what students there resisted was schooling defined as *busy work*. What they insisted as their person right was a high school education as a ticket to the outside world of cultural and economic mobility (see Miron & Lauria, 1995). Within the postmodern analytical categories of collective identities, students in both schools resisted the representation of Blacks as devaluing education and a high school diploma. Student culture then both aids in the social construction of racial-ethnic identities in inner-city schools and is shaped by dominant representations of identity.

THE SOCIAL CONSTRUCTION OF RACIAL-ETHNIC IDENTITY

Race, and racial identity in particular, constitutes a *hybrid*. It is both a social and historical process and "the product of encounters between and among differently located human beings" (McCarthy & Crichlow, 1993, p. xv). As this study illustrates, inner-city African-American students experience race differentially, owing both to structural factors (class and ideology) as well as lived student culture, both generated by students themselves and reified in the history, traditions, and the academic content of the school. Racial-ethnic identity formation, then, is always incomplete. Which factors prevail in shaping its development in the context of inner-city public schooling—cultural, social, and/or historical—is both a structural (relational) and strategic (Bondi, 1993) question. I also assert that students' unique set of academic experiences also matters.

In a prior analysis of the interviews of City and Neighborhood High students, I hypothesized that high school students, regardless of the kinds of schools they attended would differentially resist schooling depending on their relative academic success (Miron & Lauria, 1995). Thus, students who averaged a grade of A or B in their course work would reap benefits from their academic performance and continue to do well. They would not overtly question the school curriculum. Students who perceive themselves as doing relatively poorly in school work, on the other hand, would have little motivation to study harder. Academically, these students would resist the formal school curriculum. To my surprise, my findings generally did not bear this out. Rather, students at Neighborhood High sharply distinguished school work from quality education regardless of academic performance. In short, they valued an education (Barbier, 1994b) that would prepare them for college and were disappointed, if not resentful, when they saw that they were not receiving the education that would accomplish this. I draw on this finding to shape the following interpretations (Miron & Lauria, 1995).

CW, a C student put it this way:

> Like some teachers try to be hard so they seem to prepare you for college. I think that's important because I know that if I get soft teacher now and when I'll be in college and they just tell me to do this and do that I won't be able to. And here the are saying I'll give you another day or something. I'll cry because I'll be sad (in college) because you know I wasn't ready yet.

MM, a C/D student shares these same feelings:

> (Getting good grades is important to me) because I want to go to college. And during these last two years (of high school), if you want to go to college or you plan to get a scholarship, that D and A does matter. They (the college) want you with an A or B rather than a D or barely making a C. So that matters to me a lot.

MM explains exactly how difficult it is to obtain the quality education and competency in specific content areas to qualify her for college admission:

> MM: I mean math is important in reaching my goal, but this is a class that I just lack in. It's just real hard for me because I like Algebra. My first year back here I took Algebra I. We didn't have a teacher for at least four weeks of school, then we had a substitute teacher who wasn't a real teacher. The grades he gave us—he threw them away. I mean that they didn't have a teacher, so they really couldn't fail me. So I just moved on to Geometry. For Geometry I had a substitute teacher again. And now I'm in Algebra II, you know it's like I just don't know it. (The teacher) said that

you should have learned this from Algebra I, but I never really had Algebra I.

KH, also a C/D student, voiced his frustration with the educational quality at Neighborhood High:

> KH: I'm thinking this teacher isn't controlling her class, so how are we going to learn. How are we going to get a education if this teacher can't control her class and teach it. Other classes teachers are more strict and they have control over their students. The class is quiet. The teacher has time to teach, and the students don't disturb. Well, . . . they have teachers that don't know how to control the class. And I think . . . teachers should not have to worry about students being bad, so I think they have . . . the students that are bad in class and stuff like disrupt class, I think those students should be put out, and let the students that want to learn, want to listen and get a good education do what they have to do.

These two accounts demonstrate how difficult it is for the Entrepreneurial Coalition to accomplish its goals for inner-city schools. Although it has endorsed the objectives of the National Education Goals Act to make U.S. students number one in the world in mathematics and science, there is a shortage of these teachers owing to market forces. Furthermore, neighborhood schools in the inner city not only cannot attract certified teachers in these subject areas, but often they do not attract certified teachers at all. The practice of employing substitute teachers on an extended basis is widespread in large inner-city school districts. These practices virtually guarantee that students will not acquire the computational skills to make them globally competitive. Students like MM resist and resent this shortcoming of the underfunded inner city school bureaucracy.

Other students from Neighborhood High intuitively sense the interrelationships among race, identity, and academic results. SI, an African-American student with an A average, summarized academic discrimination, a result of the hidden curriculum in the school:

> SI: Some teachers might think that, well, if that student is white, well they are better than the rest. You know the rest of them in the classrooms. And you know another (African-American) person makes the higher grade than them, the teachers might say, 'well she probably had a bad day'.

172 Chapter Five

White students are not the only ones who benefit from teachers' higher expectations. Many valedictorians and salutatorians in this school district are Vietnamese (the district is 95% minority; 90% of the total enrollment is African-American):

> SI: Well there's ESL problems from the moment (the Vietnamese students) get here and most of their 12th-grade year. But when it's time for graduation ceremonies to be handled, they move up to that Val or Salutatorian slot, and then they don't take regular classes. And most of the (majority African-American) students are upset about that cause if you're taking ESL, how are you going to get above someone who's been in other classes?
>
> David: So what you're saying is the ESL classes are not as hard as the general classes?
>
> SI: I don't know if they're hard or not. But if a student is taking ESL and they're in that class for almost three and one half or four years, and then they could come up and just move into a higher spot than someone whose worked really hard for it, I think that's wrong. If you are in ESL and you don't understand, how are you going to be able to do it?

Although the school administration at Neighborhood High espouses a policy of equal treatment for all races, and the students universally embrace the ideology of *no difference*, African-Americans fall into the category of unintended victims:

> David: So, you see no difference at all in how anybody is treated by anyone else, blacks, whites?
>
> CH: It's just that everybody is treated good, but the blacks is treated fair.
>
> David: What do you mean by that?
>
> CH: Good is good and fair is a li'l under good. Alright the difference between good and fair. Good, you just, they don't watch you, you know, but fair is like they got to watch you and make sure you don't do nothing, like they to me, you know. Some of the teachers back here, they don't know me. See some of them could act bad just because they might see me, you know I have got golds in my mouth, you know different things. You know they gone expect bad of me, you know.

White teachers at Neighborhood High do discriminate by racial groups in the classroom. Administrators may take a hands-off approach; however, both teachers as a professional group and students as racial groups fall prey to the racial conflicts in the school:

> SI: I think the African-American students are treated fairly by the administration. I mean, that if they do something wrong, they'll just have to suffer the consequences. (African-American students treat Asian-American students) very differently. I mean they would make fun of them you know because of the language that they talk. . . . and cause they can't speak fluent English, other students would talk to them about that. And I'm like saying well there's no need to do that because if you came from another country and you couldn't speak fluent English either, you wouldn't want anybody doing that to you. (the other African-American students) don't seem to care.
>
> AH: (being a student at Neighborhood High) is more difficult because of all the fights . . . we're not able to do anything or hold any pep rallies or what we would usually have like assemblies. They (the administration) don't hold them anymore, and the reason is that they have too many fights. But I never heard of having a fight in an assembly before.

These narratives appear to reinforce Everhart's position cited earlier regarding the students' relative powerlessness. Traditionally, empirical research of the lived culture of the school, despite the theoretical insights derived from studies of the state's political economy (Poulantzas, 1978), remains at the level of macro power relations. Put differently, studies of student culture did not push the boundaries of marginality sufficiently. Focusing on the displacement of students from the center, such studies (Anyon, 1980; Apple, 1985; Everhart, 1983; Willis, 1977) undermined the very culture these theorists sought to uncover. SI put this issue as a civil right:

> SI: Making the grade is what is important to me. If there is a verbal confrontation (with a teacher), then I'll go get my parents. And if my parents can't handle it, they'll go to the administration. And if they don't do anything about it, they'll just take it up higher.

In the citywide high school, a 100% African-American enrollment, students from the same kinds of lower socioeconomic neighborhoods experience high expectations from their teachers. Teachers, and especially the school administration, groom African-Americans to enter elite colleges and universities. Being *African* American in this school of high academic standing is a qualitatively different phenomena then being *African* American at Neighborhood High. CT talks about how expectations are shaped by "first impressions," obviously not by race or the interplay of race and class. The school climate fosters mutual respect for successful African-American students:

> CT: If you walk in the class and you say, "hello", how are you doing? Then you sit down and do your work the first day, that's what they (the teachers) gonna expect you to do the rest of the year. But if you go in there like, with a pencil in your ear or walking in there slouchy and the teacher is talking and you are talking to your friends, she's going to expect that out of you the whole year. So, she's going to treat you a different way than the other students.

Difference is defined by academic expectations, not racial stereotyping.

JW, an African-American male, summarizes what it feels like for students to escape the stigma of the troubled generation of male, African-American high school students in this school district (see Garibaldi, 1988):

> JW: The teachers (at the citywide high school) are very helpful because if we have a problem, they are not only our teachers, but they are also a friend and a counselor to us. They'll help us during class if we need help. That's like the major thing. if we need help during class, they'll take time out during class period and pull you out on the side and talk to you and not too many teachers can offer you that. And if the teachers can't help us, we also have the vice-principal or our counselors to talk to. You get involved with a lot of community activities. You are looked as successful. Especially for a young black male like myself, you get a lot of prestige and a lot of pushing from your teachers and the principal. I really enjoy that, especially from the principal. It's a sort of love here, and it really helps a whole lot of children. It really does.

WT agrees:

WT: We treat each other with respect because I mean everyone else in society tends to look down upon us because we are black, so we treat each other with respect. It's like a family. And it's like they (the teachers) educate us. We are black. They educate us about where we've been, where our ancestors have been at.

According to CW:

CW: Being a student here is excelling in your academics, being involved in a lot of activities. Also, being a student here is like you have a bond with everybody else. It's a sort of a family here. We have a family environment. Since we are all African-Americans here, the teachers treat us very fairly. (How students are individually treated by other students) depends on who you are, where you belong, and what grade level you're in. You know, the older people get the most clout in the school and the freshmen are still trying to work their way up.

School culture is partially shaped by the simple fact that City High is 100% African-American. The family bond that fosters the sense of caring is inseparable from the issue of race. In addition, the school has historically created a strong sense of African-American pride that shapes the formation of racial/ethnic identity, both personally and collectively.

JM stated this paradox of racial identity:

The great majority of students here treat each other with respect. There are a select few who don't take that Afro-American pride as seriously as they ought to. And I'm shocked to say this, but in the majority of cases you find that among the women instead of the men. Usually it be the man who would be derogatory, but now it's turning the tide and we're having a select few females who are downgrading the males and other females, too. But other than that, everyone seems to get along real well.

SUMMARY OF IDENTITY/CULTURAL POLITICS

The unfolding of students' identity politics in the dramatic discourse of Hood High and City High hinges on the interaction between school/student culture and the broader social relations outside of the schools and classrooms. Put differently, as sites of cultural and identity politics, schools both shape students' sense of enduring and imagined self (see Chapter 6) and reproduce the dominant representations of identity. It is the dominant representation of low-income African-Americans as "deviant" that students most tacitly resist at Neighborhood High (Anfara, 1995).

At City High, active, overt resistance is actually brought along by the school in the conduct of everyday activities. City High is more integrated into the social fabric of the city than is Neighborhood High. Students feel connected to the wider society. As one student tersely remarked "we are part of that (demographic) statistic." Students at City High feel a genuine sense of racial/ethnic pride.

The empirical data I collected at both of these schools vividly illustrate both the reproductive and the productive (cultural and pedagogical) roles of the school (Coleman, Hoffer, & Kilgore, 1982). Social reproduction characterizes Neighborhood High—students there are vividly antagonistic to the expectations of teachers that low-income African-Americans do not care about receiving a quality public education. Ironically, however, the A/B and B/C students I interviewed went on to complete high school; many successfully competed for entrance into the college or university of their choosing.

SCHOOL WORK, DEMOCRACY, AND THE POLITICS OF SCHOOL VIOLENCE

Henry Giroux (1991, 1993), and many other radical scholars writing the critical postmodern perspective (Aronowitz, 1994; Britzman, 1993), have argued that schools serve as potential host sites of *deep democracy*. Passionately arguing for such radical pedagogues as antiracist education, multiculturalism, and cultural studies, these scholars point to the connections between the authority relations in the classroom and pedagogy and radical democracy. However, without altering the existing power relations within the classroom and the school, critical pedagogy (broadly defined) has the real potential to foster the undesirable consequence of reproducing dominant social relations. In the rhetoric of *liberation and emancipation*, such practices remain dangerously utopian, unless attention is given to the *deep structural* relations of inequality (Miron, 1991), institutional racism and, of late, the social construction of school violence. Orner (1989) wrote passionately on this issue:

> Demands for student voice in the educational writings of critical and Anglo-American feminists theorists presuppose subject positions for teachers and students which are highly problematic when seen through the lenses of feminist post-structuralist theories. Student voice, as it has been conceptualized in work which claims to empower students, is an oppressive construct—one that I argue perpetuates relations of domination in the name of liberation. . . . Calls for student voice contain realist and essentialist epistemological positions regarding subjectivity, identity, language, context, and power, which are central to deconstructivist work in other areas, such as literary theory, philosophy, and religion, and have much to offer the field of education. (p. 75)

As I have illustrated, these dangers are pervasive in the call for deep democracy in inner-city schools. Here I noticed acute differences in schooling generally, and the curriculum and pedagogy particularly at Neighborhood High and City High. At Neighborhood High:

> David: If you had to pick a number one goal in your life what would it be?
>
> AH: A number one goal—meaning on the outside in the world or in school?
>
> David: Whatever.
>
> AH: Well, to manage in life. To be able to handle the things on my own instead of depending on someone else. Like anybody, well mainly my mama or whatever cause that's the only person who would really do for you. You know your parents or at least your family. I want money to be able to take care of myself.

Whereas AH expressed general contentment with the curriculum (English classes help her "speak well" and "be very respectable just like on the outside"), I noted earlier that she felt bitter because she could not trust teachers with information about her personal life.

There is a profound irony at work here. Democratic practices cannot exist in the classroom without open, public sharing of information and knowledge (Argyris, 1980; Argyris, Putnam, & Smith, 1985; Argyris & Schon, 1978; Habermas, 1970). AH (see above), however, disclosed the private conversations that take place in the teachers lounges and elsewhere throughout the school building. In the classroom, there is deep silencing about the issues of genuine concern to students and teachers as well. Several students at Neighborhood High commented at the beginning of the interview that the researchers "didn't mention anything about the violence, but we have violence everywhere. . . . One week we had four fights in one day." And, listen to MM, about one killing several years earlier:

> MM: Now it's just like everybody is always bringing up guns or you know, you're in class and you see dogs walking around you know. Guard dogs, you know and they come sniff you sometimes. But I don't know . . . I never saw them sniff you, but they bring them back here, and I don't know if that's just to scare you or what. I don't know. I mean like ever since the boy got killed back here, it's like, you know.

At City High, the all African-American family contributes to a feeling of trust between most of the teachers and the students. Schooling gets defined as preparation for entry into elite colleges and universities; and the students, participating in school cultural activities and community services, feel connected to life on the "outside." WT noted that student "cliques" organize around extracurricular activities—Future Business Leaders of America, the Art Club, the National Honor Society:

> WT: (The groups) that I named are based around school activities. Some of them are classes and stuff, extracurricular things.

As most of the students I interview noted, "there are no fights here as they are in most schools." African-American students at City High learn to express themselves verbally for academic purposes. Most of them also are not afraid to discuss personal affairs as most teachers are there to counsel as well as to teach. Listen to JT:

> JT: My sociology class helps me a lot. At first I kept asking myself 'why do I have to take this class? but you learn how to deal with persons and teach them and talk to them and you know things of that nature, so all of my classes basically prepare me for reaching my goals (to travel the world and to give talks as I travel). The teachers and administration like to see students talk well and do things like that. So (they

are) happy when you do that. The teachers give you a lot of commendations when you have the courage to stand up and say what you have to say.

Learning is *not* busy work at City High. It is enjoyable, and although students occasionally resist the constant stress on achieving success, they see a vivid connection between what is learned in the classroom, and reinforced through the school's hidden curriculum, and their future identities as professionals. According to WT, going to school, then, is "like a reward as far as the teachers and the administrators and stuff because they really try to help you. I've never had as many teachers as I do here who are interested in my learning. They make learning fun." Learning is also relevant to their future aspirations. WT wants to become a child psychologist. He related his English class to that goal:

WT: As a psychologist, sometimes you might have to write down what we did. How we went about solving this problem. How we advised them and you know those things are formal. That's the skills I learned in English.

Calls for the deepening of democracy in urban schooling need to be tempered by these pervasive social realities. Elsewhere I have used the term *situated restructuring* (see Miron & St. John, 1994) to describe the complex relationship between social and economic conditions in the cities and the activities designed to restructure schools located in urban centers. Although these data reveal there is plenty that schools can do to make institutional life more democratic, it is plain that teachers need a clearer understanding of students' identity work. They also need to feel safer to take pedagogical risks and to nurture students.

CONCLUSION: THE LINGERING QUEST FOR DEMOCRACY

In this study I have sought to investigate the claim that public schools in the inner city are sites for the struggle for racial-ethnic identity. The findings provide strong empirical support for this claim. Although other descriptive works, along with my own prior study, have laid out the interrelationships among school culture, resistance, and structural relations, none has systematically probed the category of racial and ethnic identity formation. Furthermore, to my knowledge no study has raised, or empirically interrogated, the wider relational linkages between identity politics and the practices of democracy in public schooling, let alone in the wider society.

Chantal Mouffe's (1988) work on the new democracy is an invaluable theoretical guide in which I can frame the analysis here. Briefly, Mouffe argues that within every social formation, collective subjects are inscribed in multiple social relations. She is worth quoting at length:

> Within every society, each social agent is inscribed in a multiplicity of social relations—not only social relations of production but also the social relations, among others, of sex, race, nationality, and vicinity. All these social relations determine positionalities or subject positions, and every social agent is therefore the locus of many subject positions and cannot be reduced to only one. Thus, someone inscribed in the relations of production as a worker is also a man or a woman, white or black, Catholic or Protestant, French or German and so on. A person's subjectivity is not constructed only on the basis of his or her position in the relations of production. Furthermore, each social position, each subject position, is itself the locus of multiple constructions, according to the different discourses that construct that position. Thus, the subjectivity of a given social agent is always precariously and provisionally fixed or, to use the Lacanian term, sutured at the intersection of various discourses. (p. 90)

This passage highlights the futility of trying to fix any given social agency (collective identity) as determined by one category, be it class, race, ethnicity, or gender. For the students I studied from two inner-city schools in the Deep South, it is plain that their sense of personal and collective identity is dynamically shaped from the interaction between macro categories (such as race and class) and school/student culture. As I previously noted, the experience of being African American in Neighborhood High, where students feel stuck "back here" is qualitatively different from the experience of being African-American in City High, where the all African-American population feel a part of (connected with) their cultural community and the wider society.

In both schools, the discourses of schooling in the inner city play a large part in shaping both student expressions of resistance (and power) and, more abstractly, collective identity and social agency. The broad theoretical question that I raised earlier, the linkages between racial and ethnic identity formation and the practice of democracy within the cultural sphere of public schooling in large inner city school districts, turns on the struggle for new democracy, which Mouffe defines as those sets of antagonisms (resistance) and struggle (the political quest for equality). I see an abundance of empirical evidence supporting student resistance to essentialist definitions of race. Mouffe (1988) theorizes that this struggle for democracy constitutes:

> resistances to the growing uniformity of social life, a uniformity that is the result of the kind of mass culture imposed by the media. This imposition of a homogenized way of life, a uniform cultural pattern, is being challenged by different groups that reaffirm their right to their difference, their specificity, be it through the exaltation of their regional identity or their specificity in the realm of fashion, music, or language. (p. 93)

One student from Neighborhood High graphically expressed this abstract quotation when he commented that "they (the wider society) got it all wrong. The color ain't black; it's brown." However, I do not wish to leave the reader with the wrong impression that African-American students from City High did not also express antagonisms over the essential definitions of African-Americans to which the school held. Obviously, the forms of resistance in this school took shape in a vastly different context: an academically successful all African-American secondary school, a school of *excellence*. I noted earlier in the example of JM, a male student at City High, that anger exists over the school's racial obsession with success.

JM is struggling with the issue of equality. In the midst of extreme academic (and later financial and social) success for its graduates, he speaks antagonistically of the class-social determiners of identity for African-American students at his school. He also wants equal treatment for African-Americans, whether they are represented as "ahead" of other African-Americans or not. JM denounces the representation of African-Americans at the citywide school as equally successful as middle-class Whites, continually striving for a competitive edge, much like SI, who wants equal treatment for African-Americans at Neighborhood High, where some of their White teachers represent them as less academically capable than Vietnamese and White students. Equality is the recurrent underlying theme in both narrative accounts from students at each school I studied. The surprising optimistic twist at City High is that fairness, in addition to equal respect for African-Americans, pops up as valued by students.

This narrative by JM at City High leaves us as researchers and advocates for democratic schooling with hope and possibility. I am surprisingly hopeful in this more theoretically driven and interpretive framework (Feinberg & Soltis, 1992) than I was at the conclusion of my first qualitative study of resistance in the same two schools (Lauria, Miron, & Dashner, 1994, p. 45). There I concluded with the observation that "democracy was nowhere to be found." That statement remains true now if framed within the discursive practices/relations of the administrative procedures/policies and classroom pedagogy. Mouffe's theoretical work on the struggle for a new democracy informs a new interpretation. The students' expressions of resistance and power now take on new meaning. Denied equality *and* difference, students at Neighborhood High demand their equal rights with varying degrees of intensity. A more creative possibility for improvement of practice is an alliance among students, teachers, and other cultural workers (i.e., performing artists; see Chapter 6). Although I remain disappointed that the discourses and material conditions in inner-city schooling institutionally seems to deny a place for ethnicity in the grand narratives of race and class, the (often loud) voices I hear in these narratives for racial equality, respect, and fairness open a slight, but significant, door for multiculturalism. This more democratic form of multiculturalism begins with a grounding in inner-city students' culture and multiple subjectivity inscribed in the myriad social relations of the school, community, and a pluralistic democratic society.

Chapter 6

Conclusion: Breaking Through

This book began with the thesis that the current crisis in urban schooling is socially constructed. I outlined and historically analyzed the twin roles of hegemonic ideologies and education policy or reform in the construction of the crisis. I argued further that the crisis is situated at the nexus of two forces: the global political economy and the new social space of ethnic identity in the inner city.

My major goal throughout the project has been to move to the foreground the lived cultural experience of students in understanding the relations between the global economy and the formation of ethnic identity. The findings from the qualitative study of two inner-city high schools provide theoretical gains that both researchers and practitioners can use to sharply focus the interpretations of the analysis of the data. Put concisely, this theoretical understanding comes down to the fundamental recognition that the terrain of identity politics opens up both social and political space for human agency. In the contest over who they are and who they seek to become, both personally and collectively, students can exercise agency and therefore power.

This finding is rather remarkable, given the previous scholarly (and ethnographic) work on resistance. As I reviewed in the previous chapter, most writers following the critical tradition[1] assumed that students were powerless. Embracing a structural-functional framework, theorists assumed that students were culturally unsophisticated. Whereas neo-Marxist scholars such as Jean Anyon, Michael Apple, and Paul Willis acknowledged the cultural and political space the school provided, allowing for "limited penetration" (Willis, 1977) of dominant practices, their studies ironically did not make the ties between the identity politics in the classroom and the broader political relations, such as person rights (see Chapter 2). Mouffe (1988) elegantly makes these important theoretical connections:

> I would like to elaborate on the relationship between antagonism and struggle and to begin with the following thesis: An antagonism can emerge when a collective subject . . . that has been constructed in a specific way, to certain existing discourses, finds its subjectivity negated by other discourses or practices. That negation can happen in two basic ways. *First, subjects constructed on the basis of certain rights can find themselves in a position in which those rights are denied by some practices or discourses.* At that point there is a negation of subjectivity or identification, which can be the basis for an antagonism. I am not saying that this necessarily leads to an antagonism; it is a necessary but not sufficient condition. The second form in which antagonism emerges corresponds to that expressed by feminism and the black movement. It is a situation in which subjects constructed in subordination by a set of discourses are, at the same time, interpellated as equal by other discourses. Here we have a contradictory interpellation. Like the first form, it is a negation of a particular subject position, but, unlike the first, it is the subjectivity-in-subordination that is negated, which opens the possibility for its deconstruction and challenging. (p. 95; emphasis added)

In this concluding chapter I wish to flesh out these broad theoretical and empirical strokes in more detail. I return and give closure to, the main thematic concerns of this book: the social construction of racial-ethnic identity in inner-city schools; the multiple inscriptions of new political and social subjectivity; the ideological origins of school reform (see Miron & St. John,

---

[1] Giroux, of course, remains a noteworthy exception.

1994); and the dialectical relationships between structure and agency. Although readers may genuinely come to expect solutions in the way of urban school reform, I resist these impulses because it is, quite literally, impossible to prescribe technical (and even political) changes divorced from the social contexts of individual schools and school districts. Instead, I suggest concrete metaphors and images borrowed from the contemporary performing arts to conclude the project. This movement represents my final border crossing in this project.

TAKING CARE OF BUSINESS

It is plain that the ideologies and values of the modern corporation and business reform groups have saturated the discourse of urban school reform. I referred earlier to the loosely organized, yet ideologically powerful, Entrepreneurial Coalition, who have won significant policy gains in public education in urban centers across America. My assertion is (and the empirical findings in Chapter 5 support this assertion)that the net result of this ideological campaign to wrestle control of education governance from school professionals and elected officials (see First & Miron, 1991) is largely irrelevant to students' identity politics. Clearly, principals and teachers do pay "lip service" to the rhetorical arguments of business groups. Furthermore, the "restructuring" that corporations listed in Fortune 500, as well as their associated economic development groups (see Miron, 1992; Peck & Tickell, 1993), have urged has shaped reform practice such as school-based management and "community" models of governance. However, the depth of this influence, insofar as the findings from Chapter 5 suggest, approach nowhere near the levels of what Tyack (1993) brands as "ideological control". This interpretation turns on the unit of analysis.

Based on data gathered locally (see Miron, 1995) and nationally (see Curcio & First, 1995), district superintendents *do* respond to the discourses of business. In New Orleans, for example, Superintendent Morris Holmes warned the district administrators during a staff development workshop that "the community will judge you on test scores and how well our graduates compete for jobs" (Miron, 1995). However, students from the neighborhood school I interviewed (see Chapter 5) generally could not identify their school-business partner, nor describe any concrete benefits from such a partnership. Furthermore, the classroom teachers in the same school complained that they did not have access to the computers the business partner had donated to the school. Often they stated that a handful of teachers usually hogged the equipment.

On the other hand, students in the all African-American college preparatory school had clearly internalized many of the values and attitudes of the free-enterprise system. They wanted to make money. City High School fostered a sense of academic competition, motivated by heavy racial overtones, that mirrored the sense of entrepreneurship promoted by corporations in the city, and indeed worldwide (Miron, 1992; Peck & Tickell, 1993). Understandably, students there exhibited less "resistance" to economic values, and the school promoted the economic aims of school as well (Spring, 1985).

Ironically, students from both Citywide High and Neighborhood High placed a premium on the value of education, specifically earning a high school diploma and gaining admission into a college or university. Moreover, many students from both schools expressed a strong desire to attend college. However, as I tried to document in the previous chapter, it is unlikely that these values, attitudes, and ambitions derived primarily from the ideology of corporations and business groups. These groups do promote well this ideology of possessive individualism. However, in the case of many of the students at Neighborhood High, the desire and (somewhat unrealistic) ambition to earn a college degree stemmed primarily from the sense of responsibility to care for one's family. Also, this "situated" ambition (Spindler & Spindler, 1994) stemmed from the realization that, as one student noted, "you have to take care of yourself." Perhaps unintentionally, business is exploiting the dire social and economic conditions in the inner city to further its own interests.

To say that inner-city students are "taking care of business" by helping to insure their financial futures is *not* equivalent to ideological control of city schooling. I contend that these students are playing it smart. Unlike the "lads" in Paul Willis's *Learning to Labour*, (1977) many of the students from Neighborhood High are not contributing to their own social reproduction. That is what I expected to find in the interviews of students from that school (see Lauria & Miron, 1994): students resisting the formal curriculum owing to weak local economic opportunities. Put plainly, students from Neighborhood High "do what they have to do" to get by, to graduate.

In this sense, they possess the two qualities Giddens (1982, 1984) theorizes are necessary for human agency—capability and knowledgability. I argue here that it is the school—as institution—that does not possess the knowledge (ethnicity, intersubjectivity) to assist students to push through the liminal stage (see Anfara, 1995). I now turn to Giddens's work to flesh out the theoretical implications for urban education of his theory of the duality of structure and its dialectical relationship with human agency.

"SITUATED" AGENCY

The Duality of Structure

In the *Constitution of Society*, Anthony Giddens (1984) outlined his theory of "structuration." At the heart of this theory is his insistence on the *duality* of structure and agency. Structure both constrains the actions of agents as well as enables them to act in the context of social systems. He argues against both the "objective" paradigm of society, in which the social world is akin to the purportedly self-regulating organism, and the "voluntarism" of extreme forms of phenomenology and hermeneutics. In his language, structure (or the theory of structuration) is both outcome and medium. Human agents, through their lack of knowledge of the prior conditions of history, unintentionally reproduce social systems, in particular institutions. Giddens demonstrates that human agents, through their social actions, reproduce institutions (schools) and, thus, are themselves implicated in maintaining the status quo.

Inner-city schools are suffering the consequences of social reproduction. In particular, the social, economic, and now ethnic divisions that have governed inner-city life since industrialization have made life in slum neighborhoods virtual permanent ghettos (see Garvin, 1994; Hirsch, 1990; Katz, 1971). Public schools located in these contemporary ghettos (e.g., public housing developments) continue to foster social conflict as an unanticipated consequence of the ideology of equal treatment for individuals of all races (see Giddens, 1982; Lauria, Miron, & Dashner, 1994). Differences in many inner-city schools, particularly those situated in desegregated social contexts, are undermined under the sameness of race. Such administrative discursive practices actually fuel racial-ethnic conflict (see Barbier, 1994b). Inner-city schools, then become potential sites for the social construction of violence. Minority students who resemble gang members are treated as such. Furthermore, such school practices may breed physical violence (see Chapter 5).

Many minority high school students in the inner city, however, already know this. Giddens (1984) calls this type of knowledge "practical consciousness" (p. 7). He argues that it is tacit knowledge that all human agents draw on to "carry on." As the findings from Chapter 5 make clear, students resist the school's construction of their own identity. At times, as Mouffe theorizes (see earlier), they actively participate in their own identity politics, challenging such typecasting as racial identity by skin color. As one student from Neighborhood High facetiously noted, "they (society) got the color all wrong; it ain't black." As institutions located in urban centers, schools both reproduce and help construct the formation of racial and ethnic identity. It is this representation of their identity by the school that urban students seem to resist. Students possess practical knowledge of who they are, as well as who society expects them to be, and strategically rely on this knowledge to survive (see Bondi, 1993).

Thus, in order to break this cycle of social reproduction, the urban school needs to draw pragmatically on the tenets of postmodernism and critical pragmatism (see Maxcy, 1991, 1995). Its teachers and principals must learn that students potentially draw on multiple identities during the (dis)course of school life and community living. Both practical consciousness as well as discursive consciousness (Giddens, 1984) of ethnicity must be part of the repertoire of the formal school curriculum. Identity marked by racial and class categorization is already a part of the hidden curriculum. (I have more to say about this later.)

Student Outcomes and Social Action

In the 1960s, as Chapter 2 illustrated, the focus of federal education policy was on strategic action to alleviate poverty in the cities. The term *urban* became synonymous with *action*. However, as Giddens's work on structuration reminds us, social action often produces unintended consequences. One of the lingering consequences of the programs of Johnson's Great Society is a profound mistrust of government among the electorate. As I disclosed in Chapter 2, the Great Society gave way to the New Federalism and subsequently ushered in a decade of private strategies (vouchers) to resolve the problems of urban public education. In the 1980s, the term *urban* becomes synonymous with *problem*.

Coupled with the rapid decline of the U.S. economy in the global market, the poor performance on standardized achievement tests by students in the inner city produced what I have characterized as the ideological campaign of the Entrepreneurial Coalition. Strategically, the focus of the Coalition's activities have centered on "community" models of education governance (see the National League of Cities, 1993). Ostensibly, redefining education governance in large urban school districts would foster the long-term goal of increasing student achievement. If such efforts remained unsuccessful, or if existing power relations at the school or district levels proved too intractable for restructuring, renewed emphasis for choice in the forms of vouchers, magnet schools, or open enrollment could bypass the governance constraints altogether.

In part, the results have proved statistically effective (Council of Great City Schools, 1993). Test scores have risen in many large urban school districts, and the governance reform movements have helped to restore public confidence in an embattled system of public education in the cities (see Miron & Brooks, 1993). Of course, there are unintended consequences as a result. Many "magnet" (or special mission) schools are overcrowded (Lauria, Miron, & Dashner, 1994). Schools situated in poor neighborhoods have to struggle just to obtain the needed financial and organizational resources to survive (Crowson & Boyd, 1992). Social inequalities have exacerbated under the reform banner in many inner-city schools (Anderson, 1993; Foster, 1993; Kozol, 1991).

I believe that improved student outcomes and accountability for the results of urban school restructuring (Fine, 1994) need to be coupled with systematic activities in community development. Elsewhere (Miron, 1995) I have detailed the political processes embedded in the forging of links between student outcomes and community development. Suffice to say here that improved student outcomes is not sufficient if local communities remain beset with crime, poverty, racism, and uninhabitable housing. The legacy of unanticipated consequences might well be the upward mobility of a few students, and their families, with the bulk of inner-city students stuck somewhere "back here" in the dreary denizens of permanent ghettos.

A Framework for Communicative Action

In their collaborative work, *Pathways to Cultural Awareness: Cultural Therapy with Teachers and Students* (1994), George and Louise Spindler illustrate the techniques they have cultivated to bring about cultural understanding in the classroom. With adaptations to the inner-city public school classroom, I believe that this technique ("cultural therapy") is useful for eliciting the kinds of social action that are appropriate for "situated agents." In particular, the Spindlers' notion of the *enduring, situated*, and *endangered* self can inform the implementation of "practical intersubjectivity" (see later discussion) that can bring forth the developmental reconstruction of public education in urban centers throughout the United States.

According to the principles of cultural therapy, classroom teachers encounter two existentially compatible, but analytically distinct impressions of self in their students. The first is the *enduring* self, which allows for "that sense of continuity one has with one's own past—a personal continuity in experience, meaning, and social identity" (Spindler & Spindler, 1994, p. 13). An enduring self emanates from strong ego development and provides for self-esteem in students. The *situated* self copes with the demands of day-to-day living and is the basis of the interpretations students bring to their lived cultural experience. It is this pragmatic, and less idealized self, that is strategically oriented toward success in the context of academic achievement and social demands of the public school. Successful negotiation of these demands in the classroom, the authors assert, leads to self-efficacy. Finally, the *endangered* self results when the academic demands, as well as the stresses of the social context outside of the school and classroom, "violate too often and too strongly" (p. 13) the enduring self. Central to my purposes, "this can occur . . . as children and youth of diverse cultural origins confront school cultures that are antagonistic to the premises and behavioral patterns of their own culture" (p. 14). In short, the stage is set for cultural assault on the enduring self owing to the mismatch embedded in this scenario.

Whether an enduring (idealized) sense of self is meaningful in the context of urban schooling is the subject of ongoing debates between modernists and postmodernists. This debate will not distract us here. I am especially concerned with the implications for communicative action for the situated and the threatened self. In the inner-city public school classroom, especially in the context of many impoverished neighborhood schools, the situated self is, indeed, a threatened self. I have argued throughout this book, and elsewhere (see Miron, 1995; Miron & St. John, 1994), that school restructuring in urban centers will fail without attention to the social conditions that embed it. By the same token, the attempts at nurturing a social identity through "practical intersubjectivity" are also doomed to failure if educators do not develop skills in the healing and caring of the endangered self. These skills are at the heart of cultural therapy.

What Spindler and Spindler (1994), together with their students and colleagues, propose is:

> A process of bringing [forward] one's own culture, in its manifold forms,—assumptions, goals, values, beliefs, and communicative modes—to a level of awareness that permits one to perceive it as a potential bias in social interaction and in the acquisition or transmission of skills and knowledge—what we later refer to as "instrumental competencies." (p. 3)

The aim of cultural therapy is to facilitate the removal of personal blame among students for the failure to gain these "requisite" skills of mainstream society or to learn the knowledge that is taken for granted in the dominant culture. The authors provide practical training in research techniques, questioning, and communication to foster a mutual understanding between ethnic minority students (endangered selves) and their (often middle-class) teachers. This training offers a vehicle to remove the taken-for-granted structural asymmetries in the public school inner-city classroom and is an affirmative move toward action through interaction of teacher and student and students with one another in a spirit of community and a respect for difference.

THE MOVE TOWARD "PRACTICAL INTERSUBJECTIVITY"

One of the implications from the analysis of student voices in Chapter 5 is that inner-city students possess a tacit knowledge of their collective identities. That identities are socially constructed, with the school playing a major role in that construction, might seem a bit strange to educators. If nothing else, educators universally embrace the ideology of liberalism. Furthermore, the

192   Chapter Six

idea that students enter the classroom as individual subjects, marked by conscious awareness of their enduring self (Spindler & Spindler, 1994), is pervasive (Biesta, 1994) among most classroom teachers (and I suspect, school administrators as well). Biesta asserts that professional educators assume as their unit of analysis "the isolated self-conscious individual subject as a starting point" (p. 301). The assumption is that this unproblematic autonomous subject (see Chapter 4) is capable of taking action voluntaristically. At the same time that educators heed the call for unconstrained action, they simultaneously embrace the confinements of social and organizational structure "that do not recognize subjects or human agency" (p. 301). In a distorted twist of Cartesian logic, students are free to pursue predetermined ends of society's making. Biesta moves away from the dichotomy of structure and agency by proposing a theory of "practical intersubjectivity." Although unacknowledged, this theory parallels Giddens's notion of the duality of structure and his theory of structuration. Biesta's (1994) applications for educators is worth quoting at length:

> The concept of "practical intersubjectivity" can be characterized by means of its two constituting elements: *intersubjectivity* and *practicality*. The first feature must be read as the programmatic assumption that we should not understand human inter subjectivity out of human subjectivity, but human subjectivity out of human inter subjectivity. Subjectivity is considered to be a function of inter subjectivity. Although this "primacy of the inter subjective" can be understood ontologically, it will suffice for the moment to understand it methodologically. The second feature means that human intersubjectivity should first of all be understood in terms of action. 'Practical' inter subjectivity thus designates a structure of communicative relations "that arises and takes form in the *joint* activity of human subjects to achieve ends set by their life needs." (p. 301; emphasis in the original)

Biesta's synthesis of the work of Dewey, Habermas, and Mead stresses the role of *action* defined as cooperative inter/actions in the construction of intersubjectivity in the classroom. Out of the cooperative interactions that subjects undertake the "asymmetrical relationships" between educator and student is undermined. The resulting implications for practice are such that student's individual autonomy (agency) grows out of the organized communicative activities that classroom teachers foster. The emphasis, then, should not center on individual academic achievement, or what Habermas (1970) would call strategic action. Classroom teachers should orient their pedagogical activities in pursuit of the *communicative* goal of common understanding through action (linguistic, pedagogic): "Identity formation takes place through the medium of linguistic communication" (Habermas, 1970, p. 58, quoted in Biesta, 1994, p. 311). The ends of public education, therefore, move toward understanding through cooperative classroom activities. Public education in the inner cities potentially is no longer a zero-sum game.

Coupled with the work of Anthony Giddens (sketched earlier), Biesta's notion of practical intersubjectivity has significant theoretical implications for a theory of urban education. There are normative assumptions that I question, such as the apparent ease by which cooperative activities might be implemented in inner-city classrooms and the unintended consequences of this subsequent denial of conflict. However, I believe that Giddens's work on structuration can resolve these issues, and in the final section in the book merge their work and move toward a new interpretation of urban schooling.

TOWARD AN INTERPRETATION OF THEORY AND PRACTICE

From the postmodern perspective, urban schooling would combine a critical pragmatic approach with the realization that there is no enduring self. Educators can no longer unproblematically assume a unitary identity for their students upon whose foundations they can rely. I assert that *all* identity is socially constructed, hence situated. As other scholarly work has illustrated (see Boyd, 1989; Cuban & Tyack, 1990; Levin, 1988), there exists an historical mismatch between the academic and social expectations of the school and the home and community resources that so-called at-risk students bring to the institution of public schooling. The practical result is underachievement on standardized tests, high dropout and "pushout" rates, and increasing school violence. I argue that the fundamental cause of this mismatch in the current context is the denial of difference, specifically differences among and within racial and ethnic groups.

The school as a social organization works against this understanding of an unproblematized self; its practices usually assume that students have an enduring self, and it is the goal of the inner-city school to assist students to break into the educational and social mainstream through various kinds of "reforms." Although these reforms have proved somewhat successful in inner-city schools and school districts in raising the levels of student academic achievement, they have not built on student voice and culture (Anfara, 1995). Moreover, in seeking to establish nonconflictual methodologies for urban school reform, the potential benefit to be derived from the celebration of differences—cultural, racial, ethnic, social class, and gender—are unintentionally denied through the attempts at building cultural harmony through a program of multiculturalism (see McCarthy & Crichlow, 1993), Accelerated Schools (Levin, 1988), the Comer Model (Comer, 1980), and the proliferation of school-business partnerships suffer from this bias. By explicitly focusing discursive attention on the cultural biases, it is conceivable that the techniques of cultural therapy *may* reverse this pessimistic trend (see Chapter 3).

UNDERSTANDING THE FAILURES OF URBAN SCHOOL REFORM

The unequal power relations that remain unaltered work to deny students a sense of their social identity by disparaging marginality. Students are individually encouraged to pursue academic, economic, and social success relentlessly. This uncritical pursuit of strategic action in the form of individual academic achievement takes the "philosophy of consciousness" (Biesta, 1994) to its ludicrous extreme in practice: It virtually seeks to make all inner-city students products of the mythical melting pot and makes pretenses that social conditions such as poverty and unliveable neighborhoods simply do not exist. Like fictitious denotations of TNT on a Hollywood set, or in the safety of social engineers' remote controls, educators and planners can simply pretend to make these social realities go away. They will not.

This postmodern analysis calls into question the viability of Giroux's call for forging a radical democratic practice in urban classrooms. Less obtainable is a districtwide effort that seeks to realign the power relations between the central office and the schools. If anything, research undertaken for this project reveals that central office administrators are most vulnerable to the rhetoric of business and the ideologies of national and international corporations. Understandably, superintendents and their governing boards do need to respond to the influences of business in order to win their approval for new millages and to remain in public office. I assert that the paradigmatical assumption cast is the idea of the unregulated self-conscious individual. Identity is, first and foremost, personal. Actions are matters of the individual, not embedded in social interactions. Radical democracy is inconceivable when placed within this framework.

Second, Giroux's patriarchy must be questioned not solely on political and ideological grounds. More consequentially, his distinction between "authority" and "authoritarian" in the context of pedagogical relations reproduces the liberal underpinnings of the philosophy of consciousness. I must also now question my own position on the moral use of power and leadership (Miron, 1991). Using authority to pursue radical democracy in the context of situated agency undermines the political opportunities made available through an alliance of cultural workers. As Biesta (1994) argues persuasively, "Education is therefore treated as an interaction between *subjects*. However, because the child apparently lacks the characteristics of full subjectivity, it is treated as not *yet* a subject" (p. 303; emphasis in original). The consequences are devastating in the inner-city classroom *because teachers' pedagogy lacks praxis*. That is, it proceeds paternalistically owing to the despair over students' marginality. Such practice fails to recognize that out of such "liminal states" (see Anfara, 1995) student agency springs. Schools simply foster education as ritual, leaving no room for liberation and emancipation, which Giroux, following Freire, seeks.

What is there to do? As I mentioned at the beginning of this chapter, I resist the impulse to offer programmatic (strategic) "solutions." I consider this unradical. Instead, I suggest we look at images from cultural studies and the performing arts as intellectual and social practices.

HITTING THE OPTIMISTIC NOTE

The place to begin is with improvisational jazz. I return to the liner notes of *In This House* I cited in the Preface. There I mentioned that theorists need to learn from the performing artists who are working in urban cultures to look for images and metaphors to reconstruct urban schooling. Wynton Marsalis is one such contemporary performer.

Classically trained jazz trumpeter Marsalis believes that contemporary jazz is more relevant to his (mostly urban) audience than is classical music. Jazz is more optimistic. Moreover, this art form holds up the respect for cultural differences in a way that many forms of multicultural education do not. In jazz, each musician rotates and improvises as he or she sees fit, to ritually give way to the next performer in the band. The composition is held together by the discipline of the art form itself, its historical and cultural grounding in the blues and, insofar as Marsalis is concerned, in swing. Improvisational jazz maintains a bounded structure and form while allowing for freedom of experimentation and interpretation (see Marsalis, in Wyckoff, 1994, pp. 51-52).

Difference is not struck out under the multicultural umbrella; rather, community is built around the value of difference and institutionalized in the form of improvisation in each piece. Marsalis gives aesthetic life to these abstract ideas in the composition *In this House, On this Morning*. I refer again to those notes as a creative educational tool for a reconstructed urban education. The key images are: interpretation, improvisation, imagination, experimentation, crossings, and grounding. As we seek to retheorize and reconstruct urban schooling, we ought to keep these images—and the gestalt of the jazz metaphor—uppermost in our minds. We ought to view the reform of urban schooling in an artistic, creative manner (see Eisner, 1994).

I agree with Cornell West's (1993b) assessment of modern jazz's approach to aesthetics/cultural studies. These artists understand well that "openness—including the mainstream—does not entail wholesale cooptation, and group autonomy is not group insularity" (p. 22). I can leave this work with no better images and metaphors.

References

Aaron, H. (1978). *Politics and the professors: The Great Society in perspective.* Washington, DC: Brookings Institute.

Abercombie, N., Hill, S., & Turner, B. (1980). *The dominant ideology thesis.* Boston: Allen & Unwin.

Alexander, L. (1991). Message from the secretary. In *America 2000* (p. 1). Washington, DC: U.S. Department of Education.

Alkin, C. (Ed.). (1992). *Encyclopedia of educational research* (6th ed., pp. 491-498). New York: Macmillan.

Anaya, R. (1992). *Albuquerque.* Albuquerque: University of New Mexico Press.

Anderson, G. (1992). Cognitive politics of principals and teachers: Ideological control in an elementary school. In J. Blaise (Eds.), *The politics of life in schools* (pp. 121-138). Newbury Park, CA: Sage.

Anderson, J. (1993). The public intellectual. *The New Yorker*, pp. 39-48.

Anfara, V. (1993). *Neo-conservatism and the educational reforms of the 1980s.* Unpublished manuscript, University of New Orleans College of Education.

Anfara, V. (1995). *The ritual and liminal dimension of student resistance to the formal culture of schooling.* Unpublished dissertation, University of New Orleans College of Education.

Annual Economic Report to the President. (1964). Washington, DC: U. S. Government Printing Office.

Anyon, J. (1980). Social class and the hidden curriculum. *Journal of Education, 162*(1), 67-91.

Anzaldua, G. (1987). *Borderlands/ la fronterea: The new meztiza.* San Francisco: Spinsters/ Aunt Lute.

Apple, M. (1985). *Education and power* (2nd ed.). Boston: ARK.

Apple, M. (1988a). Social crisis and curriculum accord. *Educational Policy, 38*(2), 191-201.

Apple, M. (1988b). *Teachers & texts: A political economy of class and gender relations in education.* New York: Routledge.

Apple, M. (1990). *Ideology and curriculum.* New York: Routledge.

Apple, M. (1992). The text and cultural politics. *Educational Researcher, 21*(7), 4-12.

Apple, M. (1993). *Official knowledge.* New York: Routledge.

Argyris, C. (1980). Making the undiscussible and its undiscussibility discussable. In R. Young (Eds.), *A critical theory of education*. New York: Teachers College Press.

Argyris, C., Putnam, R., & Smith, D. (1985). *Action science.* San Francisco: Jossey-Bass.

Argyris, C., & Schon, D. (1978). *Organizational Learning.* Reading: Addison-Wesley.

Aronowitz, S. (1994). The situation of the left in the United States. *Socialist Review, 23*(3), 48-55.

Astuto, T., & Clark, D. (1988). State responses to the new federalism in education. *Educational Policy, 2*(4), 361-375.

Astuto, T., & Clark, D. (1992). Federal role, legislative and executive. In M.C. Alkin (Eds.), *Encyclopedia of educational research* (6th ed., pp. 491-498). New York: Macmillan.

Baca, L., & Cervantes, H. (1989). *The bilingual special education interface.* Columbus, OH: Merill Hill.

Ball, A., & Heath, S. (1993). Dances of identity: Finding an ethnic self in the arts. In S. Heath & M. McLaughlin (Eds.), *Identity and inner-city youth: Beyond ethnicity and gender* (pp. 69-94). New York: Teachers College Press.

Ball, S. (1987). *The micropolitics of the school: Towards a theory of school organization.* London: Methuen.

Barbier, S. (1994a, August 25). Racial tension grips Avondale school. *Times-Picayune,* p. B.2.

Barbier, S. (1994b). Teens offer work: Most choosing college instead. *Times-Picayune,* p. B-2.

Barfield, C. (1981). *Rethinking federalism: Block grants and federal, state, and local responsibilities.* Washington, DC: American Enterprise Institute.

Bell, T. (1986). Education policy development in the Reagan administration. *Phi Delta Kappan, 67*(7), 487-493.

Bell. T. (1995, March 15). The charter-school plus: Greater corporate involvement can be a byproduct of competition Washington, D.C. *Education Week*, p. 40.
Berger, P., & Luckmann, T. (1966). *The social construction of reality.* Garden City, New York: Anchor.
Bernal, M., & Knight, G. (1993a). Introduction. In M. Bernal & G. Knight (Eds.), *Ethnic identity: Formation and transmission among Hispanic and other minorities* (pp. 1-11). Albany: State University of New York Press.
Bernal, M., & Knight, G. (Ed.). (1993b). *Ethnic identity: Formation and transmission among Hispanics and other minorities.* Albany: State University of New York Press.
Beyer, L., & Liston, D. (1992). Discourse or moral action: A critique of post modernism. *Educational Theory, 42*, 371-393.
Biesta, G. (1994). Education as practical intersubjectivity: Towards a critical-pragmatic understanding of education. *Educational Theory, 44*(3), 299-319.
Blaise, J. (1992). *The politics of life in schools.* Newbury Park, CA: Sage.
Boaz, D. (1988). Educational schizophrenia. In D. Boaz (Eds.), *Assessing the Reagan years* (pp. 291-303). Washington, DC: Cato Institute.
Bogotch, I., Miron, L., & Garvin, J. (1993). Meeting national goals through community involvement: A case study. *Louisiana Educational Research Journal, XIX*(1), 63-69.
Bolman, L., & Deal, T. (1991). *Reframing organizations: Artistry, choice and leadership.* San Francisco: Jossey-Bass.
Bondi, L. (1993). Locating identity politics. In M. Keith & S. Pile (Eds.), *Place and the politics of identity* (pp. 84-102). New York: Routledge.
Bourdieu, P., & Passeron, J.C. (1977). *Reproduction in education, society, and culture.* London: Sage.
Bowles, S., & Gintis, H. (1976). *Schooling and capitalist America: Educational reform and the contradictions of economic life.* London: Routledge & Kegan Paul.
Boyd, W. (1989). What makes ghetto schools work? In *Conference on the Truly Disadvantaged, October 19-21.* Evanston, IL: Northwestern University.
Bredo, E. (1989). Ideological dichotomies and practical realities in educational reform. *Urban Review, 21*(3), 127-144.
Bridges, T. (1993, May 11). Creoles in Los Angeles. *New Orleans Times-Picayune*, p. A:1.
Brinkley, A. (1989) The New Deal and the idea of the state. In S. Fraser & G. Gerstle (Eds.), *The rise and fall of the New Deal order, 1930-1980.* Princeton, NJ: Princeton University Press.

Britzman, D. (1993). The ordeal of knowledge: Rethinking the possibilities of multicultural education. *The Review of Education, 15*, 123-135.

Buriel, R., & Cardoza, D. (1993). Mexican American ethnic labeling: An intrafamilial and intergenerational analysis. In M. Bernal & G. Knight (Eds.), *Ethnic identity: Formation and transmission among Hispanics and other minorities* (pp. 197-209). Albany: State University of New York Press.

Butler, O. (1988). Foreword. In M. Levine & R. Trachtman (Eds.), *American business in the public schools.* New York: Teachers College Press.

Carnoy, M. (1993). School improvement: Is privatization the answer? In J. Hannaway & M. Carnoy (Eds.), *Decentralization and school improvement: Can we fulfill the promise?* (pp. 163-201). San Francisco: Jossey-Bass.

Carnoy, M., Daley, H., & Ojeda, R. (1993). The changing economic position of latinos in the U.S. labor market since 1939. In F. Bonilla (Eds.), *Latinos in a changing U.S. economy: Comparative perspectives on growing inequality.* Newbury Park, CA: Sage Series on Race and Ethnic Relations.

Cherryholmes, C. (1988). *Power and criticism: Post structural investigation in education.* New York: Teachers College Press.

Chilcote, R. H., & Edelstein, J. C. (Ed.). (1983). *Latin America: The struggle with dependency and beyond.* New York: Wiley.

Chubb, J., & Moe, T. (1986). No school is an island: Politics, markets and education. *Brookings Review, 4,* 11-27.

Chubb, J., & Moe, T. (1990). *Politics, markets, & America's schools.* Washington, DC: Brookings Institution.

Clark, D., & Astuto, T. (1986, October). The significance and permanence of changes in federal educational policy. *Educational Researcher,* pp. 4-13.

Clark, D., & Astuto, T. (1989). The disjunction of federal educational policy and national educational needs in the 1990s. In D. Mitchell & M. Goertz (Eds.), *Education politics for the new century* (pp. 11-25). London: Falmer.

Clegg, S. (1989). *Frames of power.* London: Sage.

Clune, W. (1989). *The implementation and effects of high school graduation requirements. First steps toward curricula reform.* Rutgers, NJ: Center for Policy Research in Education.

Coleman, J. (1966). Equal schools or equal students? *The Public Interest, 4,* 70-75.

Coleman, J., Hoffer, T., & Kilgore, S. (1982). *High School achievement: Public, Catholic, and private schools compared.* New York: Basic Books.

Comer, J. (1980). *School power.* New York: The Free Press.

Comer, J. (1985). *The school development program: A nine step guide to school improvement.* New Haven, CT: Yale Child Study Center.

Comer, J. (1988). *A brief history and summary of the school development program.* New Haven, CT: Yale Child Study Center.
Committee for Economic Development. (1995). *Putting learning first: Governing and managing the schools for high achievement.* New York: Author.
Committee of Health and Human Services. (1980). *Head Start in the 1980's: Review and recommendations: A report requested by the President of the United States.* Washington, DC: U.S. Department of Health and Human Services.
Cook, C.C., & Lauria, M. (1995). Urban regeneration and public housing in New Orleans. *Urban Affairs Quarterly, 30*(4), 538-557.
Council of the Great City Schools. (1992). *National urban educational goals: Baseline indicators.* Washington, DC: Author.
Cronin, J. (1992). Reallocating the power of urban school boards. In P. First & H. Walberg (Eds.), *School boards: Changing local control* (pp. 37-71). Berkeley: McCutchan.
Crowson, R. (1992). *School-community relations, under reform.* Berkeley: McCutchan.
Crowson, R., & Boyd, W. (1992). Urban schools as organizations: Political perspectives. In J. Cibulka, R. Reed, & K. Wong (Eds.), *The politics of urban education in the United States* (pp. 87-105). London: Falmer Press.
Cuban, L. (1994, June 15). The great school scam. *Education Week*, p. 44.
Cuban, L., & Tyack, D. (1990). *Mismatch: Historical perspectives on schools and students who don't fit them.* Stanford: Stanford University Press.
Cummins, J. (1993). Empowering minority students: A framework for intervention. In M. Fine & L. Weis (Eds.), *Beyond silenced voices: Class, race, and gender in United States schools* (pp. 101-119). Buffalo, NY: State University of New York Press.
Curcio, J., & First, P. (1993). *Violence in the schools: How to proactively prevent and defuse it.* Newbury Park, CA: Corwin.
Dashner, D. (1992) *Hegemonic ideologies and resistance in the New Orleans Public Schools.* Unpublished master thesis, University of New Orleans.
Davis, B., & McCaul, E. (1991). *The emerging crisis: Current and projected status of children in the United States.* Orono, ME: Institute for the Study of At-Risk Students.
Delany, S. (1991). Street talk/straight talk. *Differences: A Journal of Feminist Cultural Studies, 3*(2), 21-38.
Department of Education, (1983). *A nation at risk: An imperative for educational reform.* Washington, DC: U.S. Government Printing Office.
Department of Education, (1991). *America 2000: An education strategy.* Washington, DC: U.S. Government Printing Office.

DeVaney, A. (Ed.). (1994). *Watching Channel One: The convergence of students, technology and private business.* Albany: State University of New York Press.

Divine, R. (1981). *Exploring the Johnson years.* Austin: University of Texas Press.

Doll, W. (1993). *A postmodern perspective on curriculum.* New York: Teachers College Press.

Dugger, R. (1983). *On Reagan: The man & his presidency.* New York: McGraw-Hill.

Eason, S. (1992). *Sources, assessment, and effects of power on resource allocation: A study of elementary schools in an urban system.* Unpublished dissertation, University of New Orleans.

Eisner, E. (1994). *What educational reformers can lear from the arts.* New York: Teachers College, Columbia University.

Ellsworth, E. (1989). Why doesn't this feel empowering? Working through the repressive myths of critical pedagogy. *Harvard Educational Review, 59*(3), 297-324.

Elmore, R. (1993). School decentralization: Who gains, who loses? In J. Hannaway & M. Carnoy (Eds.), *Decentralization and school improvement* (pp. 33-55). San Francisco: Jossey-Bass Publishers.

English, F. (1993). *Theory in educational administration.* New York: Random House.

Everhart, R. (1983). *Reading, writing and resistance.* New York: Routledge.

Excellence in Education Committee. (1992). Minutes. New Orleans, LA.

Fainstein, S. S. (Ed.). (1983). *Restructuring the city: The political economy of urban redevelopment.* New York: Longman.

Fainstein, S. S. & Fainstein, N. (1983). Regime strategies, communal resistance and economic forces. In Fainstein (Ed.), *Restructuring the city: The political economy of urban redevelopment.* New York and London: Longman, 246-282.

Feinberg, W. (1982). A review of: Ideology, culture and the process of schooling. *Journal of Education, 164*(1), 109-111.

Feinberg, W., & Soltis, J. (1992). *Schools and Society* (2nd ed.). New York, NY: Teachers College Press.

Fine, M. (1989). Silencing and nurturing voice in an improbable context: Urban adolescence in a public school. In H. Giroux & P. McLaren (Eds.), *Critical pedagogy, the state and cultural struggle* (pp. 152-173). Albany: State University of New York Press.

Fine, M. (1991). *Framing dropouts: Notes on the politics of an urban public school.* New York: SUNY Press.

Fine, M. (1993). A diary on privatization and public possibility. *Educational Theory, 43*(1), 33-41

Fine, M. (1994). *Chartering urban school reform: Reflections on public high schools in the midst of change.* New York: Teachers College Press.

Finn, C. (1988). Education policy and the Reagan administration: A large but incomplete success. *Teachers College record, 82,* 77-100.

Finn, C. (1992). Reinventing local control. In P. First & H. J. Walberg (Eds.), *School Boards: Changing Local Control* (pp. 21-27). Berkeley, CA: McCutchan.

First, P., & Miron, L.F. (1991). The social construction of adequacy. *Journal of Law and Education, 20*(4), 421-444.

First, P. F. & Walberg, H. (1992). *School Boards: Changing local control.* Berkeley, CA: McCutchan Publishing Corporation.

Fishman, J. (1976). *Bilingual education: An international sociological perspective.* Rowley, MA: Newbury House.

Fordham, S. (1993). Those loud black girls: (Black) women, silence, and gender "passing" in the academy. *Anthropology and Education Quarterly, 24*(1), 3-32.

Foster, M. (1993). Resisting racism: Personal testimonies of African-American teachers. In L. Weis & M. Fine (Eds.), *Class, race, and gender in United States schools* (pp. 273-288). Albany: State University of New York Press.

Foster, W. (1986). *Paradigms and promises: New approaches to educational administration.* Buffalo, NY: Prometheus Books.

Foster, W. (1989, April). *School leaders as transformative intellectuals: A theoretical argument.* Paper presented at the conference of the American Educational Research Association. San Francisco.

Foucault, M. (1969). What is an author. In Adams, H. & Searle, L. (Eds.) Critical theory since 1965. Gainesville: University Presses of Florida.

Foucault, M. (1972). *The Archaeology of knowledge.* New York: Pantheon.

Foucault, M. (1977). *Discipline and punish: The birth of the prison.* New York: Pantheon Books.

Frazier, L. (1993, October 6). Education matters. *Times-Picayune,* p. B1.

Freedman, S. (1990). *The real world of a teacher, her students, and their high school.* New York: Harper & Row.

Freire, P. (1973). *Pedagogy of the oppressed.* New York: Seasbury Press.

Fullan, M. (1990). *The meaning of educational change* (2nd ed.). New York: Teachers College Press.

Gans, H. (1969). Culture and class in the study of poverty: An approach to anti-poverty research. In D. Moniyhan (Ed.), *Our understanding poverty: Perspectives from the social sciences.* New York: Basic Books.

Garibaldi, A. (1988). *The black male: A moral and civic imperative.* New Orleans, LA: New Orleans Public Schools.

Garvin, J. (1994) *Public housing and social isolation in New Orleans: A case study*. Unpublished dissertation, University of New Orleans.

Giddens, A. (1974). *Positivism and society*. London: Heinemann Educational Books, Ltd.

Giddens, A. (1982). *Profiles and critiques in social theory*. Berkeley: University of California Press.

Giddens, A. (1984). *The constitution of society*. Berkeley: University of California Press.

Giddens, A. (1987). *Social theory and modern sociology*. Stanford: Stanford University Press.

Gilligan, C. (1993). Joining the resistance: Psychology, politics, girls, and women. In L. Weis & M. Fine (Eds.), *Beyond silenced voices: Class, race, and gender in United States schools* (pp. 143-169). Albany: State University of New York Press.

Gintis, H. (1980). Communication and politics. *Socialist Review, 10*, 189-232.

Ginzberg, E., & Solow, R. (Ed.). (1974). *The Great Society: Lessons for the future*. New York: Basic Books.

Giratelli, F. (1993). What can I do? Foucault on freedom and the question of teacher agency. *Educational Theory, 43*, 416-433.

Giroux, H. (1981). *Ideology, culture, and the process of schooling*. Philadelphia: Temple University Press.

Giroux, H. (1983). *Theory and resistance in Education*. South Hadley, MA: Bergin and Garvey.

Giroux, H. (Ed.). (1991). *Post modernism, feminism, and cultural politics: Redrawing educational boundaries*. Albany: State University of New York Press.

Giroux, H. (1992). Rewriting the politics of identity and difference. *The Review of Education, 14*, 305-316.

Giroux, H. (1993). *Border crossings: Cultural workers and the politics of education*. New York: Routledge & Kegan Paul.

Giroux, H., & McLaren, P. (Ed.). (1989). *Critical pedagogy, the state and cultural struggle*. Albany: State University of New York Press.

Gittell, M. (1981). Localizing democracy out of schools. *Social Policy, 12*(2), 4-11.

Glickman, C. (1993). *Renewing America's schools: A guide for school-based action*. San Francisco: Jossey-Bass Publishers.

Glucksman, C. (1982). Hegemony and consent. In A. Sasoon (Eds.), *Ap-proaches to Gramsci* (pp. 116-127). London: Writers and Readers.

Goldner, V. (1993). Power and hierarchy: Let's talk about it. *Family Practice, 32*, 157-162.

Gore, J. (1993). *The struggle for pedagogies*. New York: Routledge.

Graham, H. (1981). The transformation of federal educational policy. In R. Divine (Eds.), *Exploring the Johnson years* (pp. 155-184). Austin: University of Texas Press.

Graham, J. (1992). Post-Fordism as politics: The political consequences of narratives on the left. *Environment and Planning D: Society and Space, 104,* 393-410.

Gramsci, A. (1971). *Selections from the prison notebooks.* New York: International Publishers.

Grossberg, L. (1993). Cultural studies and/or new worlds. In C. McCarthy & W. Crichlow (Eds.), *Race, identity, and representation in education* (pp. 89-105). New York: Routledge.

Habermas, J. (1970). Toward a theory of communicative competence. *Inquiry, 13,* 205-218.

Habermas, J. (1975). *Legitimation crisis.* London: Heinemann Educational Books. Hall, S. (1980). Popular democratic vs. authoritarian populism: Two ways of taking democracy seriously. In A. Hunt (Eds.), *Marxism and democracy* (pp. 150-170). London: Lawrence and Wishart.

Hall, S. (1988). The toad in the garden: Thatcherism among the theorists. In C. Nelson & L. Grossberg (Eds.), *Marxism and the interpretation of culture* (pp. 58-75). Urbana: University of Illinois Press.

Hall, S. (1991). Ethnicity, identity and difference. *Radical America, 13*(4), 10-16.

Hannaway, J. (1993). Decentralization in two school districts: Challenging the standard paradigm. In J. Hannaway & M. Carnoy (Eds.), *Decentralization and school improvement: Can we fulfill the promise?* (pp. 135-162). San Francisco, CA: Jossey-Bass Publishers.

Hannaway, J., & Carnoy, M. (Eds.). (1993). *Decentralization and school improvement: Can we fulfill the promise?* San Francisco, CA: Jossey-Bass.

Harvey, D. (1992). Social justice, postmodernism and the city. *International Journal of Urban and Regional Research, 16*(4), 588-601.

Hartle, T., & Holland, R. (1983). The changing context of federal education aid. *Education and Urban Society, 15*(4), 408-431.

Haynes, L.A. (1993). *Redefining equity for at-risk students.* Presented at Chapter One Meeting, Madison, WI.

Haynes, N., Comer, J., & Hamilton-Lee, M. (1988). The school development program: A model for school improvement. *Journal of Negro Education, 57*(1), 11-21.

Heath, S., & McLaughlin, M. (Ed.). (1993). *Identity & inner-city youth: Beyond ethnicity and gender.* New York: Teachers College Press.

Herr, K., & Anderson, G. (1992). The struggle for voice: Institutional deafness and student diversity [mimeographed report]. Paper presented at the Teachers College Winter Roundtable. New York, Teachers College.

Herr, K., & Anderson, G. (1993). Oral history for student empowerment: Capturing student's inner voices. *Qualitative Studies in Education*, (No. 41230).

Hill, P., & Bonan, J. (1992). *Decentralization and accountability in public education* (R-4066-MCF/IET) Santa Monica, CA: Rand Corporation.

Hirsch, A.R. (Ed.). (1990.) *Creole New Orleans: Race and Americanization.* Baton Rouge: Louisiana State University Press.

Hirsch, A. R. (1983). *Making the second ghetto: Race and housing in Chicago, 1940-1960.* New York: Cambridge University Press.

Hirschman, A. (1970). *Exit, voice, and loyalty: Responses to decline in firms, organizations, and states.* Cambridge, MA.: Harvard University Press.

hooks, b. (1993). *Sisters of the yam: Black women and self-recovery.* Boston: South End Press.

Hopfenberg, W., & Levin, H. (1993). *The accelerated schools resource guide.* San Francisco: Jossey-Bass.

Hugg, P., & Miron, L. (1991). A hybrid theory for educational reform. *Loyola Law Review, 36*(4), 937-980.

Illich, I. (1971). *Deschooling society.* New York: Harrow Books.

Jeffrey, J. (1976). *Education for the children of the poor: A study of the origins and implementation of the Elementary and Secondary School Act of 1965.* Columbus: Ohio State University Press.

Jencks, C. (1972). *Inequality: A reassessment of the effect of family and schooling in America.* New York: Harper & Row.

Jencks, C. (1979). *Who gets ahead?* New York: Basic Books.

Jencks, C. (1987). *What is postmodernism?* (2nd ed.). New York; St. Martin's Press.

Jencks, C., Smith, M., Acland, H., Bane, M., Cohen, D., Gintis, H., Heyns, B., & Michelson, S. (1973). *Inequality: A reassessment of family and schooling in America.* New York: Harper Colophon.

Jetter, A. (February 21, 1993). Mississippi learning. *The New York Times Magazine*, pp. 28-50.

Johnson, L. (1971). *The vantage point: Perspectives of the presidency, 1963-1969.* New York: Holt, Rinehart and Winston.

Johnson, L. (1986). *Public papers of the Presidents of the United States: Lyndon B. Johnson, 1965.* Washington, DC: U.S. Government Printing Office.

Joyner, E. (1991). *The school planning and management team.* New Haven, CT: Yale Child Study Center.

Kantor, H. (1991). Education, social reform, and the state: ESEA and federal education policy in the 1960s. *American Journal of Education, 100*(1), 47-83.

Katz, M. (Ed.). (1971). *School reform: Past and present.* Boston, MA: Little, Brown.

Kelly, D., & Liu, J. (1993). Deconstructing cultural barriers: New paradigms for a pedagogy of possibility. *The Review of Education, 15,* 21-27.
Kiziltan, M., Bain, W., & Canizares, A. (1990). Postmodern conditions: Rethinking public education. *Educational Theory, 40*(3), 353-354.
Knight, G. (1993). Family socialization and Mexican American identity and behavior. In M. Bernal & G. Knight (Eds.), *Ethnic identity: Formation and transmission among Hispanics and other minorities* (pp. 105-131). Albany: State University of New York Press.
Kozol, J. (1991). *Savage inequalities: Children in America's schools.* New York: Crown Publishers.
Lamorte, M. W. (1989). Courts continue to address the wealth disparity issue. *Educational Evaluation and Policy Analysis, 11*(1), 3-15.
Lauria, M., Miron, L., & Dashner, D. (1994). *Student resistance to the entrepreneurial coalition's drive for ideological hegemony in public schooling* (No. 28). New Orleans: University of New Orleans, College of Urban and Public Affairs.
Lemann, N. (1991). *The promised land.* New York: Knopf.
Levi-Strauss, C. (1968). *Structural anthropology.* London: Allen Lane.
Levin, H. L. (1987). New schools for the disadvantaged. *Teacher Education Quarterly, 14*(4).
Levin, H. L. (1988). *Accelerated schools for at-risk students.* Stanford, CA: Center for Policy Research in Education, Stanford University.
Levine, M. (1985). *The private sector in the public school: Can it improve education?* Washington, DC: American Enterprise Institute for Public Policy Research.
Levine, M., & Trachtman, R. (1988). *American business and the public school: Case studies of corporate invlovement.* New York: Teachers College Press.
Levitan, S. (1969). *The Great Society's poor law: A new approach to poverty.* Cambridge: Harvard University Press.
Levitan, S. (1976). *The promise of greatness.* Cambridge: Harvard University Press.
Lewis, D.A., & Nakagawa, K. (1995). *Race and educational reform in the American metropolis: A study of school decentralization.* Buffalo: State University of New York Press.
Lewis, O. (1961). *The children of Sanchez.* New York: Random House.
Lewis, O. (1966). The culture of poverty. *Scientific American, 215,* 19-26.
Liston, D. (1990). *Capitalist schools.* New York: Routledge.
Logsdon, J., & DeVore, D. (1991). *Crescent city schools.* Lafayette: University of Louisiana Press.
Longstreet, W. (1987). *Aspects of ethnicity.* New York: Teachers College Press.

Maeroff, G. (1988, May). Withered hopes, stillborn dreams: The dismal panorama of urban schools. *Phi Delta Kappan*, pp. 633-638.

Malen, B., & Ogawa, R. (1988). Professional-patron influence on site-based governance councils: A confounding case study. *Educational Evaluation and Policy Analysis, 10*(4), 251-270.

Mannheim, K. (1936). *Ideology and Utopia*. New York: Harcourt, Brace & World.

Marcus, G., & Fischer, M. (1986). *Anthropology as cultural critique*. Chicago: University of Chicago Press.

Marcuse, P. (1981). The targeted crises: On the ideology of the urban fiscal crisis and its uses. *International Journal of Urban Research, 5*(3), 330-355.

Marsalis, W. (1994). *In this house. On this morning. Excerpts from liner notes*. New York: Columbia Records.

Maxcy, S. (1991). *Educational Leadership: A Critical Pragmatic Perspective*. New York: Bergin & Garvey.

Maxcy, S. (Ed.). (1994). *Postmodern school leadership: Meeting the crisis in educational administration*. Westport, CT: Praeger.

Mazzoni, T. (1987). The politics of educational choice in Minnesota. In W. Boyd & C. Kirchner (Eds.), *The politics of excellence and choice in education* (pp. 217-230). New York: Falmer Press.

McCarthy, C. (1988). Rethinking liberal and radical perspectives on racial inequality in schooling: Making the case for nonsynchrony. *Harvard Educational Review, 58,* 265-279.

McCarthy, C. (1990). *Race and curriculum: Social inequality and the theories and politics of difference in contemporary research on schooling*. Philadelphia: Falmer Press.

McCarthy, C., & Crichlow, W. (Ed.). (1993). *Race, identity, and representation in education*. New York: Routledge.

McGuire, C., McLaughlin, M., & Nachtigal, P. (1986). *The public education fund interim evaluation report*. Pittsburgh, PA.

McLaren, P. (1989). *Life in Schools: An Introduction to critical pedagogy in the foundations of education*. New York: Longman.

McLaren, P. (1994). *Life in schools: An introduction to critical pedagogy in the foundations of education* (2nd edition ed.). New York: Longman.

McLaughlin, M. (1975). *Evaluation and reform: The Elementary and Secondary Act of 1965, Title I*. Cambridge, MA: Ballinger.

McLure, H., & Fischer, G. (1969). *Ideology and opinion making: General problems of analysis*. New York: Columbia University Bureau of Applied Social Research.

Mead, L. (1986). *Beyond entitlement: The social obligations of citizenship*. New York: Free Press.

Mercanto, P. (1970). *School politics in the metropolis*. Columbus, OH.: Merrill.

Milliband, R. (1969). *The state and capitalist society*. New York: Basic Books.

Miron, L.F. (1991, Fall). The dialectics of school leadership: Post structural implications. *Organizational Theory Dialogue*, 1-5.

Miron, L.F. (1992). Corporate ideology and the politics of entrepreneurism in New Orleans. *Antipode, 24*(4), 263-288.

Miron, L.F. (1995). Pushing the boundaries of urban school reform: Linking student outcomes to community development. *Journal of a Just and Caring Education, 1*(1), 98-114.

Miron, L.F., & Brooks, C. (1993). Great Expectations: A critical analysis of the lessons of a grassroots movement to reform an urban school board. *The International Journal of School Reform, 2*(3), 242-248.

Miron, L.F., & Elliott, R. (1990). The moral exercise of power. *Review Journal of Philosophy & Social Science, 16*(1), 31-42.

Miron, L.F., & Elliott, R. (1994). Moral leadership in a post structural era. In S. Maxcy (Ed.), *Postmodern school leadership: Meeting the crisis in educational administration*. Westport, CT: Praeger.

Miron, L.F., First, P., & Wimpelberg, R. (1992). Equity, adequacy & educational need: The courts and urban schools finance. In J. Cibulka, J. Reed, & K. Wong (Eds.), *The Politics of urban education in the United States* (pp. 181-193). London: Falmer Press.

Miron, L. F., & Lauria, M. (1995, June). Identity politics and student resistance to inner city public schooling. *Youth & Society, 27*(1), 29-54.

Miron, L.F., & St. John, E. (1994). *The urban context and the meaning of school reform* (No.7. DURPS Working Paper Series). University of New Orleans College of Urban and Public Affairs.

Miron, L.F., & Wimpelberg, R. (1989). School business partnerships and the reform of education. *Administrators Notebook, 33*(1), 1-4.

Miron, L.F, & Wimpelberg, R. (1992). The role of school boards in the governance of education. In P. First & H. Walberg (Eds.), *School Boards: Changing local control* (pp. 151-175). San Pablo, CA.: McCutchan.

Morales, R., & Bonilla, F. (1993). Restructuring and the new inequality. In R. Morales & F. Bonilla (Eds.), *Latinos in a changing U.S. economy*. Newbury Park, CA: Sage.

Mosteller, F., & Moynihan, D. (Ed.). (1972). *On equality of educational opportunity*. New York: Vintage Books.

Mouffe, C. (1988). Radical democracy: Modern or postmodern? In A. Ross (Eds.), *Universal abandon?: The politics of post modernism* (pp. 31-45). Minneapolis: University of Minnesota Press.

Mouzelis, N. (1992). Marxism or post-Marxism? *New Left Review, 3*(167), 107-123.

Moynihan, D. (1993, Winter). Defining deviancy downward. *The American Scholar*, pp. 17-30.

Mueller, V., & McKeown, M. (Ed.). (1985). *The fiscal, legal, and political aspects of state reform of elementary and secondary education.* Cambridge, MA: Ballinger.

Myrdal, G. (1944). An American dilemma: The Negro problem and modern democracy. In A. Schlesinger (Eds.), *The national experience: A history of the United States* (pp. 46-71). New York: Harcourt, Brace and World.

Nathan, J. (1990). Progress, problems, and prospects of state educational choice plans. In W. Boyd & H. Walberg (Eds.), *Choice in education: Potential and problems* (pp. 263-287). Berkeley, CA.: McCutchan.

National Commission on Excellence in Education. (1983). *A nation at risk.* Washington, DC: U.S. Government Printing Office.

National League of Cities (1993). *The civic index.* Denver, CO: National Civic League.

New Jersey auditor general poised to take over school district. (1993, May 16). *New York Times.*

Nicholson, C. (1989). Postmodernism, feminism, and education: The need for solidarity. *Educational Theory. 39*(3), 204.

Noblit, G.W., & Pink, W.T. (1995). Mapping the alternative paths of the sociology of education. In G. Noblit &. W. Pink (Eds.), *Continuity and contradiction: The future of the sociology of education* (pp. 3-31.). Cresskill, NJ: Hampton Press.

Noddings, N. (1984). *Caring: A feminine approach to ethics and moral education.* Berkeley: University of California Press.

Noddings, N. (1994). *Towards an ethics of care in the schools.* New York: Teachers College Press.

O'Connor, J. (1973). *The fiscal crisis of the state.* New York: St. Martin's Press.

Oakes, J. (1985). *Keeping track: How schools structure inequality.* New Haven, CT: Yale University Press.

Ocampo, K., Bernal, M., & Knight, G. (1993). Gender, race, and ethnicity: the sequencing of social Constancies. In M. Bernal & G. Knight (Eds.), *Ethnic identity: Formation and transmission among Hispanics and other minorities* (pp. 11-31). Albany: State University of New York Press.

Ogbu, J. (1974). *The next generation: An ethnography of education in an urban neighborhood.* New York: Academic Press.

Ogbu, J. (1988). Class stratification, racial stratification, and schooling. In L. Weis (Eds.), *Class, race, and gender in American education* (pp. 46-71). Albany: State University Press of New York.

Olsen, L. (1994). *The road not taken: Implementing a community-specific multi-cultural curriculum.* Unpublished dissertation. New Orleans: University of New Orleans.

Omi, M., & Winant, H. (1986). *Racial formation in the United States: From the 1960s to the 1980s.* New York: Routledge.

Omi, M., & Winant, H. (1993). On the theoretical concept of race. In W. Crichlow & C. McCarthy (Eds.), *Race, identity and representation in education* (pp. 3-11). New York: Routledge.

Orner, M. (1989). Sit up and speak: Exploring the meanings of student voice and silence. Paper presented at the American Educational Studies Association Convention, Chicago.

Osborne, D. (1993, April). How to reinvent government. Metrovision Partnership Conference, New Orleans, LA.

Osborne, D., & Gaebler, T. (1992). *Reinventing Government.* Reading, MA: Addison Wesley.

Pancrazio, S. (1992). State takeovers and other last resorts. In P. First & H. Walberg (Eds.), *School boards: Changing local control*. Berkeley, CA.: McCutchan.

Patterson, J. (1981). *America's struggle against poverty, 1900-1980.* Cambridge, MA.: Harvard University Press.

Paulston, C. (1980). *Bilingual education: Theories and issues.* Rowley, MA: Newbury House.

Peck, J., & Tickell, A. (1993). *Business goes local: Dissecting the 'business agenda' in post-democratic Manchester.* In Ninth Urban Change and Conflict conference, University of Sheffield, England.

Peters, G. (1978). *The politics of bureaucracy: A comparative perspective.* New York: Longman.

Peters, T.J., & Waterman, R. H. (1984). *In search of excellence.* New York: Warner Books.

Peterson, P. (1979). *School politics, Chicago style.* Chicago: University of Chicago Press.

Pierce, N. (1993, May 31). Philadelphia tries a bit of reinventing government. *New Orleans: Times-Picayune,* p. B5.

Pinar, W.F., & Bowers, C.A. (1992). Politics of curriculum: origins, controversies and significance of critical perspectives. *Review of Research in Education, 18,* 163-191.

Popkewitz, T. S. (1979). Schools and the symbolic uses of community participation. In C. Grant (Eds.), *Community participation in education* (pp. 262-280). Boston: Allyn and Bacon, Inc.

Popkewitz, T. S. (1982). Educational reform as the organization of ritual: Stability as change. *Journal of Education, 164*(1), 5-28.

Popkewitz, T. S. (1990). Whose future? Whose past? Notes on critical theory and methodology. In E.G. Guba (Eds.), *The paradigm dialog* (sic). Newbury Park, CA: Sage.

Popkewitz, T.S. (1991). *A political sociology of educational reform: Power/ knowledge in teaching, teacher education, and research.* New York: Teachers College Press.

Poulantzas, N. (1969). The problem of the capitalist state. *The New Left Review, 59,* 53-59.

Poulantzas, N. (1978). *Classes in contemporary capitalism.* London: New Left Books.

President Johnson's design for a "Great Society." (1965). *Congressional Quarterly.*

Racism in the academy. (1993). *New York Times*, p. Y-17.

Rainwater, L. (1969). The problem of lower-class culture and poverty-war strategy. In D. Moniyhan (Eds.), *Our understanding poverty: Perspectives from the social sciences* (pp. 16-35). New York: Basic Books.

Rand Report on educational governance. (1992). (No. 14352). Santa Monica, CA: Rand Corporation.

Raskin, M. (1986). *The Common good.* New York: Routledge.

Ravitch, D. (1974). *The great school wars.* New York: Basic Books.

Ravitch, D. (1985). *The schools we deserve.* New York: Basic Books.

Ravitch, D. (1995). *National standards in American education: A citizenuide.* Washington, DC: Brookings Institution.

Reed, A. (1988). The black urban regime: Structural origins and constraints. *Comparative Urban and Community Research, 1,* 138-189.

Rosaldo, R. (1989). *Culture and truth: The remaking of social analysis.* Boston: Beacon Press.

Rulon, P. (1981). *The compassionate samaritan: The life of Lyndon Baines Johnson.* Chicago, IL: Nelson-Hall.

Sarason, S. (1982). *The Culture of the school and the problem of change* (2nd ed.). Boston: Allyn & Bacon.

Sarason, S. (1990). *The predictable failure of educational reform.* San Francisco, CA: Jossey-Bass Publishers.

Schlechty, P. (1990). *Schools for the 21st century: Leadership imperatives for educational reform.* San Francisco: Jossey-Bass.

Shanker, A. (1992, January 10). Why Clinton chose? *The New York Times*, p.23.

Shanker, A. (1995, March 12). A citizen's guide. *The New York Times*, p. 7.

Shelley, F. (1994b). Local control and financing of education: A perspective from the American state judiciary. *Political Geography, 13*(4), 361-376.

Sizer, T. (1983). *A celebration of teaching: High schools in the 1980s.* Reston, VA.: National Association of Secondary School Principals and Commission on Educational Issues of the National Association of Independent Schools.

Sizer, T. (1995, Spring). *Newsletter.* Coalition of Essential Schools. Providence, RI: Brown University.

Smith, M. P. (1974). The ritual politics of suburban schools. In M. P Smith (Ed.), *Politics in America* (pp. 110-126). New York: Random House.

Smith, M. P. (1980). Critical theory and urban political theory. *Comparative Urban Research, 7,* 5-23.

Smith, M.P. & Feagin, J.R. (Ed.). (1987). *The capitalist city: Global restructuring and community politics.* Oxford, England & New York: Basil Blackwell.

Smith, M. P., & Judd, D. (1983). The production of ideologies. *Urban Affairs Annual Review, 26,* 173-196.

Smith, M. P., & Keller, M. (1983). Managed growth and the politics of uneven development in New Orleans. In S.S. Fainstein (Ed.), *Restructuring the city: The political economy of urban development* (pp. 136-166). New York: Longman.

Smith, M. P. (1992). Post modernism, urban ethnography, and the new social space of ethnic identity. *Theory and Society, 21*(4), 493-531.

Soja, E., & Hooper, B. (1993). The spaces that difference makes: Some notes on the geographical margins of the new cultural politics. In M. Keith, & S. Pile (Eds.), *Place and the politics of identity.* London and New York: Routledge.

Spindler, G., & Spindler, L. (1994). *Pathways to cultural awareness: Cultural therapy with teachers and students.* Thousand Oaks, CA: Corwin.

Spring, J. (1985). *American education: An introduction to social and political aspects* (3rd ed.). New York: Longman.

St. John, E., Miron, L., & Davidson, B. (1992). Teacher inquiry and school transformation: An examination of exemplary schools. *Louisiana Social Studies Journal, 24*(1), 9-16.

Stack, C.S. (1993). *Education and modernism: A postmodern problem.* Paper presented at the Louisiana Philosophy of Education Society Annual Meeting. Lafayette, LA.

Stack, C.S. (1995). *A critical analysis of selected educational reform policies in Louisiana and their effects on students in two parishes.* Unpublished dissertation. University of New Orleans.

The statement by the president and the goverors. (1989, October 1). *New York Times.*

Statistical Abstracts of the United States. Annual Volumes (1960-1992). Lanham, MD: Bernan Press.

Steiner, G. (1976). *The children's cause.* Washington, DC: The Brookings Institute.

Stone, C. N. (1989). *Regime politics: Governing Atlanta, 1946-1948.* Lawrence: University of Kansas Press.

Swanstrom, T. (1985). *The crisis of growth politics.* Philadelphia: Temple University Press.

Swanstrom, T. (1988). Semisovereign cities: The politics of urban development. *Polity, 21*(1), 83-110.

Thomas, N. (1975). *Education in national politics.* New York: David McKay.

Thompson, J. (1976). *Policymaking in American public education.* Englewood Cliffs, NJ: Prentice-Hall.

Troyna, B., & Hatcher, R. (1991). Racist incidents in schools: A framework for analysis. *Journal of Educational Policy, 6*(1), 17-31.

Tyack, D. (1974). *The one best system.* Cambridge, MA: Harvard University Press.

Tyack, D. (1993). School governance in the United States: Historical puzzles and anomalies. In J. Hannaway & M. Carnoy (Eds.), *Decentralization and school improvement: Can we fulfill the promise?* (pp. 1-33). San Francisco, CA: Jossey-Bass.

Tyack, D., & Hansot, E. (1982). *Managers of virtue: Public school leadership in America, 1820-1980.* New York: Basic Books.

Tyler, R. (1974). The federal role in education. In E. Ginzberg & R. Solow (Eds.), *The Great Society: Lessons for the future* (pp. 164-187). New York: Basic Books.

U.S. Department of Education. (1994). *Goals 2000 background paper.* Washington, DC: Government Printing Office.

Valentine, J. (1979). Head Start, a retrospective view: The founders, Honorable Sargent Shriver. In J. Valentine (Eds.), *Project head start: A legacy of the war on poverty* (pp. 49-67). New York: The Free Press.

Verstegan, D. (1987). Two hundred years of federalism: A perspective on national fiscal policy in education. *Journal of Education Finance, 12,* 516-548.

Wallerstein, I. (1980). *The Modern world system: Mercantalism and the consolidation of the European world economies, 1600-1750.* New York: Academic Press.

Waters, M. (1994). *Modern sociological theory.* Thousand Oaks, CA. Sage.

Weick, K. (1976). Educational organizations as loosely coupled systems. *Administrative Science Quarterly, 21,* 1-16.

Weis, L., & Fine, M. (Ed.). (1992). *Beyond silenced voices: Class, race, and gender in United States schools.* Albany: State University of New York Press.

West, C. (1993a). *Keeping faith: Philosophy and race in America.* New York: Routledge.

West, C. (1993b). The new cultural politics of difference. In W. Crichlow & C. McCarthy (Eds.), *Race, identity and representation in education* (pp. 11-24). New York: Routledge.

West, C. (1993c). Race matters. New York: Vintage Books.

Westinghouse Learning Corporation. (1969). *The impact of Head Start: An evaluation of the effects of head Start on children's cognitive and affective development.* Athens: Ohio University.

Wexler, P. (1988). Symbolic economy of identity and denial of labor: Studies in high school number one. In L. Weis (Ed.), *Class, race, and gender in American education* (pp. 302-311). Albany: State University of New York.

Whelan, R. K., Young, A. H. & Lauria. M. (1994). Urban regimes and racial politics in New Orleans. *Journal of Urban Affairs, 16*(1), 1-21.

Whitt, J. (1982). *Urban elites and mass transportation.* Princeton, NJ.: Princeton University Press.

Whitt, J. (1984). Structural fetishism in the new urban theory. In M. P. Smith (Ed.), *Cities in transformation* (pp. 75-91). Urban Affairs Annual Review.

Wilensky, H. (1975). *The welfare state and equity: Structural and ideological roots of public expenditures.* Berkeley: University of California Press.

Williams, R. (1961). *The long revolution.* London: Chatto & Windus.

Willis, P. (1977). *Learning to labour.* Westmead, UK: Saxson House.

Wilson, J. W. (1992). Race, class, and poverty in urban neighborhoods: A comparative perspective. In the Conference on Building strong communities: Strategies for urban change. Cleveland, Ohio.

Wilson, W. (1987). *The truly disadvantaged: The inner city, the underclass, and public policy.* Chicago, IL: The University of Chicago Press.

Wimpelberg, R.K., & Teddlie, C., & Stringfield, S (1989). Sensitivity to context: the past and future of effective schools research. *Educational Administration Quarterly, 25*(1), 82-107.

Wines, H. (1993, September 19). New Jersey auditor general poised to take over school district. *New York Times*, p. 1A.

Wong, K. (1992). The politics of urban education as a field of study: An interpretive analysis. In J. Cibulka, R. Reed, & K. Wong (Eds.), *The politics of urban education in the United States* (pp. 3-27). London: Falmer Press.

Wyckoff, G. (1994, December). An offbeat interview with Wynton Marsalis. *New Orleans: Offbeat*, pp. 48-53.

Yin, R.K. (1989). *Case study research: Design and methods.* Newbury Park, CA: Sage.

Young, R.E. (1988). *A critical theory of education.* New York: Teachers College Press.

Zigler, E. (1985). Assessing head Start at 20: An invited commentary. *American Journal of Orthopsychiatry, 55*, 603-609.

Zigler, E., & Muenchow, S. (1992). *Head Start: The inside story of America's most successful educational experiment.* New York: Basic Books.

Zigler, E., & Rescorla, L. (1985). Social science and social policy: The case of social competence as a goal of intervention programs. In R. Kassochau, L. Rehmm, & L. Ullmann (Eds.), *Psychology research, public policy and practice: Towards a productive partnership* (pp. 62-94). New York: Praeger.

Author Index

A

Aaron, H., 30, *197*
Abercombie, N., 70, *197*
Acland, H., 37, *206*
Alexander, L., 92, 93, 96, *197*
Alkin, C., 39, *197*
Anaya, R., 24, *197*
Anderson, G., 10, 13, 109, 110, 123, 127, 134, 140, 141, 143, *197, 205*
Anderson, J., 122, 189, *197*
Anfara, V., 44, 147, 151, 176, 187, 194, 195, *197*
Annual Economic Report to the President, *198*
Anyon, J., 136, 173, *198*
Anzaldua, G., 144, *198*
Apple, M., 2, 3, 6, 8, 10, 11, 12, 13, 14, 15, 20, 21-22, 23, 34, 36, 42, 44, 47, 48, 58-60, 61, 70, 72, 73, 74, 75, 85, 86, 96, 98, 140, 143, 147, 149, 173, *198*
Argyris, C., 177, *198*
Aronowitz, S., 108, 135, 136, 140, 143, 176, *198*

Astuto, T., 41, 42, 43, 47, 48, *198, 200*

B

Baca, L., 108, *198*
Bain, W., 56, *207*
Ball, A., 134, *198*
Ball, S., 112, 140, 141, *198*
Bane, M., 37, *206*
Barbier, S., 170, 188, *198*
Barfield, C., 39, *198*
Bell, T., 43, 44, 69, *198, 199*
Berger, P., 17, 19, *199*
Bernal, M., 103, 106, 141, *199, 210*
Beyer, L., 55, 56, 57, 135, *199*
Biesta, G., 102, 109, 115, 122, 136, 192, 193, 194, 195, *199*
Blaise, J., 140, *199*
Boaz, D., 44, *199*
Bogotch, I., 88, 94, *199*
Bolman, L., 140, *199*
Bonan, J., 9, *206*
Bondi, L., 109, 164, 169, 188, *199*
Bonilla, F., 75, *209*

Bourdieu, P., 158, *199*
Bowers, C.A., 10, 13, 16, 54, 85, 116, *211*
Bowles, S., 10, 117, *199*
Boyd, W., 8, 16, 42, 47, 83, 88, 92, 189, 193, *199, 201*
Bredo, E., 73, *199*
Bridges, T., 106, *199*
Brinkley, A., 32, *199*
Britzman, D., 111, 113, 144, 176, *200*
Brooks, C., 8, 76, 98, 130, 189, *209*
Buriel, R., 110, *200*
Butler, O., 79-80, 85, *200*

C

Canizares, A., 56, *207*
Cardoza, D., 110, *200*
Carnoy, M., 4, 67, 71, 83-84, 98, *200, 205*
Cervantes, H., 108, *198*
Cherryholmes, C., 8, 12, 34, 56, *200*
Chilcote, R.H., 77, *200*
Chubb, J., 8, 50, *200*
Clark, D., 41, 42, 43, 47, 48, *198, 200*
Clegg, S., 140, *200*
Clune, W., 46, *200*
Cohen, D., 37, *206*
Coleman, J., 36-37, 176, *200*
Comer, J., 89, 90, 194, *200, 201, 205*
Committee for Economic Development, 71, *201*
Committee of Health and Human Services, 53, *201*
Cook, C.C., 143, *201*
Council of the Great City Schools, 93, 189, *201*
Crichlow, W., 103, 113, 169, 194, *208*

Cronin, J., 83, *201*
Crowson, R., 42, 47, 83, 88, 90, 92, 99, 189, *201*
Cuban, L., 3, 70, 87, 193, *201*
Cummins, J., 67, 68, 108, *201*
Curcio, J., 122, 185, *201*

D

Daley, H., 67, *200*
Dashner, D., 21, 42, 43, 108, 118, 139, 142, 150, 182, 187, 189, *201, 207*
Davidson, B., 88, 89, 133, *213*
Davis, B., 20, *201*
Deal, T., 140, *199*
Delany, S., 113, *201*
Department of Education, 91, 95, *201*
DeVaney, A., 85, 119, *202*
DeVore, D., 24, *207*
Divine, R., 35, *202*
Doll, W., 55, 63, 137, *202*
Dugger, R., 42, 43, *202*

E

Eason, S., 17, *202*
Edelstein, J.C., 77, *200*
Eisner, E., 196, *202*
Elliott, R., 77, 99, 115, 118, 137, *209*
Ellsworth, E., 122, *202*
Elmore, R., 71, 83, 98, *202*
English, F., 56, *202*
Everhart, R., 6, 118, 134, 136, 138, 143, 155, 173, *202*
Excellence in Education Committee, 98, *202*

F

Fainstein, N., 7, 20, 42, 71, *202*

Fainstein, S.S., 7, 14, 42, 71, *202*
Feagin, J.R., 85, *213*
Feinberg, W., 97, 182, *202*
Fine, M., 19, 68, 72, 73, 74, 136, 189, *202, 214*
Finn, C., 8, 42, 43, 44, 50, *203*
First, P., 21, 96, 98, 122, 185, *201, 203, 209*
Fischer, G., 20, *208*
Fischer, M., 23, 68, 136, 169, *208*
Fishman, J., 108, 125, *203*
Fordham, S., 112, *203*
Foster, M., 113, 189, *203*
Foster, W., 12, 99, 116, 118, 122, *203*
Foucault, M., 19, 50, 118, 133, 137, 140, *203*
Frazier, L., 126, *203*
Freedman, S., 20, *203*
Freire, P., 129, 144, *203*
Fullan, M., 7, 94, *203*

G

Gaebler, T., 9, 23, *211*
Gans, H., 30, *203*
Garibaldi, A., 163, 174, *203*
Garvin, J., 15, 23, 88, 94, 133, 143, 187, 199, *204*
Giddens, A., 22, 33, 46, 50, 61, 73, 77, 102, 112, 114, 125, 126, 128, 139, 187, 188, *204*
Gilligan, C., 134, 136, 138, 140, *204*
Gintis, H., 10, 35, 49, 117, 199, *204, 206*
Ginzberg, E., 27, *204*
Giratelli, F., 137, *204*
Giroux, H., 6, 10, 13, 14, 55, 60, 62, 65-66, 101, 109-110, 111, 112, 115, 116-117 (n.4), 118, 119, 120, 121, 124, 125, 126, 126 (n.8), 128, 129, 130, 135, 136, 138, 140, 144, 176, *204*
Gittell, M., 38, *204*
Glickman, C., 14, 90, *204*
Glucksman, C., 14, *204*
Goldner, V., 116, *204*
Gore, J., 104, 117 (n.5), *204*
Graham, H., 35, *204*
Graham, J., 122 (n.7), *205*
Gramsci, A., 3, 20, 68, 85, *205*
Grossberg, L., 103, 108, 135, 136, 138, 142, 145, 150, *205*

H

Habermas, J., 5, 98, 102, 122, 177, 193, *205*
Hall, S., 111, *205*
Hamilton-Lee, M., 90, *205*
Hannaway, J., 4, 98, *205*
Hansot, E., 72, *214*
Hartle, T., 38, 45, *205*
Harvey, D., 122 (n.7), *205*
Hatcher, R., 122, *214*
Haynes, L.A., 14, 80, 88, *205*
Haynes, N., 90, *205*
Heath, S., 68, 96, 134, 198, *205*
Herr, K., 109, 111, 123, 127, 134, 141, 143, *205, 206*
Heyns, B., 37, *206*
Hill, P., 9, *206*
Hill, S., 70, *197*
Hirsch, A.R., 187, *206*
Hirschman, A., 75, 145, *206*
Hoffer, T., 176, *200*
Holland, R., 38, 45, *205*
hooks, b., 112, *206*
Hooper, B., 160, *213*

Hopfenberg, W., 87, 88, *206*
Hugg, P., 67, 82, 83, *206*

I

Illich, I., 122, *206*

J

Jeffrey, J., 32-33, *206*
Jencks, C., 10, 31, 37, 63, *206*
Jetter, A., 70, *206*
Johnson, L., 29, 31, 35, *206*
Joyner, E., 89, *206*
Judd, D., 7, 27, *213*

K

Kantor, H., 28, 38, *206*
Katz, M., 187, *206*
Keller, M., 14, 15, *213*
Kelly, D., 62, 66, 144, *207*
Kilgore, S., 176, *200*
Kiziltan, M., 56, *207*
Knight, G., 103, 104, 106, 141, *199, 207, 210*
Kozol, J., 4, 11, 17, 42, 47, 67, 92, 189, *207*

L

Lamorte, M.W., 67, *207*
Lauria, M., 42, 43, 65, 69-70, 71, 108, 118, 119, 135, 139, 141, 142, 143, 147, 149, 150, 159, 169, 170, 182, 186, 187, 189, *201, 207, 209, 215*
Lemann, N., 11, 17, *207*
Levi-Strauss, C., 77, *207*
Levin, H.L., 4, 8, 11, 87, 88, 193, 194, *206, 207*
Levine, M., 80, *207*
Levitan, S., 28, *207*
Lewis, D.A., 9, 79, *207*
Lewis, O., 29, *207*
Liston, D., 55, 56, 57, 122 (n.7), 135, 144, *199, 207*
Liu, J., 62, 66, 144, *207*
Logsdon, J., 24, *207*
Longstreet, W., 142, *207*
Luckmann, T., 17, 19, *199*

M

Maeroff, G., 8, *208*
Malen, B., 78, *208*
Mannheim, K., 18, *208*
Marcus, G., 23, 68, 136, 169, *208*
Marcuse, P., 11, *208*
Marsalis, W., 196, *208*
Maxcy, S., 6, 12, 56, 99, 110, 188, *208*
Mazzoni, T., 39, 73, *208*
McCarthy, C., 103, 108, 113, 169, 194, *208*
McCaul, E., 20, *201*
McGuire, C., 79, *208*
McKeown, M., 45, *210*
McLaren, P., 12, 121, 139, 144, *208*
McLaughlin, M., 68, 79, 96, *205, 208*
McLure, H., 20, *208*
Mead, L., 30, *208*
Mercanto, P., 78, *208*
Michelson, S., 37, *206*
Milliband, R., 13, *208*
Miron, L.F., 5, 8, 11, 12, 16, 21, 24, 27, 37, 40, 41, 42, 43, 44, 65, 67, 69, 70, 72, 74, 75, 76, 77, 80, 81, 82, 83, 84, 85, 88, 89, 94, 96, 98, 99, 108, 115, 118, 119, 121, 130, 133, 134, 135, 137, 139, 141, 142, 144, 147, 149, 150, 151, 159, 169, 170, 176, 179, 182, 184-185, 186, 187, 189, 191, 195, *199, 203, 206, 207, 209, 213*

Author Index 221

Moe, T., 8, 50, *200*
Morales, R., 75, *209*
Mosteller, F., 34, *209*
Mouffe, C., 65, 103, 105, 112, 114-115, 121, 139, 180, 181, 184, *209*
Mouzelis, N., 114 (n.3), 129, *209*
Moynihan, D., 5, 6, 21, 34, 75, *209*
Mueller, V., 45, *210*
Muenchow, S., 50, 53, 215
Myrdal, G., 104, 105, 106, *210*

N

Nachtigal, P., 79, *208*
Nakagawa, K., 9, 79, *207*
Nathan, J., 73, *210*
National Commission on Excellence in Education, 70, *210*
National League of Cities, 38, 98, 189, *210*
Nicholson, C., 57, *210*
Noblit, G.W., 17, *210*
Noddings, N., 116, *210*

O

O'Connor, J., 24, 77, *210*
Oakes, J., 10, *210*
Ocampo, K., 103, 106, 141, *210*
Ogawa, R., 78, *208*
Ogbu, J., 87, 112, *210*
Ojeda, R., 67, *200*
Olsen, L., 112, 141, *210*
Omi, M., 104, 105, 107, 143, *210, 211*
Orner, M., 176-177, *211*
Osborne, D., 9, 12, 20, 23, *211*

P

Pancrazio, S., 82, *211*
Passeron, J.C., 158, *199*
Patterson, J., 31, *211*
Paulston, C., 108, 134, *211*
Peck, J., 185, 186, *211*
Peters, G., 29, 38, 52, *211*
Peters, T.J., 69, *211*
Peterson, P., 79, *211*
Pierce, N., 69, *211*
Pinar, W.F., 10, 13, 16, 54, 85, 116, *211*
Pink, W.T., 17, *210*
Popkewitz, T.S., 2, 3, 8, 9, 33, 34, 68, 73, 75, 83, 87, 96, *211*
Poulantzas, N., 14, 60 (n.4), 98, 173, *211*
Putnam, R., 177, *198*

R

Rainwater, L., 30, *212*
Rand Report, 8, *212*
Raskin, M., 96, *212*
Ravitch, D., 16, 50, 78, *212*
Reed, A., 129, 143, *212*
Rescorla, L., 53, *215*
Rosaldo, R., 59, *212*
Rulon, P., 26-27, 28, 31, 32, 34, 35, *212*

S

Sarason, S., 7, 83, 94, *212*
Schlechty, P., 121, *212*
Schon, D., 177, *198*
Shanker, A., 10, 71, 94, *212*
Shelley, F., 83, *212*
Sizer, T., 92, *212*
Smith, D., 177, *198*
Smith, M., 37, *206*
Smith, M.P., 1, 5, 6, 7, 11, 14, 15, 21, 22, 23, 27, 56, 59, 61, 62, 63, 65, 68, 77, 85, 98, 102, 105, 107, 109,

222 Author Index

110, 111, 114, 120, 136, 138, 139, 169, *212, 213*
Soja, E., 160, *213*
Solow, R., 27, *204*
Soltis, J., 182, *202*
Spindler, G., 102, 108, 109, 186, 190, 191, 192, *213*
Spindler, L., 102, 108, 109, 186, 190, 191, 192, *213*
Spring, J., 186, *213*
St. John, E., 8, 11, 16, 24, 72, 75, 81, 88, 89, 121, 133, 179, 184-185, 191, *209, 213*
Stack, C.S., 55, 63, 137, 148, *213*
Statistical Abstracts of the U.S., 46, *213*
Steiner, G., 52, *213*
Stone, C.N., 70, 71, 129, 143, *213*
Stringfield, S., 36, *215*
Swanstrom, T., 27, 71, 85, *213*

T

Teddlie, C., 36, *215*
Thomas, N., 31, *213*
Thompson, J., 47, *213*
Tickell, A., 185, 186, *211*
Trachtman, R., 80, *207*
Troyna, B., 122, *214*
Turner, B., 70, *197*
Tyack, D., 69, 72, 83, 84, 87, 121, 139, 185, 193, 201, *214*
Tyler, R., 28, *214*

U

U.S. Department of Education, 16, 95, *214*

V

Valentine, J., 51, 52, *214*

Verstegan, D., 38, 45, 46, *214*

W

Walberg, H., 21, *203*
Wallerstein, I., 14, *214*
Waterman, R.H., 69, *211*
Waters, M., 18, 151, *214*
Weick, K., 15, 150, *214*
Weis, L., 68, *214*
West, C., 104, 106, 112, 113, 125, 196, *214*
Westinghouse Learning Corporation, 30, 52, *214*
Wexler, P., 134, 140, 143, *214*
Whelan, R.K., 69-70, 71, 143, *215*
Whitt, J., 74, 84, *215*
Wilensky, H., 38, 49, *215*
Williams, R., 57, *215*
Willis, P., 6, 13, 20, 58 (n.3), 136, 143, 173, 184, 186, *215*
Wilson, J.W., 9, 144, *215*
Wilson, W., 6, 7, 9, 17, 67, 106, 133, *215*
Wimpelberg, R., 5, 8, 36, 80, 83, *209, 215*
Winant, H., 104, 105, 107, 143, *210, 211*
Wines, H., 82, 215
Wong, K., 8, 9, 15, 77-78, 81, *215*
Wckoff, G., 196, *215*

Y

Yin, R.K., 145, 146, *215*
Young, A.H., 69-70, 71, 143, *215*
Young, R.E., 1, 98, *215*

Z

Zigler, E., 50, 53, *215*

Subject Index

A

abuse of power by adults over students, 122
academic competition mirroring corporation values, 186
academic competition/social cooperation climate, 165
academic excellence, 157
academic failures, constructed measures of student, 21
academic success, desire for, 166
Accelerated Schools Process (ASP), 87-89
accountability, 69, 70, 76
acculturation, 102-103
accumulation, 11, 12
achievement, student, U.S. compared to Japan and Germany, 7
ACT-UP, 142-143
action
  as cooperation, 192
  focus on, 4, 22
  meaning, 112
administration, incorpoartion of dominant ideologies in, 23

administrative discretion, 71-72
administrators, central office, most vulnerable to business ideologies, 194-195
African American Infusion Program, 16
African Americans, 65
African-American
  100% enrollment at City High, 175
  different qualitative experiences in being, 142
African-American awareness weeks, 125
African-American oral language traditions, 125
African-American school, trust, respect and support in, 157
African-Americans, middle-class, aspirations, 143
African-Americans
  political power, 143
  underclass, marginalized, 143-144
agency, situated, 187-191

224 Subject Index

agency; see human agency
ahistoricity, 56, 68
AIDS, 142-143
Alexander, Lamar, 92, 95
Algebra Project, 70
All Congregations Together, New Orleans, 143
alternative assessment practices, 88-9
amelioration, 24
AMERICA 2000, 92-93, 95-96
American Book Company, Channel One, 85
American culture, romanticized homogeneous vision of, 6
American Dilemma, An,, 104-105
American Federation of Teachers, 70
American identity, single, 3
anthropology, 59
Anti Defamation League, 119
antibias pedagogy, texts, 129
antibias pedagogy as cultural politics, 128-132
antirepresentationalism, 56
arrests, 163
artistic, creative manner, urban school reform viewed in, 196
ASP; see Accelerated Schools Process (ASP)
assimilation, 125-127
assimilation, schools in, 104
assimilationist position, 104-106
assumptions, modernist and postmodernist, 60-62
attention span, 6
authoritarian populism, 74-76
   free market, 77

authority versus authoritarianism, 122
autonomy, group, not group insularity, 196
"back here", 180

B

banking notion of education, 122
beliefs
   of dominant social groups furthered in classroom, 11
   middle-class, about work place and correct behavior, 12-13
   middle-class teachers, 12
beliefs, students; see students, belief
Bell, Terrel, 43, 44
benign neglect, 15
Bennett, William J., 43
bilingual community education, Milwaukee, 16
Bilingual Education, 64, 124-125
bilingual/bicultural education, 108
Black history, 168
Black on Black crime, 21
Black students; see students, Black
Black, "not really," 131-132
Blacks
   as collective political agents against undemocratic schools, 129
   inordinate suspensions of, 16
Blacks; see also African-American
blame for poor schools and student achievement, 75
blaming students for ignorance of mainstream culture, not,

Subject Index 225

191
blues music, 196
board waivers, 75
border crossing, difficulties of, 132-133
Border Crossings: Cultural Workers and the Politics of Education, 116-117
border pedagogy, 65-66, 112
  discourse as praxis of, 122
brain trust, 35
Brazil, critical literacy in, 129
breaking through, 183-196
brown color instead of black, 181
Budget, Bureau of the, 35
budget, school, discretionary authority over, 79
building on strengths, 87
bureaucracy, bloated, negative characteristics, 120
bureaucratic isolation, 15-16
Bush, George, 91-92
business groups, principals and teachers paying lip service to arguments of, 185
business, exploiting dire inner-city conditions, 186
business, hegemonic influence over public schooling aims, 85-86
business and industrial leaders, early 20th century, 69
business involvement; see private sector
business management policies, U.S., 7
Business Roundtable, 7, 70, 75
Business Task Force, New Orleans, 149
busy work, 155, 156
Butler, Owen, 70, 79-180

C

California Achievement Test (CAT), 11, 145-146
capability for human agency, 187
capitalist marketplace, 109-110
capitalist social relations, 74
capitalist societies, advanced, connected through information technology and media, 85
CAPs; see Community Action Programs
care, fostering trust, 160
caring for students by teachers and staff, 157-160
centralization, 83
centralized fragmentation, 69
Chambers of Commerce, 70, 93
change, assumedly for the better, 10
changes, divorced from individual school and district contexts, impossible, 185
Chapter One, 4, 30
Chelsea, MA, school district, 86
Children's Defense Fund, 53
children
  as oppressed, 57
  putting first, 98
Children of Sanchez, The, 29-30
choice
  as measure of freedom, 109
  politics of, 73-74
Christian academies, all-white, 73
Cities in Schools project, New Orleans and Shreveport, 80-81
citizenship rights and respon-

226 Subject Index

sibilities, 93
City High School
  integrated into city social fabric, 176
  Louisiana, 135-182
city schools, disadvantaged position of, 46-47
city social and economic conditions related to school restructuring activities, 179
citywide enrollment, 157
Civil Rights Act of 1965, 51
Civil Rights Act Title IV, 36
Civil Rights Movement, 143
class, 10
class, race and gender, intersection of, 139
classical music, 196
classism, and New Right, 124
classroom as political, 116
classroom teachers; see teachers
client oriented, 120
climate, school social, 89-90
cliques, student 162
Coalition on Educational Alternatives, 75
coalitions achieving educational improvement, 10
Coleman Report, 36-37
collective identity, 112, 141
collective identity, toward notion of, 108-110
college aspirations, underachieving students, 166
college preparatory courses, 45
colonization, 106
  legacy of, 128
color, people of; see race; racial minorities
Comer Model, 89-90

Committee for Economic Development (CED), 7, 70-71, 75, 79-80
common good, 96
common sense, 18
  new, 115
communicative action, 190-191
communicative goal of common understanding, 193
community built around value of difference, 196
community development, need for coupling with school restructuring, 189
community models of governance, 185
community, new politics of, 91-96, 121
Community Action Programs (CAPs), 51, 52
community boards in Chicago, 8, 16
community development view of urban schooling, 24
community involvement, 90
  broad, 95-96
community praxis, 24
community, spirit of, 191
competition, high school graduates for jobs, 185
compromise, 70
computers business partner donated being hogged, 186
conflict
  active engagement of, 141
  social and racial, 157
conflict; see also racial-ethnic conflict
conflicts
  glossing over, 140
  student verbal, 164
connectedness to local commu-

Subject Index 227

nities and wider society, 166, 167
conscientization, 129
consciousness, philosophy of, 102
consensus building and Entrepreneurial Coalition, 69-72
consensus decisions, 90
conservative, category of difference, 124
conservative ideologies, 47-50
conservative restoration, 2, 4-5, 8, 22
and The New Federalism, 38-40
constructed objectivity, 19
constructed reality, measures of, in urban schools, 20-22
consumerism, 73
contested character of inner-city schooling social regulation, 13, 98
"Contract With America", 54
Cooke, Robert E., 50-51
cooperation, in fighting, 164
cooperative classroom activities, understanding through, 193
cooptation, 196
core subject competency, 93
corporal punishment and verbal abuse, 133
corporate and political elites, consensus among, 8
corporate downsizing and restructuring, 76
corporate model of city schooling in global economy, 97
corporate policies and practices, failures of, 74
corporate regime, 71
corporate values, little effect

on student culture, 151
corruption, 120
Council of Great City Schools, 93
counterhegemonic strategies, 117
creative, artistic manner, urban school reform viewed in, 196
Creole, 107
crime, 2-3
criminality, being African-American and poor not synonymous with, 143
crisis
  current, forms of, 24
  privatization of answers to, 38-40
  problems focus, 24
  social construction of, 22
  understanding forms of, 1-24
critical literacy, texts, 129
critical pedagogy, 12, 15, 128, 144
critical pragmatism, 12
  to break social reproduction cycle, 188
critical social theory, 137
cultural articulations, 120
cultural backgrounds, multiple, 127
cultural channels, 111
cultural conflict, denying, 112
cultural deficits, 126
cultural determinism, 29-30
cultural diversity, 112
cultural mobility, 169
cultural pathology, supposed, 106
cultural politics, hidden, fostering accomodation in school, 134

cultural praxis and liberation, 119
cultural reproduction and resistance, 10
cultural therapy, 190
cultural understanding in classroom, 190
cultural workers, 119
cultural workers, alliance, 182
cultural/identity politics, 21, 175-176
culture, deficit model of, 106
culture of poverty thesis, attacks on, 29-30
curricula
  cafeteria-style, 45
  formal and hidden, 136
curriculum
  antibias, 119
  changes, school-business partnerships, 81
  hidden, racial and class categorization, 188
  incorporation of dominant ideologies in, 23
  multiethnic, New Orleans, 16
  multiethnic/multicultural movements, 24
  national goals, 91-92, 115
  as political text, 85
  private regulation of, 12
  recreating unequally responsive economy, 12
  viewed as depoliticized texts, 116
customers (parents and students), 69

D

decentered, 115
decentralization, 4, 9, 15, 41, 71, 76, 83-84
Detroit, 78
  loosening bureaucracy, 98
  unlikely to lead to democratic practices, 120
Deep South, racial politics in cities, 143
delegating authority, 69
democracy
  as a luxury, 144
  dangers of deep in inner-city schools, 177
  deepening in inner-city schools, 144
  deepening, 121
  education, and social relations, 114
  in classrooms, 117
  lingering quest for, 179-182
  nowhere to be found, 182
  radical, when inconceivable, 195
  struggle for new, 181
  using authority to pursue radical, 195
democracy, crisis of, less urgent than school crime, 133
democracy, school work, and school violence politics, 176
democratic change, giving equal value to erasing injustices for all, 114
democratic praxis, 6, 12
democratic struggles, linking diverse, 114-115
democratizing public schooling, 111
Department of Education, 42-43
deregulation, 42
deskilling of teaching, 15
despair, discourse of, 16, 54

determinancy, 101
developmental needs of children, 89
deviance
 behavioral, perceived, 5,6
 descendant levels of, 75
 difference as social, 124
 new, 21
devolution, 41, 83
Dewey, John, 69, 88
dialectics between lived and organizational cultures, 23
dialects, ethnic, 126-127
difference
 artificial (socially constructed), 124
 as defined by academic expectations, 174
 as postmodern category, 124
 as resource, 104
 as social deviance, 124
 denial of, cause of mismatch, 193
 politics of, 124
 radical conceptions of, 126-127
 respect for, 191
differences
 celebration of, 194
 respect for cultural, in jazz, 196
different, right to be, 181
diminution, 42
discipline, 2-3, 14
 incorporation of dominant ideologies in, 23
discourse shaping the world, 110
discourse, concrete versus abstract, 57-58
discrimination, academic, 171
disestablishment, 42
dislocation and removal, poor Black families, 123
Doggett, Rebecca, 82
dominant groups, 20
double coding, 63
dropout rate, 93
dropouts, 16, 20
dropouts and test scores, 19
drugs in schools, 10, 21, 93
duality of structure, 187-188

E

"ear'oles", 58, 61
ECIA; see Education Consolidation and Improvement Act
economic decline and low student achievement, 147
economic mobility, 169
economically underprivileged, the, 57
economic competitiveness, 7, 8
economic planning, 96
education, as way out of poverty, 126
education; see also public education
educational ideologies, 43
educational market as equalizer, 48-49
educational opportunities, new inequality in, 90
educational productivity, perceived low, 2
Education Consolidation and Improvement Act (ECIA), 39, 41
Education Revenue Sharing Act of 1971, 38
Elementary and Secondary Education Act of 1965 (ESEA), 31, 32, 64
elite schools, minority students in, 109
elitism, 168

230 Subject Index

emancipation, 195
empirical data, socially constructive, 21
employable skills as end of education, 71
empowerment, parent/student/community, 15, 71, 95-96
empowerment coupled with responsibility, 87
English
  Black, 125
  dialects of, 108
  standard, 125
English-as-a-second-language, 108
entrepreneurial classes, strategies of, 23
Entrepreneurial Coalition, 3, 7, 10, 20, 40, 53, 65
  and consensus building, 69-72
  difficulty accomplishing inner-city school goals, 171
  history, 147
  ideological control of urban schooling, 67-99
  ideological hegemony in Louisiana, drive for, 147-150
  ideological strategies, themes, 95-96
  ideological strategies of, 72-90
  impact on Louisiana education policy, 150
  irrelevant to student identity politics, 147
  leadership for global economic growth, 68
  and Republican Party, 98
  marginally successful in Louisiana, 147
  significant education policy gains in American cities, 185
  undermining school empowerment, 88-89
epistemology, 18
equality redefined, 48
equality wanted for all races in school, 181
equality wanted regardless of academic success, 181
equivalence, democratic, 118
ESEA; see Elementary and Secondary Education Act of 1965
essentialism, 56
ethnic acculturation, naturally progressive view of, 104
ethnically affirming or denying school strategies, 6
ethnic difference, postmodern understanding of, 24
ethnic difference, urban schooling as, 65-66
ethnic expression, new forms of, 15
ethnic identities
  critically reimagining how they can be redefined, 113
  imagining how they were constructed, 113
ethnic identity, 2,3,6-7, 13, 14, 68
  arts programs and, 134
  as fixed product of acculturation and descent, 102
  as means of resistance and accomodation, 136
  as relational social process, 111
  as self-concept, 102-104
  as social process, 110-112
  assumed to be a shared cul-

tural heritage, 106
constantly changing, 139
European immigrant model, 104-105
formation, collective, 112
group, relations with other groups, 111
modernist view of, 102-108
new social space of, 16, 23
part of social formation, 110-112
recasting politics of, 108-116
reformed owing to historical conditions, 110
socially constructed, 110
struggle for, 21
ethnic identity; see also identity; urban ethnicity
ethnic minorities, giving up parts of identity to acculturate, 103
ethnicity, 10, 22
as collective lived cultural experience, 111
as contested cultural terrain, 112
embracing, 112-114
postmodern, social space of, 21
ethnic minorities
behavioral differences from white middle-class students, 6
learning deficiencies of, 6
ethnic minorities disenfranchised in schools, 57
ethnicity, race and class, 182
Ethnograph (Version 4.0), The, 146
ethnographic research, 13
ethnography, 10, 58-62
ethnography of school culture, previous critical, 143
European immigrant model, based on White experience, 106
European immigrant model of ethnic identity, 104
everyday school life, 151-155
everyday, understanding of the, 101
excellence, 181
excellence, financial incentives to accomplish, 70
Excellence in Education Committee, New Orleans, 9
excellence, teachers pushing students toward, 168
exit interviews with principals, present study, 146
expectations of findings, present study, 146
expectations, White middle class, of schools, 87
exploitation, 57
extirpation, virtual, Native Americans, 106

F

failures of urban school reform, 194
fairness valued, 182
family, responsibility to care for, 186
family, students, teachers and staff as, 160
fashion specificity, 181
feminism, 116, 117
synthesized with postmodernism and modernism, 117
Fernandez, Joseph, 8
field dependent learning, 6
fighting in school, 154, 157
fights, lack of, 162
financial incentives to accom-

232   Subject Index

plish excellence, 70
first impressions, 174
Food and Drug Administration, 142
foreign languages, as linguistic handicaps, 125
fragmented centralization, 84
fraternities, segregated, 130-132
Free Enterprise and Computer Literacy, graduation requirement, 148-149
free enterprise, courses in, 119
freedom and social justice for all groups, 24
free market, excesses of, 40-47
free market tool, urban schooling as, 65
funding, increased, 8
funding and technical expertise, school-business partnerships, 81

G

gang members, students resembling treated as such, 188
gender, 10, 56
gender relations, 151
gender, race and class, intersection of, 139
gender; see also women
generic strategy, dangers of, 93-94
Germany
  economic dominance, 3
  student achievement, 5, 55
ghettos, permanent, 187
Girl Scouts, 81
Giroux, Henry, controversial writings, 116
global economy, 7
competitive, and educated workforce, connections between, 80
competition in, 93
dispositional skills embedded in, 83
emerging, changes caused by, 67
and urban ethnicity linked, 68
global fiscal crisis, 24
global political economy, 14
goal of project, 183
Goals 2000, 70, 93, 95, 96
gossip, 161-162
governance
  altering, 20
  community models of, 185, 189
  crisis, deconstructing, 7-13
  crisis of legitimacy of, socially constructed, 22
  self-, 23
  urban school failures of, 9
governance and management teams, 89-90
governance reform
  as common sense, 8-10
  contradictions of, 10
governance, shared; see shared governance
government elites' interests in schooling crises, 64
government, mistrust of, 189
governments, legitimation crisis of, 5
grade level prestige, 175
graduation rates, disproportionate negative effects on minority students, 150
graduation requirements, changes in Louisiana, and Entrepreneurial Coalition,

Subject Index 233

148-149
Great Society, 3, 22-37, 64
  call to action, 26-28
  in cities, classrooms, countryside, 27
  significance of, 26-28
growth machine, 71
guard dogs, 178

H

Head Start, 3, 30, 50-54, 64
  evaluations of, 52-53
Health, Education and Welfare, Department of, 34-35
hegemonic practices, 15, 62
hegemony, competition for, 98
hegemony never certain, 20
Heller, Walter, 28-31
hermeneutics, 187
high school education, as ticket to outside world, 169
high school graduation, 93
high schools in present study, characteristics of, 145
historical and cultural connection, 143
Holmes, Morris, 185
human agency, 126-127
  and school/classroom micropolitics, 140-141
  and structural relations, 137-138
  and student power, 183
  and student resistance, 141
  evidenced by resistance, 141
  necessary qualities, 187
  relationships among school culture and student resistance, 138
  tied to discourse, 137
  versus institutional structures, 114
human agents
  lack of historical knowledge, 187
  maintaining status quo by reproducing institutions, 187
human development, ongoing, 24
hybridity, 103, 169

I

identities
  multilayered and fractured construction of, 126
  multiple, 105
  student, collective, 141
identity
  as autonomous, unitary, 136
  as personal, 195
  as process, 110-112
  as relational and in process, 109
  dynamically shaped from interaction of macro categories and school/student culture, 180
  economically functional, student resistance to assuming, 7
  forged in discourse, 105
  how social context constructs, 126
  no essential origins, 142
  politics, 90
  psychological, 110
  shaped through language use, 126
  social, knowledge of, 140
  socially constructed, 136
  subaltern, 103
  underlying conception of, 102
identity politics
  and racial formation, 142
  and student resistance, 136-141

in classroom, 108
opening space for human agency, 183
rise of, 143
social context of, 147
identity politics and school democracy, relationship, 180
identity politics, postmodernism, and student resistance, 135-182
identity work, 134, 143
teachers need to understand students', 179
identity, collective; see collective identity
identity; see also ethnic identity
ideological control of urban schooling, 67-99
ideological roots of crisis, 23
ideologies, dominant, 23
ideology, types, 18
illiteracy sustaining poverty, 129
imaginary unities, 112
immigrant analogy, 104
In This House, on This Morning, 195-196
individual; see self
inefficiency, 120
inequality, deep structural relations of, 176-177
Inequality: A Reassessment of Family and Schooling in America, 37
inequality, school reproduction of educational and social, 85
inner-city conditions, dire, exploited by business, 186
inner-city ethnic minorities not exercising political rights, 78
inner-city schooling

cultural politics of, 13-16
ideological control over, 84-86
ideological patterns in, 2-7
possible reconfiguration, 133
social regulation of, 5, 13
inner-city schools; see also schools
inner-city schools
as identity politics sites, 135
believed inferior, 10
dangers of deep democracy in, 177
deepening democracy in, 144
historically abandoned, 15
investigating sites of, 138
relationship between democracy and social space of urban ethnicity in, 138
relative autonomy of, 14-15
sites for racial-ethnic identity work, 179
undeniable problems, 16
worsening conditions, 7-8, 11, 21, 67
inner-city social structure, deterioration of, 9
Inquiry method, 87-88
institutional structures versus human agency, 114
instructional technicians to cultural pedagogical workers, transition from, 122
instrumental competencies, 191
integrated school change, 87
intervention as progress, 9
interview data from high schools, 24

J

Japan

Subject Index 235

economic dominance, 3
student achievement, 5, 50
jargon, 57
jazz, 195-196
jazz, historical and cultural grounding, 196
Jesuit Order, 130, 132
job preparation as educational goal, 5
job prospects, inner-city families, 14-15
Job Training and Partnership Act (JTPA), 81
Johnson, Lyndon B., 3, 26-36
  education-related bills, 32
  hopes for Great Society and education improvements, 32, 64

K

Kennedy, John F., 26
key images for reconstructed urban education, 196
knowledgability for human agency, 187
knowledge
  and information, sharing, 177
  about employability and economic survival, 97
  acceptable and official, 12-13
  authentic, 18
  cumulative, 56
  defined, 17
  new forms of unofficial, 15
  official, 3
  political uses of, 3
  positive use of, 33-34
  and power, 56
  social division of, 13
  social production of, 96-97, 117
  student production of, 123
  transmission of, 122
knowledge; see also self-knowledge
KOS (Kids of Survival), 121
"lads", 58, 59, 60-1

L

language pluralism, 56
language specificity, 181
layoff of middle managers, 76
leadership, intellectual and moral, 70
  provided by dominant groups, 85
learning deficiencies, 6
Learning to Labour, social reproduction in, 58-62
learning, enjoyable, 179
legitimation, 11-12, 15
  defined, 19-20
  of ideas, 19-20
legitimation crisis of governments, 5
liberal ambivalence on race, 125-126
liberal, category of difference, 124
liberalism and educators, 191
liberation, 195
liminal states, 195
limited English speakers disenfranchised, 57
limited English-speaking families, migration of, 67
literacy, 93
literacy, critical, 128-129
lived cultural experience of students, 183
local community values; see values and needs, local community
local cultures, modifying domination structures, 101
local education agencies

(LEAs), 39-40
local history and culture, 70
local ideologies, 120
local school boards
　accountability, 76
　politically vulnerable, 72
　reform of, 76
local social movements,
　strength of countervailing,
　70
Los Angeles Unified School
　District, ethnic conflict in,
　15
Louisiana Association for
　Business and Industry, 149
Louisiana Educational
　Assessment Program
　(LEAP), 145-146
Louisiana Educational Policy,
　148
Louisiana Handbook for School
　Administrators (The
　Handbook), 147-149
Louisiana State Board of
　Elementary and Secondary
　Education, 148
love for students from teachers
　and staff, 174
Loyola University, New
　Orleans, 130-2

M

magnet schools, 6, 18, 23
　as form of choice, 189
　New Orleans, 17
　overcrowded, 189
　reproducing classism and
　　racism, 118
mainstream, school helping
　students to break into
　through reforms, 194
making ethnic differences
　invisible, 97
managers of virtue, 71

man and social world, interaction, 19
marginality
　culture of, 24
　despair over students', 195
　disparaging, 194
marginalization, 63
market economy, 73-74
market incentives, 7-8
Marsalis, Wynton, 134, 195-196
mass culture imposed by media,
　181
math
　abstract, 12
　basic, 12
math and science
　competition, 93
　specialized course offerings
　　in, 6, 70, 87
meaning, created through culture, 137
meaning and knowledge, constraints on classroom production, 119
meaning, how students construct, 118-119
meaning ascertained through
　analysis of local practices,
　56
media coverage fueling social
　construction, 18
melting pot, mythical, 194
metal detectors, 133
metanarratives, 56
micropolitics, school/classroom, and human agency,
　140
micropolitics of school, 136,
　137
minority ethnic population
　becoming a majority, 68
minority students, in elite

schools, 109
mismatch
  caused by denial of difference, 193
  cultural, 190
  school expectations and home/community resources, 139, 193
mission priorities, 69
modernism, 25, 56
  assumptions of, 102
Moffett, James "Jim Bob", 81
money, students wanting to make, 186
moral leadership, 12
moral necessity to disregard state's bureaucratic wishes, 137
Moses, Robert, 70
multiculturalism, 104, 182
multiethnic urban culture, 67-68
multiple cultural backgrounds, 127
multiple subjectivity, 182
music specificity, 181
mutual understanding, ethnic minority students, 191

N

National Assessment of Educational Progress, 94
National Commission on Excellence in Education, 7
national education goals, discourses excluding teachers, parents and students, 94-95
National Goals panel, 96
National Head Start Association, 53
National Institutes of Health, 142-143
Nation at Risk, A, 43, 48
neat organization impossible, 15
negative feelings about school, 152-154
negative self-images, reinforcing, 21
neighborhood enrollment, 157
Neighborhood High School students, college entrance, 176
Neighborhood High School, Louisiana, 135-182
neighborhoods, unliveable, 194
neo-Marxists, 116
neoconservative and neoliberal groups, 75
neopopulism, 23
neutrality, flawed assumptions of, 85
New Federalism, 188-189
new political subjects
  from ethnicity to, 114-116
  in multiethnic milieu, 129
  teachers and minority students, 115
New Right, and Entrepreneurial Coalition, 147
Newark, NJ, schools, state regulation, 82
New Federalism, 25, 65
  and conservative restoration, 38-40
new politics of community, 72
New Right, The, 40-41, 44, 54
  ascent of, 47-50
  legitimated by schools, 12
New York City, high school graduation rate, 8
news, students watching to get involved in society, 167-168
NHSA; see National Head Start Association
no fault, 90

O

objectivation, 19
objective paradigm of society, 187
objectivity, 56
Ocean-Hill Brownsville, teachers' firings in, 78
Office of Economic Opportunity (OEC), 51
openness not cooptation, 196
oppressed, the, 57
oppression, grounding literacy teaching in circumstances of, 129
oppression and exploitation, Whites responsible for, 125
optimism, cautious, 65
optimistic music, 196
oral history
  analysis of students' ethnic awarenesses to reconceptualize urban schooling, 134
  examining which voices privileged in history books, 129
organizationally driven, 120
other, 97
  orientation to the, 57
Outcome-Based Education, St. Charles Parish, LA, 80
out-of-control bureaucracy, New Orleans, 16

P

panaceas
  educational, 87
  technological, 117
Panhellenic Council, 133
parent, rights versus teachers' rights, 78
parent committee membership by principal's invitation, 79
parent councils, Chicago, 79
parents
  altering governance in Chicago, New Orleans and Cleveland, 98
  inability to influence school policy and practices, 81
  influencing school direction, 99
  input, 90
  interactions with school professionals, 90
  keeping school social calendar, 90
  as tutors or aides, 90
parents and community groups in large cities, 15
partnership, government and private sector, 5
passing classes, 156
paternalism in classroom, 195
patriarchy, 117
  and New Right, 124
patronage, 120, 129-130
patronization, 63
pedagogical intervention, empowerment via, 68
Pedagogy of the Oppressed, 129
pedagogy, antibias, as cultural politics, 128-132
peer-defined status, 111
people of color; see race; racial minorities
people, learning how to deal with, 178
performing arts, images and metaphors from, 134
personnel matters, limits on parents' authority in, 78
person rights, 48
phenomenology, 187
plan of the book, 22-24
pluralism, schools in, 104

police state, modern, high school campus as, 133
political ideological movements, 23
political subject
 decentered, 115
 Marxist or liberal theories of, 114
politicians, minority, benefitting from racism, 129-130
politics of organizational decline, 83
politics of urban schooling and postmodernism, 101-134
poor families, students of, disenfranchised, 57
populist reform movements, 71
portfolios, student; see alternative assessment practices
positive feelings about school, 154-155
positivism, 2, 4, 22
 assumptions of, 33-34
 critiques of, 36-37
 excesses of, 57
 legacies of, 33-37, 49-50
possessive individual, 73-74
possessive individualism, democracy, 77
postcolonial perspective, 104
postmodern analysis, emphasis, 62-63
postmodernism, 2, 13, 16, 22, 23, 55-8
 and politics of urban schooling, 101-134
 as morally bankrupt, 135
 current climate, 25
 identity politics, and student resistance, 135-182
 possibilities for deep democracy, empirical assessment of, 135
 tenets of, 56-58
 to break social reproduction cycle, 188
 use of term, 55-56
postmodern method, emancipatory possibilities in, 66
poststructuralism, 13, 16, 23
 concerned with micropolitics, 140
potential control over knowledge, 97
poverty; see also war on; culture of; Johnson, Lyndon B.
poverty
 causes of, 29-30
 collective expressions of, as student resistance, 138-140
 decentered and present everywhere, 136
 consensus for federal action, 31
 denying, 194
 limits of federal action to end, 32- 33
 route out of, 31-33
power and knowledge, 56
power and leadership, moral use of, 195
power relations, central office and schools, 194
power relations unequal between teachers and students, 122
power relations, 136
power, schools applying productively, 118
power/knowledge, situating in urban schools, 117-120
practical consciousness, 188
practical intersubjectivity, 109, 190

prayer, school, 44
pregnancy, teen, 20
pride, 154, 155
   racial/ethnic, 176
principal
   decision-making authority of, 76
   selection or dismissal of, 79
prisoners, 57
Private Industry Councils (PICs), 81
private inner-city schools, Milwaukee, vouchers, 72-73
private schools, increase in per-pupil funding, 67
private sector
   government partnership, 5
   as major policy actor, 5
privatization, 83-84, 98
   tools of, 41
problems, substituting for "urban", 2
problem solving as scientific and professional action, 34-35
producing students desired by the economy, 69
production, 11, 12-13
progress; see also scientific progress
progress
   as intervention, 9
   meliorative view of, 10
   symbolic political and cultural, 9
progressive social movements, oppression in, 128
property rights, 48
prosperity, risking, to attack poverty, 28-29
public confidence, restoring, 189
public education, developmental reconstruction of, 190
public education, goals of, 5
public education; see also education
public housing
   dilapidated, 128
   violent crime in, 143
public housing as ghettos, 187
public housing, schools and neighborhoods attached to, 17, 23
public life, reconstruction of, by deepening democracy, 120-121
pullout remedial programs, 4

Q

quality of life, inner city, affected by global economy, 67

R

race
   experienced differentially by Black students, 169
   liberal ambivalence on, 125-126
   negative labeling of, 129
race and ethnicity, deconstructing social determinants of, 124
race, 10, 56, 65
   as separate category of socially constructed identity, 106
   pervasiveness of, 105-8
   reduced to component of ethnic identity, 106
race, class and gender, intersection of, 139
racial formation, 142, 143
racial identity, 126
racial minorities

common differences consists in permanent racial difference and nonincorporation, 107
distinctiveness from majority not altered by adopting white norms and values, 107
racial-ethnic conflict, administration fueling, 188
racial-ethnic identity
cultural struggles for, 24
formation always incomplete, 169
social construction of, 169-175
struggle in city, 142
racial-ethnic identity; see also ethnic identity
racial quotas, 17
racism
and New Right, 124
as explanation for inequality of Blacks, 106
determining social identities of students, 120
history of, 125
individual narratives related to properties of, 130
institutional, deep structural relations of, 176
pervasive, 102
structural causes of, 130
students resisting, 118-119
taught and learned, 128
radical critical theorists, 144
radical left and identity politics, 142
radical pedagogues, 176
radical, category of difference, 124
radical democracy in schools, 116

radical democratic society, reconfiguration of, 66
rainbow coalition needed, 57
rappin' and cappin', 21
rationality, 24
rationality of material and social structures, assumed, 22
reactionary discourse, 124
reading achievement increase, inner-city students, 94
Reagan and Bush administrations, 117
Reagan, Ronald, 39-46, 48
realism, 56
realities, multiple, 57, 62
reality, 17, 56,
as political production, 113
socially constructed, 19
reason, alleviating school distress, 102
reform, concept of, undefined, 3
reform, educational
and corporation values, 185
failures of, 194-195
piecemeal approach, 87
social conditions embedding, 191
somewhat successful but not built on student culture, 194
reform, historically unequal power relations undermining, 11
regional identity, 181
reinventing schooling, 20, 98
reinvention of government, 23
relevance of jazz over classical music, 196
remedial education, 11, 81
Republican-dominated Congress, 75

242 Subject Index

Republican Party and Entrepreneurial Coalition, 98
research design, present study, 145-146
resistance
   and anxiety, 138
   as expression of power, 138
   as identity work, 140
   cultural, 21, 24, 58-62
   earlier study of in same two schools, 182
   influenced by student culture, 151
   previous scholarly and ethnographic work on, 184
   student collective expressions of power, 138-140
   student collective ideologically organized, 141
   student collective ideologically organized, from capacity for human agency, 139
   student, identity politics and postmodernism, 135-182
   student, individual and collective, 139
   student, interpreting, 166-169
   student, relationships among school culture and human agency, 138
   student, space to foster, 141
   student, tacit, 151
   student, to busy work, 167
   student, to essentialist definitions of race, 181
   students, of school constructing their identity, 188
   students, to formal curriculum, 186
   teacher and student, 15
   to representation as deviant and at risk, 90
respect, and school violence, 162
responsibility to care for family, 186
romanticizing actual worsening conditions, 16
romanticizing cultural formations of inner-city schooling, 23

S

Schafly, Phyllis, 44
school
   assemblies suspended, 165
   racial conflicts in, 173
school climate as ordered social relations in class, 157-164
school culture, relationships among student resistance and human agency, 138
school life as disclosed by students, 141
school reform, need for coupling with community development, 189
school work findings, present study, 155-156
school work, democracy, and school violence politics, 176
school, as cultural/identity politics site, 116
school, the, lacking knowledge of ethnicity and intersubjectivity to help students, 187
school, walks to, dangerous, 128
school-based management, 4, 9, 75, 76, 87, 185
school benefits, unequal distribution of, 10
school boards

Subject Index

curriculum changes, 81
curriculum intervention, 80
elites seizing control of, 8
funding and technical expertise, 81
ideological strategy of Entrepreneurial Coalition, 68
local, defensiveness, 20-21
local, financial excuses, 20-21
local election of, 9
newly configured, New Orleans and Atlanta, 9
New Orleans, parent movement to elect, 8
prevalent in Chicago and New Orleans, 81
replacement or abolition of, 9
restoration of school facilities, 80
school choice, 5, 6, 9, 23, 75
  ideological strategy of Entrepreneurial Coalition, 68, 72-73
school councils, local, Chicago, 9
school culture, 6-7
School Development Program (SDP), 89-90
school finance, 4-5
school governance, fundamental tension in, 83
school improvement ideas, authority to propose, 79
school incentive programs, 75
school intervention, 86-90
  ideological strategy of Entrepreneurial Coalition, 68
school readiness, 93
school-business partnership, students believing they did not benefit from, 150
school-business partnerships
  constraining meaning and knowledge, 119
  cultural biases, 194
  Louisiana, 149-150
school/student culture and outside social relations, interaction, 175-176
schooling as preparation for elite college entrance, 178
schools
  as active producers of knowledge, 124
  historically authoritarian, 144
  inner-city, historically undemocratic, 133
  radical democracy in, 116
  rigidly organized, 128
  underfunded, 128
schools and teachers, ideological constraints on, 102
schools in present study, enrollment, 157
schools in present study, student bodies, 136
schools' informal culture
  reproducing inequality, 13
  resisting dominant school ideologies, 13
schools; see also inner-city schools
schools
  institutionally separate from economics, 14
  neighborhood, traditional, 18
  noninstructional purposes of, 10-11
  resistant to change, 7
school-to-work transition,

facilitation of, 80
science; see also math and science
scientific and technical knowledge, minimal, 149
scientific principles, alleviating school distress, 102
scientific progress, 56
Scott, John, sculptor, 134
SDP; see School Development Program
segregation in desegregated schools, 24
self
    as autonomous and isolated, 102
    endangered, healing and caring for, 190-191
    enduring, 109
    enduring, endangered and situated, 190
    enduring, nonexistent, 193
    fixed, unitary, 103
self-concept, 102-103
self-efficacy, 190
self-knowledge, 140
self-realization, 103
sexism; see patriarchy
Shanker, Albert, 70
shared decision making, 75
shared governance, 23, 76-79
    contradictory practices of, 77
    ideological strategy of Entrepreneurial Coalition, 68
    impediments to implementation, 77-79
    large urban school districts, examples, 77-78
    parent participation in, 78-9
    Salt Lake City, 79

site-based management, 71
situated agency, 187-191
situated and threatened selves, communicative action for, 190
situated human agency, 195
situated restructuring, 179
skilled workforce to enhance job creation for poor students and families, 97
skills of mainstream society, requisite, 191
skin color, 113
slavery, 106
    legacy of, 128
small sample size, present study, 146
social action, capacity for, 104
social action; see also action
social competition, tense climate, 165
social conflict, consequence of ideology of equal treatment, 187-188
social construction, 18
Social Construction of reality, the, 17
social construction of urban schooling, federal shaping of, 26
social context of urban schooling, 25-66
social isolation, 133
social life, uniformity of, 181
social problem perspective, 20
social production of knowledge, 117
social reality, constructing, 17-18
social reality, ideology and, 18-19
social reconstruction, 24
social regulation, reemergence

of, 7, 8, 22
social relations, how constituted, student understanding of, 123
social relations, multiple, 180
social reproduction in Learning to Labour, 58-62
social reproduction, 165
social reproduction, unintended consequences of, 128
social space, new, of ethnic identity, 6, 22
social studies goals and objectives changes in Louisiana, 149
social world as given, 18-19
socialization agents, nonfamilial, 104
Society of Jesus; see Jesuit Order
sociology class, 178
sociology, historical, 18
sociology of knowledge, 17, 18
Socrates, 116
solutions, programmatic, unradical, 195
somebody, becoming, 111
sororities, segregated, 130-132
Southern Christian Leadership Council, 3
Sputnik, 87
staff development activities, 89-90
standardized test scores, 11, 19, 45, 57
   reading and math, 93
   rising, 189
   underachievement, 193
standardized tests, national and international norm-referenced, 22-23
Stanford University.

Accelerated Schools Process, 87
state education policy, marginally affecting students' lives, 151
state fiscal control, 83
state government, constraining meaning and knowledge in classroom, 119
state regulation, reemergence of, 45-46, 65
state regulation/state takeover, 82-83
   ideological strategy of Entrepreneurial Coalition, 68
state regulations, professional leeway in complying with, 137
state responsibility for low achievement of inner-city students, 74
state takeover of inner-city students and schools, 23, 82
stations in life, assigned, 13
statistically underachieving; see underachieving
statistics versus calculus, 149
status quo versus reform, 10
stereotyping by students of each other, 165-166
storytelling as cathartic, 123
storytelling; see oral history
strategic action, 193
structural asymmetries, taken-for-granted, removing, 191
structural functionalism, 13
structural relations
   and human agency, 137
   impermanent, 137
structuralism
   and culturalism, 22

246 Subject Index

as self-fulfilling prophecy, 22
structural relations versus lived cultural experience, 68
structuration 73-74
  as outcome and medium, 187
  duality of, 187-188
structure and agency, dialectical relationships between, 185
structures, ahistorical, 137
student
  agency and resistance, 141
  culture, connectedness to wider society, 166
  identities, multiple, 118
  representation in school governance and discipline, 14
  as represented by identity, 6
  school roles, 139
student achievement, long-term goal of increasing, 189
student activities suspended, 153-154
student behavior, control of deviant, 8
student culture, 58-62
  differences between schools, not within schools, 168-169
  Louisiana high schools, 151-155
student cultures, distinct, 151
student narratives; see oral history
student outcomes and social action, 188-189
student resistance; see resistance, student
student voice, 177
students

academic experiences, unique set of, 169
African-American, 7
agitating for greater control, 115
AIDS victims, 8
at-risk, 2
awareness of others' ethnicity, 109
belief in equal treatment for all races, 172
belief they did not benefit from school-business partnership, 150
Black and/or rural, corporal punishment and verbal abuse of, 133
Black middle-class, 131-132
Black public housing dwellers, 131-132
Black, perception of who is Black, 131-132
college preparation, lack of, 170
college, desire to attend, 186
community service, 178
coping strategies, 109
cultural unsophistication assumed, 184
disadvantaged, 11
disappointed and resentful at not being prepared for college, 170
disenfranchised, 8
disruptive, 171
doing what they have to do to graduate, 186
educated inner-city, as employable in global economy, 86
ESL, 172
ethnic awarenesses analyzed

to reconceptualize schooling, 134
ethnic minority, mutual understanding, 191
exercising power, 118
free enterprise values internalized, 186
future identities as professionals, 179
harsh circumstances, 128
human agency, capacity for, 139
identity work most important, 110-101
individual autonomy (agency), 192-193
inner-city, validating knowledge and cultural experience of, 14
interviewed in present study, 145-146
knowledge of who society expects them to be, 188
knowledge of who they are, 188
lived cultural experiences, critical reflection of, 123
lived culture, 136
minority, instilling business values in, 81
Neighborhood High, not contributing to own social reproduction, 186
not blaming, 191
power from exercising agency, 183
powerlessness assumed, 184
production of knowledge, 123
pushing through liminal stage, schools not helping, 187
relative powerlessness, 173
respecting each other, 163
seeking upward mobility, 10
stereotyping each other, 165-166
taking out into local commmunities, 120
underachieving, 19, 20
underachieving, college aspirations, 166
underclass, 6
verbal expression, encouragement in, 178-179
who they are in class, 108
writing own texts, 129
students' needs, concern with meeting, 140
subaltern identity, 108
subject, child treated as not yet a, 195
subjectivity, new political and social, multiple inscriptions of, 184
subjects, interaction between, 195
subordinate groups, 20
subordinate subjectivity, 103
substitute teachers, 170-171
substitute teachers, extended basis, 171
suburban schools, increase in per-pupil funding, 67
success
  racial obsession with, 181
  redefining student, 14
success, encouraging relentless individual pursuit of, 194
success, stress on, resisting, 179
superintendents
  benefits from responding to business, 195
  responding to business discourse, 185

248 Subject Index

survival, schools in poor neighborhoods, 189
suspension of Blacks, inordinate, 16
swing music, 196
switching, cultural and linguistic, 108-109
symbolic meaning, 22
symbolic universes, 10
symbols, intrusive use of, 140

T

Taiwan, student achievement, 50
taking care of business, 185-186
taking care of self, 177, 186
talents, performing arts or math and science, 17
Taylor, Pat, 81
teacher role redefining, 122
teacher-student bond, 158, 160
teachers
  allying with other cultural workers, 133
  as friends and counselors, 158
  as public intellectuals, 122
  betraying student confidences, 161
  certified, attracting, 171
  evaluation of, 79
  fostering students' ethnic identity and awareness of others' ethnicity, 118
  gossiping about students, 161
  high expectations of Black students, 174
  higher expectations of non-Blacks, 172
  informal authority, 87
  interest in students' learning, 179
  joining with parents, 115
  lack of control over class, 171
  need for safety to take pedagogical risks and nurture students, 179
  not talking in class, 159
  power use, 118
  racism, dealing with their, 130
  refusal to help students, 167
  rejecting all forms of totalizing narratives, 128
  rights versus parents' rights, 78
  threatening to fail students, 160
  treating Blacks differently, 159
  treating students fairly, 175
  unions, 5, 78
teachers and staff caring for students, 157-160
teachers and students, relational assymetry, 192
teachers, oppressed, 115
technical workforce facing stiff competition, 149
technology, alleviating school distress, 102
test scores, 17
test scores; see also standardized test scores
textbooks, 119-120
texts locked in understaffed warehouses, New Orleans, 16
themes, main, of book, 184-185
theory and practice, 193-194
thesis of book, 183
thought influenced by social

Subject Index

context, 18
tight coupling, classroom practices, 84, 86
Title One; see Chapter One
top down intervention strategy, 4
Total Community Action, 51-52
tracking, 11
transformation, 65
trust, 160-161
   evolving into positive communication, 160

U

underachieving, 23
unequal educational outcomes, 23
unions; see teachers unions
unitary self, 101
United States Congress and AIDS research, 142-143
unity of purpose, 87
upward mobility, 117
   for Blacks, 157
urban
   meaning, 3, 25, 50, 64
   synonymous with action, 188
   synonymous with problem, 189
urban centers' restructured economic position, 14
urban education, situatedness of, 128
urban ethnicity, 6-7
urban ethnicity; see also ethnic identity
urban ethnicity and global economy linked, 68
urban ethnic politics, milieu of, 15-16
urban ethnography, 23
urban ethnography; see also ethnography
urban pedagogy, theory of, 116-123
urban pedagogy; see urban schooling
urban school boundaries, 132-134
urban school crisis, social reality of, 16-20
urban school districts, large, 15
urban schooling
   actions for more just society, 101
   community development view of, 24
   contemporary source of ideological control, 84
   as drain on domestic economy, 101
   as ethnic difference, 65-66
   as free market tool, 65
   as governmental intervention, 64
   history, 2-7
   ideological control of, 67-99
   images and metaphors to reconstruct, 195-196
   key images for reconstructed, 196
   new vision of, 24
   political economy of, 11
   politics and postmodernism, 101-134
   problematic meaning of, 2-7
   social construction of, 17, 24
   social context of, 22, 25-66
urban school reform; see reform, educational
urban schools
   changing demographics in, 111

V

values
- radical democracy in, 120
- situating power/knowledge in, 117-120

values
- economic development, transformation of, 98
- free enterprise, internalized by students, 186
- middle class, imposed on socially disconnected populations, 11
- and needs, local community, 96, 98-99
- reproduction of dominant, 13-14
- transformation by parents, 98

values and attitudes, working class, 60-62
valuing college admission, 186
valuing high school diploma, 186
valuing public education, not, 169
variance in student responses within schools, little in present study, 151-152
violence
- gang, 164
- school practices breeding, 188
- in schools, 16, 93, 122, 178
- corporal punishment and verbal abuse, 133
- fear of, 10
- increasing, 193
- politics of, democracy and school work, 176-179
- and respect, 162-166
- social construcion of, 188
- deep structural relations, 176-177

voluntarism, 187
vouchers, 23, 75, 98, 189

W

War on Poverty, ideological and economic bases for, 28-30
weapons, students carrying to school, 134
women, 57
women; see also gender
worker productivity, 7
workers, passive, 117
workplace, ever-changing, 149-150
work training, 81